AF208578

Niclas Timmerby

$$IH \dashrightarrow C \dashrightarrow EH : (E = potential^\infty) \dashrightarrow R = P$$

THE FORMULA FOR PROFITABILITY, GROWTH AND DEVELOPMENT

FOR ALL TEAMS, INDUSTRIES AND ORGANIZATIONS

When you, as a leader, shift your focus to culture instead of concentrating on targets, magic happens right before your eyes.
Niclas Timmerby

© 2025 Niclas Timmerby

Graphics and layout by Niclas Timmerby

Förlag: BoD · Books on Demand, Östermalmstorg 1,
114 42 Stockholm, bod@bod.se
Tryck: Libri Plureos GmbH, Friedensallee 273,
22763 Hamburg, Tyskland

Image of nebula on cover created by Thomas Budach

ISBN: 978-91-8080-918-4

Table of Contents

Reflection pages for you as a leader:
A: 33-34, B: 58, C: 87, D: 121, E: 170, F: 362, G, 389-390.
Chapter 2: 214, Chapter 3: 246, Chapter 4: 270, Chapter 5: 291,
Chapter 6: 322, Chapter 7: 348.

FOREWORD

Money can determine what you do.
Your passion determines how you do it.
Niclas Timmerby

This book has been in my mind and has accompanied me for the last fifteen years. Gradually, the thoughts have become more concrete, and through reflections and notes, they have evolved into ideas. From these ideas, a methodology emerged that I began to use in coaching conversations. Consequently, a process with specific steps was developed to make the methodology applicable and repeatable, even after I have completed my part.

For the past twelve years, I have employed the methodology in a structured manner in training programmes for both small and large groups, as well as in lectures accompanied by various tools and workshops. I have applied the methodology in companies, government bodies, municipal organisations, trade unions, vocational schools, and sports clubs.

Now is the time to formalise this into a theory on paper (or digitally, if you choose that option). I have experienced immense joy when I have seen leaders discover a whole new way to lead—leading with a structured methodology that genuinely comes from the heart.

If you find the courage to lead from the heart, you genuinely touch people; when you touch people, the person in front of you changes. When individuals in a team change, it simultaneously affects the culture/atmosphere in the shared working environment where you spend time, collaborate, and share knowledge and experiences.

This influence shapes and molds all the individuals involved. It alters the way of communicating, the relationships, and the overall dynamics within the team.

"Culture eats strategy for breakfast."
- Peter Drucker

When the culture changes, the team's shared values and the informal rules are simultaneously reshaped into something new, leading to changes in behaviors, attitudes, and levels of trust, reliability, performance, morale, and principles.

When you, as a leader, systematically employ the methodology in this book, you will discover significant synergy effects on many levels in your professional life. My ambition is that this book will also encourage you to reflect on yourself as an individual, where you too have various teams such as family, friends, acquaintances, peer groups, networks, associations, and more.

To make the various concepts that can describe "a group of people working together" more tangible, I will use the term "*entity*" throughout the book.

"Entity" is employed as a composite term to refer to organisations, companies, participants, sports teams, work teams, departments, associations, institutions, and other units that collaborate to achieve common goals and ambitions.

My ambition with this book is to present a theory and methodology that suggests that if a leader focuses on creating and maintaining a corporate culture that values participation, trust, and safety, this methodology has a greater potentia to foster and sustain long-term profitability, quality in daily work, and efficiency within an entity than if the leader concentrates solely on target figures and objectives. Job satisfaction and reduced employee turnover are added benefits.

INTRODUCTION

People are like flowers;
in the right environment, anyone can flourish.
Niclas Timmerby

*Regardless of the type of entity you operate within, **culture** exists as something invisible to the eye that influences people's will, desire, and energy, and it is so strong that you cannot shake it no matter how strong or powerful you are.*

A good culture cannot be purchased regardless of how many billions are put on the table; it is also impossible to buy a machine that creates a good and sustainable culture, nor can a speaker or educator quickly "fix" the culture.

Let us start from the beginning.
The word culture comes from the Latin word *"colere"*, later *"cultura"* which can be translated to cultivation. The word has evolved from describing agriculture to being used during the Roman Empire to describe intellectual and aesthetic activities such as art, literature, music, and theater, as well as education and development. In the 1960s, researchers and business leaders began to take an interest in the impact that the entity's values, norms, and behaviors had on performance and employee well-being.

The concept of "*corporate culture*" was created and quickly became popular in the following decades. For many years, it has been an important part of business management and organizational theory. Over time, the meaning of the word has expanded, and today it is also used to describe social and intellectual activities of a group or community (an entity).

Today, the term "corporate culture" is commonly used to describe the shared values, norms, traditions, working methods, interactions, behaviours, and attitudes that characterise a company and its employees.

Research and studies also demonstrate the importance of continuously promoting and maintaining a positive culture, regardless of the entity.

Here are five examples:

1. A study from Harvard Business Review shows that companies with a strong corporate culture have higher productivity, better customer satisfaction, and lower employee turnover than companies with a weak corporate culture.

2. A research report from MIT Sloan Management Review indicates that companies with a strong corporate culture are better equipped to handle changes and challenges in a rapidly changing business environment.

3. A study from Deloitte shows that companies with a strong corporate culture have a higher degree of innovation and are more adaptable to changes than companies with a weak corporate culture.

4. A study from Gallup shows that companies with a strong corporate culture have a higher level of engagement among their employees, leading to higher productivity, lower absenteeism, and lower employee turnover.

5. A survey from Glassdoor indicates that companies with high ratings on corporate culture on Glassdoor.com (a platform for reviewing employers) have higher stock returns than companies with low ratings on corporate culture.

The synergy effect of placing a strong emphasis on values and/or a shared foundation of values has also been demonstrated.

Here are three examples of studies and reports that demonstrate the effect of working with a values-driven leadership to positively influence corporate culture:

1. A study published in the journal "Organization Science" examined companies that had implemented a strong values-based corporate culture. The results showed that these companies had higher profitability and better financial performance compared to companies that did not have as strong a values-based culture.

2. A report from the Corporate Leadership Council studied over 50,000 employees in various organizations and found that companies with a strong corporate culture based on shared values had higher employee engagement and better financial performance.

3. A study published in the "Journal of Business Ethics" examined companies that had a clear and communicative value base. The results showed that these companies had higher profitability and better financial performance compared to companies that did not have as clear and communicative foundation of values.

All employees are looking to the leader, sometimes with a critical eye, as the leader must provide clear direction and demonstrate how the entity will achieve its goals.

What essential conditions are reasonable for the leader to establish for each team member in order to set expectations and maximise the potential of both individuals and the entity?

Here are concepts that I will gradually explain in the book:

- Where do we want to go (*the entity's vision*)?

- How will we get there together (*the leader's mission*)?

- What are the rules we have established among team members (*the team's shared foundation of values*)?

- Has the leader communicated *emotional information* in the form of *motivation*, *mutual expectations*, and *a clear direction*?

- Do we genuinely have an open culture supported by an accepted *feedback culture*?

- Is there a structure for *tailored coaching* to assist team members in their personal and professional growth?

- Do we trust each other enough to be willing to "run through fire for one another"? In other words, does the leaders practise a *trust-based*, *values-driven* leadership that fosters *a culture of development*, enabling everyone to grow in their roles and as individuals within our entity?

So, what do you nurture as a leader every day in every physical and digital meeting, during brief spontaneous conversations, and in longer planned discussions, in performance reviews, and when you communicate via email, text, or your organisation's intranet?

What do you cultivate when you enter a room through the hormones you relentlessly and constantly emit without uttering a word, and what do you leave behind in that space?

What do you nurture that propels your team forward when you speak in front of several team members or in situations where you encounter team members outside of work hours?

In summary, how do you influence your organisation through your character and personality?

Are you influenced by others in your leadership style, or are you shaped by your own genuineness?

The word shaped originally comes from the Latin word *imprimere* which in Ancient Rome described the action of pressing something onto a material. Much later in Germany, the word *prägen* (later *preigen*) described how someone or something is shaped or influenced by various factors.

Self-awareness is your most important tool as a leader.

Dare you to be genuine? Regardless, you as a leader influence the culture in your entity at every moment.

It's very simple: either your team thrives or it does not.

A

Situational leadership

_____

A leader without passion is like a dancer without body language.

Niclas Timmerby

As a leader, you will often find yourself in various situations that require you to make both straightforward and challenging decisions. I would like to suggest that the four choices outlined below are among the most important, *as they will govern the decisions you make and the evaluations you will need to conduct in the future.*

- Focus on influencing results or focus on influencing culture.
- Control systems or passion and will.
- Result-oriented leadership or value-driven leadership
- Assessment culture or development culture.

The foundation, regardless of your choices above, is to consciously engage in situational leadership.

If you are unaware of the current phase your organization is in, you will lack a clear understanding of how to lead effectively.

Therefore, this section addresses this crucial aspect. Here, you will receive the fundamentals, a process for how you as a leader can concretely begin to apply this theory, a proposal for a workshop that you can implement within your organization, as well as relevant studies related to this theory.

Situational leadership is grounded in research derived from studies and observations of leadership behaviors and their effects on employee performance and the work environment.

Paul Hersey and Ken Blanchard initially conducted research and observations to identify different leadership styles and their impact on employee motivation and performance.

They identified four main leadership styles: directive leadership, supportive leadership, participative leadership, and delegative leadership. These are sometimes reformulated as; authoritative, supportive, coaching, and delegative.

The four components of situational leadership.

What is your organization's overall maturity level, and in which phase is it currently situated regarding competence and engagement, both individually and as a group? Reflect on how you, as a leader, can influence and change these dynamics.

1. **Directive leadership**: This style is employed when the organization is newly formed or has a low maturity level. In this phase, the team requires clear instructions and guidelines to get started and to understand their roles and responsibilities. The leader provides explicit directives and takes control of the situation to guide the team in the right direction. *Summary: This approach is utilized when team members are inexperienced or possess low competence in the task at hand.*

2. **Supportive Leadership:** This style is employed when the organization has begun to develop and has reached a certain level of maturity. At this stage, the team can operate more independently but requires support and encouragement to continue growing. The leader provides feedback, encouragement, and assistance to enhance employees' confidence and motivation. *Summary: This approach is used when employees have some experience but still need support and persuasion to effectively perform their tasks.*

3. **Participative leadership (Coaching)**: Participative leadership is utilized when the entity has a high level of maturity and is capable of contributing its ideas and opinions. At this stage, the entity is self-driven and needs to be involved in decision-making to feel included and engaged. The leader promotes open communication, delegates responsibility, and encourages collaboration and creativity.

An additional aspect that has evolved within this concept is coaching leadership, which began to gain traction in business during the 1990s, notably through the work of Sir John Whitmore in his 1992

"The deeper you get to know your team members' emotions, values, motivations, drives, obstacles, goals, and dreams - the more they will contribute and be passionate about you as a leader."
- Niclas Timmerby, on the importance of tailored coaching

book "Coaching for Performance." This work emphasised the significance of employing coaching techniques and methods in corporate management to foster employee development and enhance performance. In this model, the leader acts as a coach or mentor, developing team members by asking questions, actively listening, providing feedback, and assisting them in identifying and achieving their goals. *Summary: This style is utilized when employees are competent and motivated but still require support and encouragement. It is important to recognize the two components: (A) "participative," which promotes open communication, delegates responsibility, and encourages collaboration and creativity; and (B) "coaching," which focuses on fostering individual development and growth by helping employees discover their own solutions and take responsibility for their personal development.*

4.**Delegating Leadership:** is employed when the group exhibits a high level of maturity, is self-sufficient, and possesses experience in their field. In this context, the group is capable of making their own decisions to achieve established goals. The leader provides support and resources as needed but grants the group responsibility and authority, along with the freedom to make decisions and take accountability for completing tasks. *Summary: This is used when the employees are both competent and motivated.*

Reflection exercise: My own entity.
Take about 15 minutes to reflect on your team members as you read the summaries again. Where do they stand today: 1, 2, 3, or 4?

Consider your own leadership journey as well. *A true leader does not merely focus on where people currently are; instead, a true leader sees it as their role to help individuals grow through their leadership.* How can you assist your team in their development?

_____
_____
_____
_____
_____
_____
_____
_____
_____
_____

Depending on where your entity is located today, it determines how you need to adapt your leadership to move your entity forward.

Before you begin your concrete work with conversations and workshops, it is important to focus on creating a sense of security for yourself.

Here, you will find the fundamentals in the form of a process description for continuously maintaining a successful culture within your entity. The purpose is to create an environment where team members thrive, perform at their highest level, and contribute to the success of the entity:

Step 1: Clear Communication and Vision.
Ensure that all team members understand the rationale behind the entity's vision. It is crucial to communicate this vision regularly and in a manner that engages and inspires; find creative ways to keep the vision ever-present, ensuring it is ingrained in everyone. The vision represents our "why." Why do we come to work every day? The answer is: We all come to work each day to collectively strive towards our common vision. *By fostering a shared understanding of the entity's vision, along with the values, goals, ambitions, and strategies that can be clearly linked to that vision, you establish the right conditions as a leader to build a strong foundation for the desired culture.*

Step 2: Create Participation and Engagement.
Involve team members in as much decision-making as possible and provide them with the opportunity to influence their work environment to promote participation and engagement. This can be achieved by organising regular team meetings, workshops, or brainstorming

sessions where everyone has the chance to contribute their ideas and perspectives in a structured manner. *By fostering a sense of ownership and shared responsibility, you cultivate a strong, loyal, and engaged culture.*

Step 3: Develop Strong Relationships.

Team members need to feel safe and motivated to elevate the culture to the next level. Encourage and support the development of robust relationships among team members, primarily through open communication. When team members can discuss anything openly with one another, knowing that conversations remain confidential within the entity (integrity), they feel secure, which gradually makes them increasingly open in their communications. This has a crucial positive effect: it reduces the risk of conflicts. Another significant benefit of fostering strong relationships is that team members become naturally motivated to come to work each day to contribute. *The passion for being in a workplace and within an entity where individuals feel safe and motivated becomes increasingly important, often surpassing the importance of salary.*

Step 4: Feedback and Development.

Later in the book, I will provide you with practical tips on how to foster an accepted feedback culture within your entity. Feedback at all four levels is fundamentally important for supporting the development of team members and is another essential step in building a strong and loyal culture. *By providing constructive and appreciative feedback on an individual basis, you cultivate a culture within the culture where team members feel valued and motivated to pursue continuous improvement.*

Step 5: Conflict Management and Problem Solving.

The more emphasis you place on Step 3 (open communication), the fewer conflicts are likely to arise within your entity. However, if conflicts do occur—which is natural in an environment where individuals are diverse—you will already have established a feedback culture (Step 4), making it easier to address conflicts early on. It is also important in your leadership role to listen and offer support when necessary to move forward constructively. As a leader, be prepared for problems and conflicts to arise, so you can address them effectively, calmly, and in an organised manner. An important point I wish to emphasise is that *the calmer and more structured you are in addressing problems and conflicts, the more respect you will earn from your team members. Even those who challenge you (as discussed later in the book) will appreciate your approach to handling conflicts and issues. Be attentive to the needs of your employees and act promptly to resolve any concerns, minimising negative effects on the culture.*

Here's how you can organise a workshop with your entity to assess whether your focus is more *task-oriented or relationship-oriented.* Understanding this balance is fundamentally important for effective situational leadership.

"Situational leadership is a key to success in today's dynamic and constantly changing work environment. By being responsive to employees' needs and adapting your leadership style, you can foster a culture of trust, collaboration, and innovation."
- John C. Maxwell

Through this interactive workshop, your entity can gain a deeper insight into the significance of balancing task focus and relationship focus in its work.

Expect a half-day for this workshop, which consists of:

Part 1: Participants will individually assess where they currently stand, determining whether they are more focused on tasks or relationships.

Part 2: A joint session where you collectively evaluate the exercise and openly discuss the insights gained. This is also an opportunity to talk about feelings and explore how to think differently about individual differences.

Part 1.

Create a cover page with the following information:

- A concise explanation of the purpose of the workshop, outlining the model from their perspective and what the workshop will entail.

- Emphasise that participants do not need to share their exact answers with anyone.

- Encourage participants to be honest and take their time to reflect before providing their ratings.

- Clarify that there are absolutely no right or wrong answers. The aim is to increase awareness of their preferences and how they can balance task focus and relationship focus in their work. Their honest responses will assist you as a leader in adapting your leadership approach more effectively to each individual and the group as a whole.

Self-Assessment Template - Task Focus / Relationship Focus

On page 29, you will find the self-assessment template. Before participants begin, clearly explain the rating process to ensure everyone understands how to assess themselves.

It is beneficial to go through Statement 1 together before allowing participants to work independently with the self-assessment template. If someone is not finished within the allotted time, do not rush them. Instead, say something like: *"Now we need to be quiet for a little while until everyone feels ready."*

Suggested Text for the Instruction Sheet:

During the workshop, you will see eight statements divided into two groups, with a line separating them. Statements 1-4 focus on task orientation, while statements 5-8 focus on relationship orientation.

You will rate yourself on a scale from 1 to 5 for each statement. The goal is to determine whether you have a more task-oriented or relationship-oriented approach to your work.

The number 3 represents a balance between task and relationship focus. Always start from the middle, i.e., "3,' to indicate balance. If you do not feel balanced, reflect on which direction you lean towards and make a choice.

The aids are (Agree) and (Disagree).

After the exercise, we will discuss the overall results together.

I want to emphasise that there are no right or wrong answers; the aim is to identify and increase awareness of your work patterns and behaviours. Please be open, honest, and engaged during the workshop to get the most out of the exercise.

Grading Scale:

1: Always the most task-focused.

2: More task-focused than balanced.

3: A balance between task focus and relationship focus.

4: More relationship-focused than balanced.

5: Always the most relationship-focused.

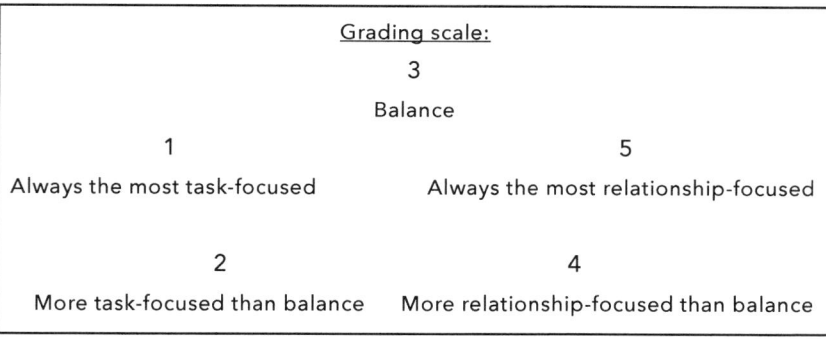

1.   I prioritise completing tasks and achieving goals above all else.

   (Agree)   1   2   3   4   5   (Disagree)

2.   I am more interested in achieving results than in building relationships with colleagues.

   (Agree)   1   2   3   4   5   (Disagree)

3.   I am more inclined to focus on details and efficiency than to take others' feelings into account.

   (Agree)   1   2   3   4   5   (Disagree)

4.   I am more focused on solving problems and making decisions than on building cooperation and strengthening relationships.

   (Agree)   1   2   3   4   5   (Disagree)

---

5. I prioritise building strong and positive relationships with my colleagues.

   (Disagree)   1   2   3   4   5   (Agree)

6.   I am more interested in creating a positive work environment than in achieving quick results.

   (Disagree)   1   2   3   4   5   (Agree)

7.   I am more inclined to show empathy and listen to others' needs than to focus on completing tasks.

   (Disagree)   1   2   3   4   5   (Agree)

8.   I am more focused on building collaboration and creating a positive work culture than making quick decisions.

   (Disagree)   1   2   3   4   5   (Agree)

Part 2.

<u>After their work is finished: Evaluation and Feedback</u>

- Ask everyone to share which number they received the most of, if they feel comfortable doing so. (Sometimes multiple numbers can share the highest score, and that is perfectly acceptable.)

- Take notes in the meantime so you can clearly convey how the data is weighted, whether it is balanced or skewed more towards one focus or the other. There is nothing wrong with this; however, it is beneficial for you as a leader in upcoming recruitment drives to have a clear picture of how your team is structured. Feel free to use the self-assessment template during interviews.

- Request evaluation and feedback from team members. Ask them how they experienced the workshop and what they learned from it, and whether they feel better equipped to manage both task and relationship focus to appreciate the benefits of diversity and their own development.

- Provide participants with the opportunity to share their insights with the group, taking careful notes so that you, as a leader, can identify concrete tools and strategies for use in future individual and group discussions.

- Read or display what scores 1+2, 3, and 4+5 signify (on the next page) so that everyone leaves with a clear understanding from the workshop.

Now that you are aware of your team's positioning, this insight can very likely lead to more open communication and a better understanding of natural differences.

(Most task-focused):
If you predominantly selected 1 and 2, it indicates a strong focus on completing tasks and achieving goals above all else. You prioritise achieving results and concentrate on details and efficiency, as you are more inclined to solve problems than to foster collaboration. You are a valuable member of the team!

(Balance):
If you predominantly selected 3, it suggests a balance between task focus and relationship focus. You prioritise both completing tasks and building relationships with colleagues. You consider both details and efficiency as well as others' feelings. You are inclined to solve problems and make decisions while also nurturing collaboration and strengthening relationships. You are a valuable member of the team!

(Most relationship-focused):
If you predominantly selected 4 and 5, it signifies a strong inclination towards building strong and positive relationships with colleagues. You prioritise creating a positive work environment and are less concerned with achieving quick results. You demonstrate empathy and listen to others' needs, focusing more on fostering collaboration and cultivating a positive work culture. You are a valuable member of the team!

Research on situational leadership.

Research shows positive effects on employees' motivation, performance, and job satisfaction. By flexibly adapting your leadership style to the situation and the needs of your employees, you as a leader can foster a positive work environment and create conditions to successful outcomes.

Three examples of contemporary studies on this theory:

1. A study from 2018 examined the effects of situational leadership in healthcare. The study showed that situational leadership was positively correlated with employee job satisfaction and performance. Source: Kuo, C. C., & Lin, C. Y. (2018).

2. One study from 2017 investigated how situational leadership affects employee performance within a technical organization. The study showed that situational leadership was positively correlated with employee performance and job satisfaction. Source: Felfe, J., & Schyns, B. (2006).

3. A third study from 2016 examined the effects of situational leadership within a military organization. The study showed that situational leadership was positively correlated with employee motivation and performance. Source: Bjugstad, K., Thach, E., & Thompson, K. (2006)

Reflection, section A

1. Reflect on your leadership style today; is it in symbiosis with your entity?

2. Consider your communication style (tone, body language, word choice, voice strength, and other factors that affect how the message is received by the recipient). Is it in harmony with your entity? Does it align with how you wish to lead? Your communication style is influenced by various factors, including personality, upbringing, cultural background, education, and experiences. Do you challenge yourself, or do you expect your communication style to be accepted and respected by everyone in your entity? Is your communication style propelling you and your entity forward?

3. Reflect on the risks you face if you lead your entity with a leadership style that is out of sync with its current state.

> For example:
>> A. What risk do you encounter if you micromanage an entity that is competent and motivated?
>> B. What risk do you face f you delegate to an entity that requires supportive leadership?

4. Your entity comprises individuals at different stages; they come from various cultures and backgrounds. Reflect on your current leadership style and consider how you can adapt your approach to better engage everyone.

5. Utilise feedback, coaching, and employee conversations to foster open individual communication, where you challenge and develop your team members in their current phase, enabling them to function better and understand their colleagues.

6. Dedicate time each month to sit in silence for an hour to reflect: Where are you and your entity headed? Are you progressing towards the vision? Is there open communication? Is there an accepted feedback culture? Are the coaching conversations forward-looking? What do you need to prioritise in the coming month?

(Tip: Use paper and pen for this personal reflection, avoiding digital tools. However, feel free to summarise digitally when you feel ready.)

B

Focus on influencing results or culture

Leadership is largely determined not by what you say,
but by how the people around you feel.
Niclas Timmerby

Now that we have laid the foundation and you have a clear understanding of where your organisation currently stands, as well as the tools available to aid each team member and the group as a whole in their growth, it is time to make your first choice.

In every thought you have at the workplace, there is a fundamental idea that drives your approach to leadership, which directly impacts how both you and your organisation feel. It centres on how you will achieve your goals and ambitions, as well as those of the organisation.

Most often, it is numbers that dominate a leader's thoughts and focus. These numbers take the form of targets, budgets, revenue, personnel costs, cash flow, liquidity, equity, debt ratios, gross profit, operating margins, capital turnover rates, and more. *This is entirely natural*; all types of entities must achieve essential key figures and generate profit to survive. At times, owners have profitability as a prerequisite for continuing to drive the organisation, or profit is necessary to create a buffer or to invest in remaining competitive. If an organisation does not achieve profitability, there is no basis for its continued operation. It is a hygiene factor.

The practice of communicating targets to motivate organisations to achieve goals has been in place for over a century.

In the 1920s, it is documented that General Electric, under the leadership of business leader and strategist Alfred P. Sloan, introduced management by objectives by setting specific and measurable goals for each division within the company to monitor and manage their performance.

Approximately 75 years ago, in the 1950s, various management by objectives systems and the use of targets became increasingly accepted in business.

Now, I want to challenge this notion and put it to the test.
There is ongoing debate surrounding the use of targets as a methodology in business and education, suggesting that they can lead to detrimental effects. Do targets genuinely measure and promote real performance, or does the focus shift towards quantity rather than quality?

There are also questions regarding whether targets can be demotivating for employees or if they can lead to narrow and limited goals that are not necessarily relevant or beneficial to the organisation as a whole.

So, are targets the appropriate factor to focus on when leading team members? In the 2020s, in today's society, culture, and climate, do they inspire motivation, will, and passion?

Is it truly targets today that encourage individuals to contribute, to energise the entity, to feel a desire to remain in the business, to instil pride, to speak positively about the entity to others, and to feel that it is progressing?

I am well aware of various concepts, such as The Performance Management Chain, which suggest that if an entity, *in simplified terms,* works with measurable goals, feedback, and coaching, it can achieve the desired results.

My opinion is that overarching targets are necessary, but the focus for achieving long-term success must be on influencing the culture.

Focusing on numbers and targets and allowing them to dictate the atmosphere in the workplace can yield excellent results in the short term. An entity can achieve short-term profitability by concentrating on targets; however, given that *what* people seek from their workplace to feel stimulated has changed dramatically over the past 20 to 30 years, there are significant risks in today's society for an entity that prioritises targets over building a positive, sustainable, and enjoyable culture.

Allow me to explain:

In the 1760s in Britain, The Industrial Revolution began, marking approximately 260 years ago. Previously, people worked on a small scale, primarily in agriculture and crafts, often within families or local communities. However, something exceptional occurred; urbanisation began as factories and other larger facilities required a workforce in significant numbers to perform specific and repetitive tasks.

"Culture is the key to unlocking the potential of every organization."
- Daniel Coyle

- People were bound to fixed working hours and specific workplaces.
- They had to work to secure a decent living.
  - (In Sweden, where I reside, the first known poorhouse was established in Stockholm as early as 1626. However, it was socially stigmatizing to rely on poor relief, and many lived in extreme poverty due to a lack of access to information. "Poor relief districts," where each parish or municipality was

responsible for assistance, were introduced in Sweden in the
late 1800s and early 1900s.)
- *Many workers were treated very poorly but adapted because they*
  needed employment to survive. Although working conditions were
  often dire and the working days long—particularly within the textile,
  mining, machinery, food, iron, and steel industries, and notably within
  the arms industry during the First and Second World Wars—workers
  (some as young as five or six years old), adapted to their
  circumstances.

A considerable time later, as the Industrial Revolution spanned
approximately 220 to 230 years, the culture within society began to
change.

Around 1980, The Information Society began to emerge as people
increasingly utilised advanced technology to control machines. The
year 1991 is widely regarded as the point at which the information
society became known to everyone, with the advent of the internet. As I
write this book in 2025, it has been only 34 years since the information
society made its entrance as a new cultural paradigm.

When a culture changes, the people within it change.
Society transforms, behaviours evolve, attitudes shift, language use
adapts, conditions and opportunities alter, and, not least, workplaces
undergo significant changes.

People in the information society no longer worked merely to survive, as
there was now a well-functioning social safety net. Instead, individuals
began to work for a better standard of living.

- *They worked to save money, to travel, and to purchase their own homes, boats, or cars.*
- *A person could switch jobs for another if the salary was slightly better, allowing them to improve their standard of living.*
- ***Targets became extremely important,*** *as achieving them meant greater opportunities for higher salaries, bonuses, or other benefits.*
- *Those born into the information society adapted to these changes but began to seek personal development at work. Consequently, well-being and the work environment became increasingly significant.*

Then, change occurred rapidly; the information society lasted only about seventeen years. By around 2008, the next culture emerged: <u>The Digital/Social Revolution</u>.

In just seventeen years, society underwent another transformation. With the digital/social revolution, technology became more accessible and affordable for everyone. Before long, individuals could use "free" technology (the internet) to learn to build a deck, listen to lectures, study geography and languages, or even master advanced coding.

"Culture is what holds the organization together and gives it a unique identity. It influences how employees feel comfortable, perform, and engage in their work."
- Unknown

The first phone with an internet connection was the "Nokia 9000 Communicator," launched in 1996. It featured a built-in browser and could connect to the internet via a built-in modem. However, it was with the launch of the "iPhone 2G" in 2007 that the internet became an integral part of daily life. Soon, as internet usage became more affordable, many people found themselves with round-the-clock access.

- Today's younger generation does not pursue quality of life as fervently as their parents; instead, they are focused on achieving a fulfilling **quality of life**. They are concerned about the environment and the well-being of the planet.
- Consequently, in the workplace, they are less interested in high salaries, which are no longer the primary motivation in this culture. **As a result, the drive for performance targets diminishes**.
- Instead, people seek a vision; they desire meaning and purpose, well-being, a healthy work environment, and opportunities for personal development. They often ask, "Where are we going so I can decide if I want to come along? How will you lead and motivate me?" It is essential to be prepared for their continuous questioning.
- They value soft attributes, such as a positive and sustainable corporate culture, effective leadership, collaboration, and strong ethics. In contrast, hard values (which you may recall from page 36) hold less significance and driving force in this culture.
- What young people primarily wish to experience in their workplaces today is **engagement**. According to The Deloitte Millennial Survey (which focuses on the generation that grew up between 1981 and 1996), the main reason they want to remain in a job is engagement.
- It is crucial for you as a leader to educate yourself about **generation-adapted leadership** to understand the opportunities and challenges associated with this generation. **By comprehending their culture, you can better understand their needs and lead them in a manner that benefits all parties involved**.

Since then, the pace of change has accelerated even further. At an almost unbelievable rate, The AI Society has emerged as the new culture.

The year 2020 is considered the starting point of the AI revolution, occurring just twelve years after the onset of the digital/social revolution. It is still too early to fully grasp how this will transform the entirety of the new culture to which we must all adapt as our new reality. What we have already observed is that AI is ubiquitous, manifesting in the form of chatbots, self-driving cars, customer service applications, social media, and virtual/digital assistants.

<u>Amidst all this, it is important to recognise that what we are witnessing is entirely natural.</u> As humans evolve and discover new technologies, societies and cultures change, and over time, more people, societies, and cultures undergo transformation as well.

As early as 1956, the first AI laboratory was established in conjunction with a conference on formal research in artificial intelligence. Researchers convened to discuss the possibilities of creating intelligent machines. During the conference, they identified several problem areas that would become the focus of their research, including machine learning, natural language processing, problem formulation and solution methods, abstract thinking, and self-correction. Thus, what we observe around us today has been developing for approximately 65 years.

Reflect briefly on the time spans thus far and consider how profoundly different people's needs have become over this period.

Reflect on your own experiences in comparison to those of younger or older colleagues, friends, parents, and relatives. Do you share the same general perspectives on various matters, especially considering that you may have been raised in different cultures? I find myself, humbly, uncertain about that.

The four most recent cultural shifts include:

- Around the year 1760, The Industrial Revolution marked the transition from agrarian societies to industrialised ones, profoundly changing economic structures and social dynamics.
- The Information Society, emerging around 1980 and becoming widely recognised with the advent of the internet in 1991, this cultural shift transformed how people accessed information and communicated.
- The Digital/Social Revolution beginning around 2008, this shift made technology more affordable and accessible, fostering a culture of learning and interaction through digital platforms.
- The AI Revolution, beginning around 2020, is marked by the rapid integration of artificial intelligence into daily life, impacting various aspects of society and individual behaviour.

These cultural shifts have shaped generational perspectives and values, leading to significant differences in how people relate to technology, work, and social responsibility.

Why are young people so different from "when I was young"?

As someone over 50 years old, I have often wondered why things generally seem so different today: What has happened to the respect for society and for others, as well as the willingness to contribute without demanding anything in return? Why is there such a challenging working environment for preschool teachers, educators, and subject teachers? Unfortunately, I hear fewer and fewer people express gratitude, and I witness an increasing number of individuals neglecting to use turn signals. Why is this the case? The answer becomes evident when considering how cultural shifts have altered people's needs. When I was growing up, my siblings and I had to adapt to various circumstances. If my mother asked me to go grocery shopping, I did so without objection. If she requested that I mow the lawn or clean the basement, I complied without hesitation. In school, students showed respect for their teachers, and if anyone was disrespectful or cheeky, it resulted in an immediate call home, leading to a mortified parent having to collect their child—without objection.

"To lead people, you as a leader need to understand people's needs.

If you understand the incredible power of culture, you understand people's needs."
- Niclas Timmerby

The key word here is "adapt." We adapted, and our parents adapted as well. We followed the culture instilled in us by our parents. What has transpired is that parenting practices have changed drastically, quite naturally, given the evolution of cultures. Instead of children being expected to adapt, they are asked, "What do you **want**? Do you **want** an ice cream? Do you **want** to eat now?*
It is commendable that the traditional view of parenting has shifted away from an authoritarian, hierarchical structure in which parents held "power" and children were expected to be obedient.

With the cultural shifts we have experienced, it is now more common for children to be involved in decision-making, with adults actively seeking their opinions and preferences. I gained insight when I studied different cultures; my strong reactions stem from my upbringing in the older "adaptation culture," which makes the "want culture" feel very foreign and even wrong to me. In simple terms, cultures are immensely powerful, rendering us as individuals somewhat powerless against the natural changes that accompany cultural shifts. Keep this in mind as you, each day as a leader, cultivate the culture within your entity; Do you engage everyone? Do you possess a deep self-awareness of how your leadership style impacts those around you?

If I may add a perspective beyond the organisational context, I have reflected on 15+1 aspects of upbringing and parenting that, regardless of culture, are crucial for parents to instil in their children from an early age. This foundation will help children navigate their personal and professional journeys more easily as they grow.

1. *Right and wrong (ethics)*

2. *Mine and yours (rules)*

3. *Cooperation (to listen and help one another)*

4. *Gratitude (to express thanks and snow appreciation for what one receives)*

5. *Contribution (to gain something in life, one must first give)*

6. *Perspective (to recognise that the world does not revolve around oneself)*

7. *Humility (to acknowledge when one has erred and to apologise). This also includes patience—waiting for one's turn.*

8. *Generosity (to share with others and offer assistance)*

9. *Economics (to understand the value of money*

10. *Care (to show concern for people and possessions)*

11. *Empathy (to demonstrate compassion for people, animals, and nature, particularly when someone is unwell or something has been harmed)*

12. *Equality (to recognise that everyone deserves to be treated kindly and that no one is more valuable than another based on gender, age, or other factors)*

13. *Setting boundaries (to ensure that parents remain consistent in their statements, e.g., "If you don't finish your meal, you won't get dessert." Additionally, to teach children to advocate for themselves and assert their right to fair treatment)*

14. *As a parent, avoid speaking ill of others, commenting on appearance or knowledge, and refrain from irony or sarcasm. This*

fosters a sense of security in children, enabling them to trust others and take responsibility.

15. Encourage self-sufficiency (to equip children to handle life's natural challenges, failures, and adversities)

15+1. Explaining life. In the free world, children grow up with an idealised vision of how life should be. It is crucial to explain to children, as they enter their teenage years, that while this ideal image is beautiful, obstacles in life are inevitable. Events and situations will cause pain, including failures, difficult challenges, setbacks, heartbreak, gossip, disappointments, and tragedies. When the ideal image shatters, the critical question is: how do you respond? Can you cultivate enough strength and insight within yourself to navigate a life that sometimes takes unexpected turns? It is important to recognise that not everything is someone's fault; sometimes, life simply unfolds as it does. Young people need to develop a gentle understanding that life changes over time, much like stones in the sea. This understanding is essential for their personal development and self-image regarding their self-concept and identity. It prepares them to embrace change rather than be overwhelmed by it. Acknowledging that the ideal image can be shattered is not cynicism; rather, it is a gift that enables one to better handle life's challenges. Facing life's challenges independently fosters a sense of inner security.

I hope you now recognise the immense power that a cultural shift brings. As cultural changes occur more rapidly than ever, they impose significant demands on your leadership.

Where do your team members currently stand, considering their age and cultural backgrounds? How is each individual coping with the rapid societal changes?

Do you understand their needs?

It is not surprising that individuals feel uncertain and anxious about the future of society. **Have the courage to address existential matters in employee conversations to foster closer connections with your team and cultivate greater trust.** *Topics may include the meaning and purpose of life, death, loneliness, fears, identity (Who am I?), morality, ethics, self-actualisation, and more. In my conversations with employees, I have often been surprised to find that those I expected to speak the least had the most profound thoughts to share.*

Dare to open up, express your emotions, and then listen, listen, listen, and listen some more. This fosters deep trust.

In your employee conversations, consider the following:

- *Why do your team members come to work? What motivates them?*
- *What do they need to feel inclined to stay?*
- *What do they require to perceive their development within the workplace?*
- *What do they need to feel that they are growing as individuals?*

Reflect on these questions yourself:

- *Why do I go to work? What is my drive?*
- *Does my team trust me?*
- *Do they feel loyalty to me and the organisation?*
- *Do they feel safe in the workplace, able to be themselves?*
- *Do they understand "why" we are all at work? (The vision, mission, shared foundation of values, goals, ambitions, etc.)*

A prerequisite for genuinely leading with a focus on influencing culture is to have an accurate and compassionate view of humanity.
If you lead authentically from your deepest values, your team will sense it. Conversely, if you do not lead genuinely, they will also feel that absence.

The most important aspect of your self-leadership is genuineness.
Being true to yourself and daring to show your authentic qualities despite stress and pressure. If you fail to lead genuinely, it will not end well in the long run; either you or your environment will suffer. Dare to be authentic by being yourself.

A genuinely good and true view of humanity acknowledges the complexity, potential, and value of your fellow human beings. *In your role as a leader, it is essential to recognise that everyone has potential.*

One of your most important, yet often unmentioned, tasks in a leader's job description is to help each individual team member gain insight into their potential, enabling them to see, understand, and desire to grow and develop.

You promote well-being, justice, equality, and diversity. You dare to demonstrate empathy, compassion, respect, and dignity. You advocate for human rights and everyone's right to be their true selves within the organisation.

"Those who gain insight into the benefits and the positive synergies of leading with a focus on culture will never want to lead in any other way."
- Niclas Timmerby

As a leader, you consistently stand up for your team.

*I once heard an incredibly wise perspective on a good and true view of humanity: **all people can and want to develop if they are provided with the conditions needed to succeed**.*

The fundamentally important "why".
What is absolutely most important for your team? Have you asked this question to your team members during job interviews, in everyday conversations, or during performance discussions? If you have established trust with your team, you will receive honest answers.

Often, we assume, guess, and interpret why others behave in certain ways without actually asking them. Instead, we continue to hypothesize, consciously and unconsciously, until our unfounded beliefs become our reality.

This reality influences how we perceive humanity. As long as you, as a leader, operate on assumptions, you cannot see or harness the potential of your entity.

A study conducted by Manpower posed the question to leaders: What is most important for your employees?

They also asked the leaders to guess what they thought the employees would respond. *Here are the top three guesses made by the leaders regarding employee priorities, in order of importance:*

1. Salary
2. Promotion opportunities
3. Job security

In contrast, here is what employees actually prioritized:

1. *To be seen*
2. *Interesting/challenging tasks*
3. *Participation*
4. *Personal development*
5. *Personal responsibility for results*
6. *Salary*
7. *Conditions (working hours, benefits, distance to workplace, etc.)*

Can you see the connection in these responses, especially in light of earlier discussions about the power of cultural shifts?
It's not surprising that employees responded this way, given that the study was conducted several cultural shifts after the Industrial Revolution.

Numerous studies demonstrate that *having too many active goals simultaneously can deteriorate performance, well-being, and results. One well-known study, "The Impact of Organizational Culture on Employee Engagement and Performance: A Meta-Analysis" by Wang and Hsieh, examined the relationship between organizational cultures and employee engagement.*

The purpose was to identify specific aspects that demonstrate what has the greatest impact on an employee's engagement and performance. Published in 2013 in the Journal of Business and Psychology, this study occurred almost exactly in the midst of the social/digital revolution and the current AI revolution.

The researchers conducted a meta-analysis, analyzing data from 87 previous studies in the field using statistical methods to compile and interpret the results.

Having read a portion of this book, you can infer what the study demonstrated, as you know what members of today's culture seek. The results revealed that four aspects of organizational culture are particularly important for promoting employee engagement and performance:

1. Strong leadership
2. Clear values and goals
3. Open communication
4. Supportive work environment

As you can see, clear goals were included in the study, and after working in both smaller and larger entities for over 30 years, I understand that. Clear goals will always be a significant part of achieving success, regardless of the field or organizational structure.

"A true leader understands that it is not the people who are "wrong".
It is the communication between them that is flawed."
- Niclas Timmerby

What I have experienced in reality is that the goals at the end of the 1980s and the beginning of the 1990s, when I started working, were <u>very few but incredibly clear and well communicated to everyone</u>.

Now, in the 2020s, the goals are almost infinite and therefore unclear. It is disheartening, as it raises the question: how can this be the case when we now know so much more, and entire departments in large companies are focused on issues related to this?

Are companies and organisations so entrenched in outdated cultures that they fail to recognise reality, understand the impact of cultural shifts on societies and individuals, and comprehend what stimulates and motivates team members today?

A study by FranklinCovey, conducted by Stephen Covey, shows that:
- With 2-3 active goals running simultaneously, you achieve 2-3 goals.
- With 4-10 active goals running simultaneously, you achieve 1-2 goals.
- With 11-20 active goals running simultaneously, you achieve 0 goals.

Solution: Clearly and formally close outdated goals.
The conclusion is that too many goals create ambiguity, leading team members to feel overwhelmed by the targets. *"What should I/we really focus on?"*

What I have observed while working in various entities is that goals are created, which is entirely natural. However, *they are rarely closed before new goals are established*.

If you want your entity to have a greater chance of achieving the goals you set, my strong recommendation is:

1. Maintain a maximum of 2-3 very clear goals active at the same time, with specific deadlines for each goal.

2. Establish two sub-goals for each main goal that are relevant and measurable for each team member; this allows you, as a leader, to state: if you achieve these two sub-goals, the organisation will reach the main goal.

3. Conduct continuous follow-ups on the progress in relation to the sub-goals and respective main goals.

4. Check in with your team members during follow-ups; is anything unclear? What obstacles are you currently facing in reaching the goals? Do you need additional resources to achieve the goal, and if so, what?

5. When the deadline for each goal arrives, formally and clearly close the goal. For example, say: *'You have worked hard on this; this is the result, and now we will close this goal. Thank you for your efforts."*

6. Evaluation: Create a simple form for inputting thoughts and feelings. *What did we do well, and what can we improve in the future?*

Later on, in the section discussing the importance of consciously leading with the vision, you will see an even clearer connection to the team members' "why."

The vision is the "why."

Summary:
Focus on influencing results or focus on influencing culture.

Everyone in an entity knows where the focus lies; <u>they become acutely aware of it from their very first day in the workplace</u>.

We have concluded that both aspects are essential within an organisation, even in the 2020s. A focus on goals is necessary, as is a focus on culture. However, the balance between these two has shifted.

In light of the rapid cultural changes we have experienced, my perspective is that having a few very clear and time-bound goals is beneficial for team members. Naturally, there should be multiple goals within the organisation that align with its long-term strategies and vision.

To foster drive, motivation, and engagement across all ages and cultures, my recommendation is to prioritise the development of a positive and genuine culture.

As a leader, you play a crucial role in creating and maintaining this culture. Everyone in an organisation seeks clarity. Everyone. Clarity reduces feelings of stress, uncertainty, confusion, and misunderstanding. It enhances motivation, engagement, trust, and confidence, and promotes effective collaboration.

Setting clear goal images that are consistently reviewed and formally concluded is a straightforward and effective methodology for establishing a fundamental, continuous structure of security within entities.

Focusing on results can certainly yield positive short-term outcomes. Focusing on culture can undoubtedly lead to favourable long-term outcomes.

Culture <u>invariably</u> influences the work environment.

<u>A results-oriented focus fosters a culture centred on achieving outcomes.</u>
<u>A culture-focused approach cultivates an environment that facilitates results.</u>

Focus on influencing results, it creates a cycle where everything begins and ends with outcomes. When a team member joins an entity, they hear about the previous results achieved and the goals set to surpass those results.

This shapes the work environment and, in turn, creates a culture of high expectations and a drive to exceed past performances. However, this can sometimes foster competition over collaboration and lead to a stressful work environment, where team members fear failure due to the pressure to constantly outperform themselves.

A significant negative consequence of such a culture is that team members may experience ongoing anxiety about failing, which stifles their creativity, willingness to take risks, and pride in the organisation.

"As long as you, as a leader, operate based on assumptions without truly understanding the 'why,' you cannot recognise and harness the potential within your organisation."
- Niclas Timmerby

A focus on past results constructs a work environment where outcomes shape a culture that influences future results.

Focus on influencing culture. By concentrating on cultivating a culture of openness, respect, trust, well-being, diversity, and happiness, an environment is established where these soft values significantly impact team members' daily lives, behaviours, attitudes, and norms.

This cultural influence affects communication and the interactions and actions of team members.

I recall visiting an organisation I led a decade ago, where I emphasised a cultural focus. We built an incredibly strong team with a wonderful work environment. Revenue increased by 73 percent in one year, despite maintaining the same products, premises, and opening hours.

I asked a long-standing team member about the culture. She replied, "It's the same as we created ten years ago—a relaxed environment filled with humour. All of us old ones are still here!" This response fills me with pride and demonstrates that the methodology is effective.

"What are the overwhelmingly most important factors for an entity to achieve good liquidity and solvency?

1. *The people in the team.*
2. *The people in the team.*
3. *The people in the team.*
4. *All other factors.*

- Niclas Timmerby

A work environment shaped by a healthy culture fosters motivation, engagement, and well-being, leading to reduced employee turnover and noticeable stress. A positive workplace culture is likely to result in increased employee engagement and higher profitability, as supported by various studies.

*Focusing on culture **constructs** a work environment where a healthy culture influences future results.*

Research on how corporate culture affects various factors.

"Which team members do you prefer: those who come to work solely for the salary, or those who come to work for the sake of the culture?"
- Niclas Timmerby

A study conducted by Harvard Business School demonstrated that companies with a strong and positive workplace culture exhibited higher productivity and profitability. These organisations also showed a greater ability to attract and retain talented employees.

A study published in the Journal of Occupational and Environmental Medicine revealed that organisations with a positive workplace culture experienced lower levels of work-related stress and better physical and mental health among employees.

Research published in the Journal of Applied Psychology indicated that organisations with a strong and positive workplace culture achieved higher levels of employee engagement, performance, and customer satisfaction. Additionally, these organisations reported lower employee turnover and absenteeism.

A study published in the Journal of Organizational Behavior found that employees who feel secure and encouraged to share ideas and think creatively are more likely to contribute to the organisation's innovation and success.

Reflection, Section B

1. Reflect on the atmosphere within your entity. If you were newly hired, how would you perceive the work environment and culture?

2. If you were newly employed, what immediate feelings arise when you hear yourself communicate? Is the focus on culture or on results? Does what is communicated during interviews and in job descriptions match reality?

3. Based on the section regarding cultural shifts, do you understand the needs and motivations of all your team members?

4. Do you consider yourself to have a genuinely good and accurate view of humanity?

5. How many active goals do your team members currently have that are not clearly and formally closed?

6. What balance do you maintain in your approach to leading and motivating? Is your predominant focus on influencing results, or is it primarily on influencing culture?

7. Reflect on how you can influence the culture in your role and within your entity. Do you have the courage to be authentic in front of your superiors and your entity?

C

Control systems or passion and will

You are the one who changes the culture, the people, and the outcomes.

It is not your words, checklists, knowledge, experience, or CV.

Niclas Timmerby

Now that we have covered section A and B, it is time to connect the next process step in **the foundation**, and I am making the steps more comprehensive now. The next choice for you as a leader is how you genuinely wish to lead your entity; with control systems or with passion and will?

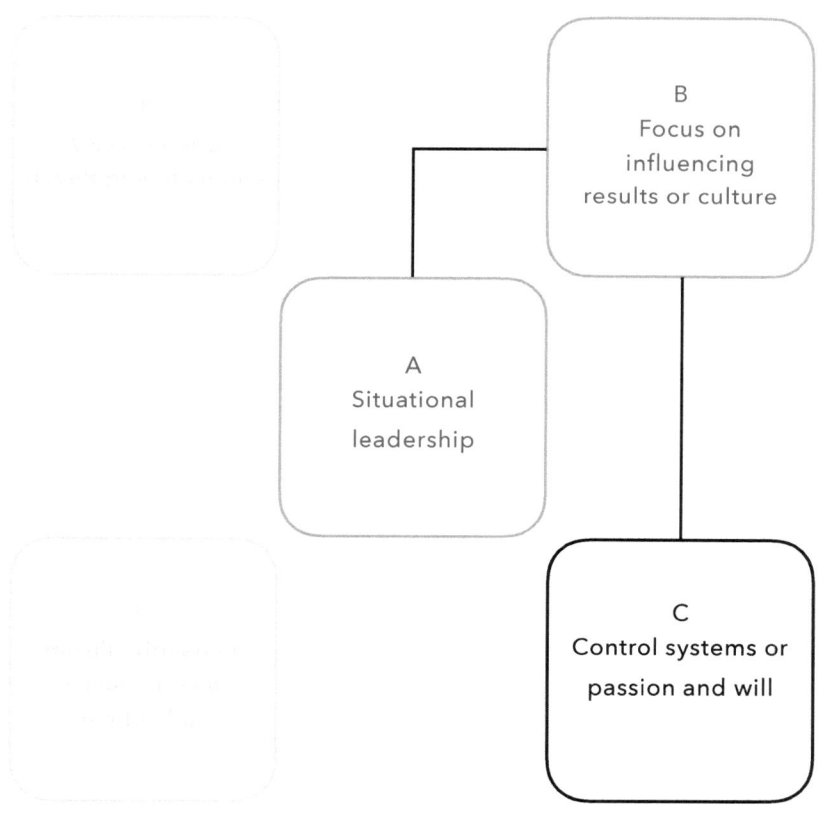

This section of the book is pivotal as you, as a leader, begin to reflect more formally and officially, with the entity's best interests in mind, on how daily work is led and perhaps actively seek to change it. How are team members motivated today, and is it worth openly reviewing whether this methodology is truly the right one in the long term?

(Later in the book, a separate chapter on trust-based leadership will be clearly linked to this section.)

This section comprises the following main parts:
1. Many companies communicate that they have a flat organisational structure, yet they still unknowingly (?) lead as if they have a hierarchical organisation.
2. Your control systems weighted towards passion and will.

First, an introduction.

Paradigms = a theory or accepted understanding that has been regarded as a truth.
I want to first highlight paradigms because an increasingly popular expression in everyday life is "paradigm shift." The term itself is used to describe a dramatic change or shift in fundamental mindsets, perspectives, or ways of thinking within a certain area.

A famous example of a paradigm shift is the scientific revolution in the 1500s and 1600s when Copernicus and Galileo Galilei questioned the then-prevailing geocentric worldview and introduced the heliocentric model of the solar system. The discovery during the same era that our planet is not flat is retrospectively referred to as a significant paradigm shift. The concepts of *paradigm*, *paradigm shift*, and *paradigm displacement* were introduced by Thomas Kuhn in his book "The Structure of Scientific Revolutions," published in 1962. Kuhn argues in the book that scientific paradigms are stable and dominant until they encounter enough anomalies and challenges that cannot be explained within the existing paradigm. Then a paradigm shift can occur, where a new way of thinking and new theories take over. As a historian of science and philosopher, his thesis was that scientific progress does not occur gradually and linearly, but rather through periodic changes and revolutions in thinking and methods. Kuhn's work has had a significant impact on the philosophy of science and has contributed to a critical understanding of scientific development and change. His theories have also been applied in areas outside of science, such as technology, economics, and social sciences.

Can you see your entity's paradigm as the correct paradigm?
After what you have read about cultural shifts, are the methodologies employed in your organisation the most appropriate, or are there other truths that are better aligned with current cultures? Are paradigm shifts or paradigm displacements relevant?

Reflect on the dramatic journey that the generation approaching well-deserved retirement has undergone:
Approximately 65 years ago, they grew up in the midst of the Cold War during the industrial revolution and culture. If they generally started working at 20 years old, it was then 1973; around 1980, the next culture (the information society) began to gradually take hold, even though it was not fully established until 1991. Around 2008, they began to adapt to the next culture (the digital/social revolution), and now, as they approach retirement, they must adapt to the AI revolution.

Considering all these significant shifts, could it be wise and insightful to review what motivates team members and organisations? I want to emphasise that I feel this is an absolute necessity, as we cannot assume that the culture that predominates today in society and drives people's needs will remain a lasting paradigm over time. History and facts show that we need to be very flexible.

Consider the synergies with situational leadership and flexible leadership, both of which are absolutely necessary as they focus on adapting leadership styles according to current circumstances and situations, and the needs that arise while highlighting the importance of being flexible to motivate team members and achieve results.

- *You have the ability to adapt and be flexible.*
- *You can be authoritative when quick decisions and clear directives are required, but also participative and supportive to accommodate the needs, creativity, and initiative of team members.*
- *You have the ability to link flexible leadership to the phase or situation your organisation and each team member is in.*

Reflecting on and discussing what motivates the team members in your entity involves insightfully and benevolently questioning outdated organisational thinking, whose theories and methods can be traced back to the early 1900s.

It has been over 100 years. It is high time to begin letting go of theories that are a century old and to focus on concepts that better align with the recent cultural shifts. We need to consider approaches that are more applicable to both older and younger individuals and that are more relevant for team members with diverse backgrounds.

What are your truths?

You are, and have always been, surrounded by paradigms your whole life; you have encountered various types of truths and have been influenced since you were a newborn. All these truths that other people have had and consciously or unconsciously "given you" play a significant role in shaping who you see yourself as today (your identity).

When a person consciously or unconsciously influences another through behaviour, values, life choices, or simply personality, this is known as imprinting. *The influence can be so strong and powerful that a single sentence can shape another person's life.*

For instance, if you have a fear of the dark, snakes, spiders, speaking in front of people, the ocean, or death, it is likely because (1) you have experienced trauma or (2) you have been imprinted by someone close to you who said, "that is scary" or "that is dangerous," usually with the best of intentions.

"To discover your truth, you must have the courage to question everything you have learned."
- Albert Einstein

Humans are born with only two innate fears: falling and loud noises. This logically implies that all other fears we develop as adults are a result of imprinting. We have heard or read "the truth" somewhere, and thus it has become our truth.

The troubling aspect of paradigms or truths is that they can be easily passed on, especially to young people, who view us adults as role models and examples. It is our duty as adults, particularly as parents and leaders, to be mindful and take responsibility for our considerable influence.

<u>All individuals constantly influence their surroundings.</u>
When I conduct leadership training or lectures, I highlight this fact at the outset so that everyone in the room can gain insight, become aware, and begin to reflect on their immense superpower:

The superpower we all possess is <u>our ability to influence others</u>, which makes us all superheroes.

I am reminded of Peter Parker's Uncle Ben, who tells him: "With great power comes great responsibility."

For those of you with leadership responsibilities, Ben's words are directed squarely at you. You are a leader; you are the superhero that everyone should follow and look up to. All eyes are on you; how do you take responsibility for what you emit and, consequently, influence your entity?

"The imprinting of our lives depends not on what happens to us, but on how we choose to react to it."
- Viktor Frankl

- *What emotions do you bring into a room?*
- *When you leave the room, what emotions do you leave behind?*
- *You don't even need to speak; you are constantly sending signals to others.*
- *When you arrive at the workplace, how do you influence people and the culture through the signals you project?*

Your superpower remains with you even after you leave the meeting, the room, or the workplace. Even when you are on holiday, it lingers at the workplace; your superpower that influences the culture and the people within it. <u>Your superpower is ever-present.</u>

What you transmit to others are signals in the form of hormones. You also have neurotransmitters, which can be described as chemical messengers that transmit information between the brain and your body. Each neurotransmitter has a unique role in your brain and body, affecting, among other things, your appetite, sleep, mood, cognitive ability, and pain perception. The chemicals secreted allow your nerve cells to communicate with each other through impulses.

When a nerve impulse reaches the end of a nerve cell, the chemical signal (the neurotransmitter) is sent to another cell. This signal is transmitted across a synaptic gap between the two cells. When the neurotransmitter reaches the other cell, it binds to receptors (structures on the surface of a cell that can bind to specific molecules) and subsequently affects the cell's activity. This can either activate the cell to carry out its function or inhibit it, temporarily halting its activity.

When these cells communicate in your brain, it ultimately influences your feelings, behaviour, and mental state. This is why certain chemicals are used as medications to treat conditions such as depression and anxiety. It also explains why drugs, smoking, and alcohol can be harmful, as the substances within them disrupt the brain's natural chemical balance. They influence the production, release, and reuptake of neurotransmitters.

Here are a few simple examples: *Alcohol decreases the production of glutamate and increases the production of GABA, leading to decreased brain function and inhibition of the nervous system. Drugs increase the release of neurotransmitters such as dopamine, which can provide a feeling of euphoria. However, this can decrease the number of dopamine receptors in the brain, leading to addiction and increased tolerance, meaning the individual needs to increase the dose to achieve the same effect. Smoking increases the production of norepinephrine* *and adrenaline, raising heart rate and blood pressure, while simultaneously decreasing dopamine production, which can negatively affect mood and the reward system. The greatest risks associated with smoking include serious lung and cardiovascular diseases, as it adversely impacts virtually all vital organs in the body.*

Be gentle with your thoughts and the words you say to yourself. Be kind to yourself, for your thoughts significantly impact how you feel.

What your surroundings perceive is fundamentally shaped by how you talk to yourself, creating an unstoppable chain reaction in your body. Some hormones are truly beneficial to give and receive in a healthy manner, such as oxytocin, often referred to as "the love hormone," and dopamine, which I call "the goal-fulfilling hormone." These hormones contribute to feelings of trust, confidence, motivation, drive, well-being, joy, increased self-confidence and self-esteem, and reduced stress.

Conversely, there are hormones that can negatively affect a person's well-being when present in incorrect doses, such as cortisol, which influences your stress response system.

It is important to understand that cortisol naturally exists in your body to regulate your reaction to stress. Cortisol is also involved in the regulation of the sleep-wake cycle, immune system functions, blood sugar levels, and metabolism. Produced in your adrenal glands, cortisol levels are highest in the morning (this is referred to as morning cortisol) and typically peak between 06:00 and 09:00. Levels then naturally decrease throughout the day, regulated by the brain and the hormonal system.

The danger for us humans arises when we expose ourselves to physical or emotional stress and chronic stress over an extended period. This can lead to prolonged overproduction of cortisol, which can have serious health effects. It can cause sleep problems and chronic fatigue, decreased immune function, weight gain, and an increased risk of cardiovascular diseases, osteoporosis, and fractures. Prolonged overproduction can also affect brain function, increasing the risk of anxiety, depression, and cognitive issues such as memory loss or difficulty concentrating.

What you think affects your emotions.
These influence your hormones, determining which chemicals are released in your body and the neurotransmitters involved. <u>This, in turn, affects your well-being, your decisions, and consequently, how you achieve your goals and ambitions.</u>

What your entity thinks influences how team members feel, how the culture is impacted, and the pace at which you achieve your ambitions.

To illustrate the power of signals, consider how your body is directly affected when someone near you says: *"There are lice at preschool," "Our son vomited a lot this morning; we hope it's not a bug," "This medicine has terrible side effects," "Many get seasick on this boat trip," "You will have a hard time sleeping tonight after all that coffee,"* or *"There is an extremely high amount of pollen this year."*

What you feel in similar situations is referred to as "the *noceo* effect", more commonly known as "the *nocebo* effect", a term derived from Italian. The opposite of this is "the *placebo* effect", which has been extensively studied. *A well-known study from 2015 (Rutherford;*

"Placebo response in antidepressant clinical trials" in the Journal of Psychiatric Research) examined the placebo effect on individuals with depression. Researchers administered a placebo to half of the participants and an active treatment to the other half. Those who received the placebo tablets experienced a significant reduction in their depressive symptoms.

*In Latin, the term **noceo** translates to "I harm", indicating the negative impact that expectations and beliefs can have on one's health or well-being. **Placebo** means "I please" or "I satisfy", highlighting the positive outcomes that can arise from the power of suggestion and belief*

What do you emit in the form of hormones, chemicals, words, tone, or body language? And regarding the roceo and placebo effects, how do you impact your surroundings, do you please or harm?

In the introduction of this section, I have briefly outlined what drives our thoughts and feelings and why we choose to act or not.
It is fundamentally important for us as humans to pause and reflect on what or who has influenced us throughout our lives, as well as the basics of how our bodies are affected by our thoughts and experiences. I believe this topic is of such significance that it should be included in education at the secondary school and high school levels, to better prepare young, impressionable individuals for life and the various influences they may encounter.
This concept is known as self-leadership, which is founded on the insight into how we actively and continuously influence ourselves and our surroundings through the signals (our superpower) that we constantly emit to ourselves and everyone we encounter.

<u>Self-leadership is divided into two fundamental parts.</u>

1. Insight: In order to understand and lead others, you must first understand and lead yourself. <u>The better you understand and lead yourself, the better you can understand and lead others.</u>

> *Your **thoughts** influence your **emotions**, which in turn affect your **actions** (do you act or react, and do you take the time to reflect beforehand?), impacting your **well-being** and whether you achieve your **goals and ambitions** in life.*

2. Work consciously and strategically on yourself with emphasis on point 1:
(<u>A</u>) You need a crystal-clear insight into *your current situation*: where are you? How well do you understand your thoughts and feelings with full self-awareness? How well can you lead yourself?

(<u>B</u>) You need a *vision* of what you strive to achieve: where are you headed (how do you want to feel, what goals do you want to reach, what ambitions do you wish to achieve)?

(<u>C</u>) You need a *clear picture of your strategies* and how you will approach them on a daily or weekly basis, namely, exactly how will you get from your current situation to your vision?

(<u>D</u>) *Reflect* on the resources you need access to in terms of time and a network of contacts.

(<u>E</u>) *Communication*: when you consciously and strategically embark on your personal journey of self-leadership, it is important to communicate this to those closest to you. Express your thoughts and feelings to create understanding about why this journey is important to you.

(F) *Most importantly in the process*: if the vision feels overwhelming, set realistic expectations for yourself. Be easygoing with yourself and break down the vision into smaller steps so you can see yourself achieve your sub-goals.

(If you wish to delve deeper into self-leadership, I have written several books, one of which has now been translated into English: "7 Steps within Self-Leadership".)

Self-reflection is a valuable tool for becoming more aware and independent. It is a simple process wherein you pause and, from a helicopter perspective, reflect on your own thoughts, feelings, and actions.

At the same time, you consider yourself from an external perspective: what am I projecting to my surroundings? *Is this what I want to emit? Am I being genuine, or am I transmitting/influencing others with something that is not my truth?*

"Just the fact that you are pausing to reflect right now is truly a significant achievement.

Many rush through life and compromise their own thoughts and feelings because they are too busy living according to the truths of others."
– Niclas Timmerby
on the importance of continually pausing in life for self-reflection.

Self-reflection fosters insight and a deeper understanding of yourself. You gain a strong awareness of patterns in your behaviour and attitude. It can also help you get closer to your true values, allowing you to live more authentically as "you."

After this necessary introduction, here is the first main part of this section: *Many companies communicate that they have a flat organisational structure, yet they still unconsciously lead as if they were a hierarchical organisation.*

The hierarchical organisation is embedded in the DNA of all organisations, and this is hardly surprising, as its heyday was during much of the 20th century, particularly during the industrial revolution.

The concept of a hierarchical organisation implies that entities are clearly structured hierarchically and possess defined lines of authority and responsibility. This was necessary in an era where mass production and efficiency were paramount. *The principles and concept were introduced in 1916 by Henri Fayol and Max Weber, over a hundred years ago.* The managers at the top made the decisions, and all information and authority flowed downwards through the hierarchy in a straight line. There were clear positions and roles, and employees reported to their immediate superiors. The hierarchical structure facilitated a clear distribution of responsibility and control over work processes.

Naturally, with the cultural shifts (which you have read about previously), society and the business world have changed. The need for more flexible and adaptable entities has increased drastically as globalisation, technological advancements, and rapid changes have created a demand for enhanced collaboration, innovation, and involvement at all levels within organisations.

As a result, so-called "flat organisations" and other alternative structures have become increasingly popular and prominent in today's society. *These structures promote open communication, shared responsibility, and decision-making at lower levels. They are entirely in line with the cultural shifts that have occurred.* The hierarchical organisation still has its place in certain industries and organisations, but its dominance has diminished in tandem with societal and business world changes.

This transformation has also led to team members taking a more active role in contributing to the success of their entity. Instead of merely following orders, they are given the opportunity to share their ideas, take initiative, and help shape the direction of the entity. This leads to increased motivation, engagement, and creativity among employees. The flat organisation also enhances the importance, and indeed the requirement, of transparent and open communication, promoting collaboration and the significance of creating involvement. *(Involvement is a key word I will return to several times.)*

According to an article published in Harvard Business Review (2019), today's organisations are increasingly embracing a flatter structure that promotes collaboration, innovation, and engagement. The traditional hierarchical structure (the line organisation), which was once the dominant model, has become less common. The study shows that in a flat organisation, businesses can be more efficient and productive, and employees experience a higher level of engagement and motivation when provided with the opportunity to take on more responsibility and be involved in the decision-making processes of the organisation. A flat organisation facilitates quicker adaptation to change and creates a more dynamic and successful organisation in today's fast-paced business world.

One of the earliest and most well-known examples of a flat organisation was W.L. Gore & Associates, an American company founded in 1958. W.L. Gore & Associates was renowned for its unique work culture and flat hierarchy, where there were no traditional managers or hierarchical structures. Instead, employees were organised into smaller teams and enjoyed significant freedom and responsibility concerning their work tasks.

Today, many companies and organisations have adopted flat structures; for example, Google and Zappos are well-known for their flat organisations that place a strong emphasis on shared responsibility and decision-making.

Several studies indicate that in today's prevailing cultures, a flat organisation is preferable to a hierarchical organisation. A 2017 study published in the "Journal of Organizational Behavior" examined how different organisational structures affected employee engagement and performance. The results showed that employees in flat organisations exhibited higher levels of engagement and performance compared to those in hierarchical line organisations. Another study from 2015 published in the "Journal of Applied Psychology" investigated how organisational structures influenced employee motivation and job satisfaction. This study found that employees in flat organisations reported higher motivation and job satisfaction compared to those in hierarchical line organisations.

What I have discovered during my work as a consultant and as an employee in various types of organisations is that, in many organisations, the official message is that it is a flat organisation, yet the structure remains hierarchical. My conclusion is that "operating as a flat organisation" is a decision from senior management, but fears prevent it from fully materialising.

Some leaders within organisations have the courage to lead with trust, maintain open communication, and genuinely listen and delegate (which means that responsibility is transferred to the team member and not micromanaged; more on this later in the book in the chapter on trust-based leadership).

Leadership is by far the most significant factor in successfully implementing a flat organisation. *The paradox I have observed is that while the message about implementation comes from management, support for higher-level and middle managers in executing the implementation is often inadequate.* There is a need for greater knowledge among management teams regarding situational leadership to particularly support and coach managers in the organisation in their change efforts.

I find that very wise decisions are made, but reasonable conditions for successfully executing the process, so that the decision aligns with the existing culture, are not always provided.

If a decision does not align with the existing culture and the prevailing values and norms, it inevitably becomes a long journey for the organisation and its entities. In all likelihood, management has no choice but to gradually ease the decision and, informally and unofficially, revert to a hierarchical organisation.

> "If a decision lacks the conditions to take root in the culture,
> management needs to reassess the process and conditions."
> – Niclas Timmerby

So how do you gradually ensure that significant/transformative decisions (such as the implementation of a flat organisation) align well with the existing culture of the entity?

Reflection for the management team:

(A)
Analyse and Understand the Current Culture. Evaluate how decisions and implementations have occurred up to now. Why do we want to change? What is the purpose, what are the benefits, and what is the vision?

"A decision has no chance of altering the culture."
– Niclas Timmerby

(B)
Brainstorm in the Group: How will this impact people as we communicate the message? How and when should we convey the decision? How do we communicate during the initial process and progressively throughout? How do we follow up, and what forms of dialogue should we have (large group, by entity)? When can we consider that we have achieved the vision? What criteria should be met?

(C)
Considering point 1, what resources do we need (Is the time frame in point 1 feasible given the resources we have)? What obstacles might arise, and how do we address/manage them? Who, how, and when might we communicate externally?

Proposal for a workshop for entities within a larger organisation to align major decisions with existing corporate culture, linked to situational leadership:

Plan for a half-day workshop comprising the following five parts:

Part 1: Introduction.
Part 2: Reflection on the Current Corporate Culture.
Part 3: Discuss the Decision Made and How It Can Positively Contribute to the Current Corporate Culture and Profitability.
Part 4: Implementation of the Decision.
Part 5: Summary, Reflection, Needs.

Part 1: Introduction.
- Welcome and present the purpose of the workshop.
- Discuss the importance of implementing decisions in line with the corporate culture, the significance of participation, a shared vision, and how it can affect well-being and the success of the entity.

Part 2: Reflection on the Current Corporate Culture.
- Invite team members to reflect on the current culture and identify its values, norms, and behaviours, as well as how this impacts individuals and the whole.
- Use the method you feel best fits the context and the current state of your entity based on what you have gathered about situational leadership. Methods may include group discussions, brainstorming, or individual reflections, ideally in combination to create as open a discussion format as possible. It is crucial that everyone has the opportunity to express their views and that this is not rushed.

- Take notes during the meeting and highlight the key factors, words, and feelings you observe at the conclusion.
- Initiate a new open discussion when you share your notes and reflections. Emphasize the importance of collaboratively discussing how, as a unit, you can work in everyday situations to facilitate the implementation of decisions within your culture.

Part 3: Discuss the Decision Made and How It Can Positively Contribute to the Current Corporate Culture and Profitability.

- Present the decision made by management.
- Discuss the purpose and goals of the decision and how it is expected to contribute to the corporate culture. Discuss the advantages linked to the entity's profitability and, if possible, in relation to competitors.
- Connect the decision to your earlier open discussion on how best to receive decisions for smoother acceptance and implementation within the culture's values, norms, and behaviours.

Part 4: Implementation of the Decision.

- If possible, divide the entity into smaller groups (ideally with a maximum of 5-6 per group) and ask them to identify how the decision can be implemented in a way that aligns with the culture.

- Ideally, everyone in the group should have a role. Suggestions include:

    - One person ensures that everyone's voice is heard and that all have the opportunity to contribute.

    - One person ensures that focus is maintained on the task during the allotted time.

- One member acts as a timekeeper and is responsible for ensuring the group completes its work within the set time.

- A group member documents the work in a way that it can be described and archived.

- The group has one or more people prepared to clearly articulate the group's conclusions.

- In the group rooms, the groups have two tasks.
    - 1. To discuss challenges and obstacles that may arise and identify strategies to overcome them. (2)
    - 2. Develop an implementation plan that considers the corporate culture and aims to ensure the decision is successfully realised.

Part 5: Summary, Reflection, Needs.

- Ask each group to present their implementation plan and share their thoughts, feelings, and conclusions.
- Note down key words and key strategies. Once everyone has presented, create a joint discussion about the challenges, lessons, and insights gained during the workshop.
- Conclude by summarising the key points, sharing your personal insights about what your entity has contributed, and how you feel the workshop was conducted. Emphasize in your summary the importance, as a leader, of adapting the implementation of decisions to the corporate culture, ensuring everyone expresses their thoughts and feelings, and fostering a sense of participation.
- As a final point, stress the importance of personal reflection and offer your support in the form of conversations should any feelings of uncertainty arise.

Summary, Main Part 1: Many companies communicate that they have a flat organisation, but they still unintentionally (?) lead as if they were a traditional hierarchical organisation.

Natural cultural shifts and their impact on entire countries and societies spread to political decisions, new legislation, institutions, larger and smaller entities, minorities, and of course to all individuals living and working in that culture. This leads to norms, behaviours, and even values changing at an increasingly rapid pace.

It is essential for all types of entities to insightfully assess how the organisation is structured: Is it predominantly a traditional hierarchical line organisation, or is it primarily a horizontal, decentralised flat organisation? Does the structure of your entity align with the prevailing cultures? And is there an awareness that the last members who operated during the industrial revolution will be working their last day before retiring in just over ten years?

"In a flat organisation, leadership is not limited to a single individual but is distributed throughout the entire organisation.

Everyone has the opportunity to be a leader and to influence."
– Linda Hill, Professor, Harvard Business School

- *Is your entity ready for the future?*
- *Is the management team in your entity prepared?*
- *Are you ready to lead future generations in tomorrow's cultures?*

"Hierarchies no longer work.
We need to move from a vertical structure to a flat organisation where everyone can contribute and be involved in decision-making."
– Tony Hsieh, Zappos

Main Part 2.

Your control systems weighted towards passion and will.

It is time to be more concrete; what are control systems in an entity?

They can include, for example:

- Employment contracts.
- RACI or role and responsibility descriptions.
- Role and responsibility areas or accountability agreements.
- Meetings and daily conversations.
- Scheduling and staffing tools.
- Competence matrices.
- MRS (management by objectives and results).
- BSC (balanced scorecard).
- Specific roles, such as nurse, airline captain.
- Qualifications and necessary experiences.
- Salary and benefits.
- Inventory.
- Procurement.
- Costs.
- Margins/Contribution margin.
- Technical systems.
- Training programmes.
- HR department handling personnel matters.

(In associations, it can also include physical status and specific roles within the team or club/association.)

After reading the points above, it is clear that this type of control tools is, to some extent, needed in an entity.

However, it is not the above points that make all team members passionate about their roles, that they feel passion and will.

That they want to contribute everything they have within them without thinking about salary, fully accept their roles, and thereby take 100 percent responsibility, feel that they would "run through fire" for their team and leader, that they want to learn new things and become self-sufficient, that they are more solution-oriented, that they run a little faster and are a little more efficient with smiles on their faces, that they are cooperative, that they take initiative, that they are focused on doing their utmost for the entity. And above all, that they demonstrate enthusiasm and spread genuine joy and engagement to others.

I am sure you want to extract what is written above in italics from your entity. I am certain you want self-sufficient and motivated team members who spread engagement while also delivering good results.

I want to refer back to my quote in the preface: *"Money can determine <u>what</u> you do. Your passion determines <u>how</u> you do it."*

Absolutely, control tools can dictate what you do; however, I am 100 percent certain that none of the standard control tools I listed on the previous page have anything to do with genuine passion. Some of the control tools can certainly foster will.

You need both will and passion to achieve long-term success in your entity, but what are the actual differences when a team member feels will or passion? It is very important for you as a leader to have insight into this in order to gauge feelings within the team and know how to motivate your entity on an individual basis. And ask yourself: why do I go to work besides striving towards the vision, out of will or passion?

Passion	Will
Emotional and deeply rooted.	Rational and conscious.
A profound feeling of joy and engagement for something that the person is passionate about.	Focused on achieving specific goals or performing specific tasks.
With genuine passion, energy, joy, and a strong motivation are created.	Necessary to do what is required and to be determined in one's role.
It provides intrinsic motivation to continue growing and developing within one's field.	Helps to overcome challenges and to reach goals.
A deep, intense feeling of joy and enthusiasm for something the person loves to do. A natural and spontaneous feeling that arises from the individual's inner drives and leads to devotion.	A conscious action that requires determination and commitment to be created. This energy that generates the necessary will often needs to come from external factors such as, for example, salary.
It gives a person perseverance and a strong will to fight even when faced with difficult challenges.	Will is often short-term since it requires a constant input of energy; it can quickly diminish when an individual encounters difficulties or obstacles.
The drive is a deeply rooted feeling of joy and inner satisfaction from doing something the person loves, preferably with like-minded individuals.	The drive is some form of goal in the shape of affirmation or reward in the form of money or status.

What Creates Motivation?

With the difference between passion and will clarified, it is appropriate to highlight which factors create motivation and drive.

The foundation for creating motivation and intrinsic drive in today's cultures is to lead with *trust-based leadership*, which you will read about specifically in section G. The reason is that *trust is a prerequisite for creating self-sufficient team members and long-term motivation in an entity today*. All team members need to feel trust toward you as a leader.

In addition to trust, there are four other essential factors that foster intrinsic, genuine motivation in a person in the workplace:

1. **Competence.** *"I need to feel deep down that I have enough competence to perform my job. This makes me self-sufficient."*

2. **Belonging.** *"I need to feel like a part of the team and that I am accepted as the unique person I am. This makes me feel secure."*

3. **Independence.** *"I don't need anyone to 'nitpick' (micromanage). Let me try and make mistakes sometimes. That is when I grow and develop the most and the fastest."*

4. **Personal Responsibility.** *"Let me feel that I am important and significant by delegating personal responsibility to me. Let me feel that I can influence the daily work, our shared work environment, the work atmosphere, the culture, and the results. This makes me feel involved."*

When you can get everyone in your entity to feel that:
- They have the necessary competence for their role,
- They feel like one of the team,
- They feel independent enough to manage their tasks, and
- They feel they have individual responsibility for moving the entity forward.

Then you have an entity that is motivated. The team members:
1. Are self-sufficient.
2. Feel secure.
3. Take initiative for the entity's development.
4. Feel involved and therefore want to contribute.

Now you have achieved an incredible foundation in your leadership that allows you to begin to ease off on control tools and instead focus on something that is much more enjoyable for you as a leader and develops both you in your leadership role and all your team members. You can now start to lay out a structure in your work where you move away from control tools and instead focus on passion and will.

Passion and will can include:
- Leading with a focus on the vision.
- Leading with your own personal mission to achieve the vision.
- Effective delegation.
- Creating an accepted feedback culture.
- Consensus through values and a shared value foundation.
- Developing people by challenging them.
- Further developing team spirit.
- Challenging them through tailored, individual coaching.
- Introducing a new, deeper dimension in performance conversations.
- Focusing more on long-term ambitions than on short-term goals.

It is precisely at this stage in your leadership that you transition from being a manager who uses necessary control tools to becoming a leader who creates engagement, passion, and will. You are now on a completely different journey with your entity, a wonderful journey driven by mutual development, trust, collaboration, and involvement.

Control systems, or passion and will – linked to situational leadership.

- You know who you have in your entity, you are aware of who is closest to balance, and you know who is most focused on tasks versus relationships.

*"The manager controls.
The leader delegates.*

*The manager focuses on talking.
The leader focuses on listening.*

*The manager praises the work done.
The leader praises the person."
– Niclas Timmerby*

- After the workshop you have guided them through, they are conscious of what it entails, as well as what and how they can develop with your help.

- You are well aware that you continually need to switch tracks in your flexible leadership when communicating with your entity. Between directing, supporting, coaching, and delegating, depending on the phase your respective team members are in (and the cultures they have operated within).

You also recognize the importance of understanding and being able to lead in a generation-adapted leadership style connected to cultural shifts.

Reflection, Section C

1. Reflect on your superpower. How do the signals you constantly send out affect your surroundings at home and in the workplace? How do you influence yourself through your emotions?

2. Reflect on who in your entity comes to work every day with will and who does so with passion. Don't forget to reflect on yourself.

3. Reflect on your leadership responsibility toward yourself. *The better you understand and lead yourself, the better you can lead and understand others.* Have you laid out a strategy connected to self-leadership? (Where are you, where do you want to go, and how will you get there?)

4. Reflect on your leadership responsibility to make your entity motivated and self-sufficient. You have a clear picture of your leadership, as well as where your entity is. You are aware that you need to use primarily control tools with an entity that is new, unmotivated, or not self-sufficient. You now know how to create intrinsic motivation, and with your insights into situational leadership, you can take your entity from its current state to one where you can guide with soft tools that foster passion and will.

5. Reflect on what strategy you should prepare when a new employee starts next time. How will you help the individual feel intrinsic motivation right away? How will you make them feel included in your entity's culture? As soon as a new team member starts or leaves, the dynamics change immediately, affecting your culture. How do you nurture the positive aspects of the culture you have built?

D

Results- or values-driven leadership

Your perception of humanity is how you view other people.
How you treat others is exactly how they see you.
Niclas Timmerby

Can you see a pattern shaping as you make your internal choices about how you want to lead your entity, where the foundation is situational leadership to better understand your entity? From your first choice (B), should your focus be on influencing results or culture? For your next choice (C), do you want to lead with control systems or create passion and desire through intrinsic motivation? Now comes your next choice.

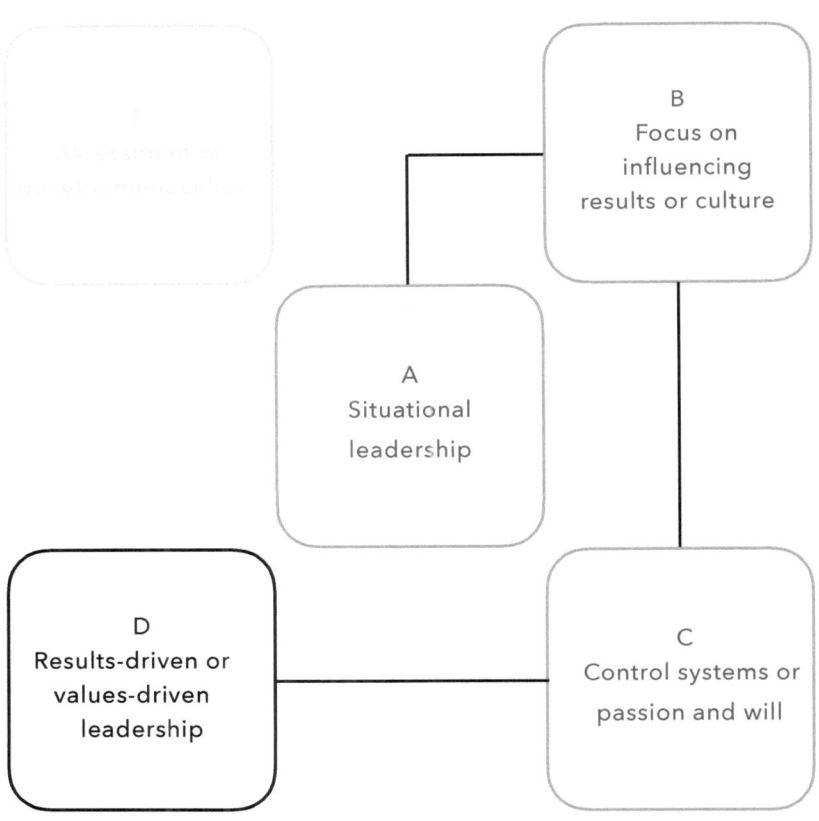

Why are you a leader?

What motivates you to lead?
- *Is it status, money, and/or power?*
- *Or is it a genuine desire from the heart to make a positive difference in people's lives, seeing it as your life's mission to help others grow internally and develop in their roles?*

What are your morals and ethics?
- *Do you find genuine happiness in achieving results after making decisions that ultimately benefit yourself, consciously disregarding potential consequences for others?*
- *Or do you find genuine happiness when you see the people you have helped grow and develop achieving results without needing praise?*

Are you authentic in your leadership?
- *Do you say "yes" without expressing your true opinion, even when you sometimes find decisions unreasonable in terms of timing or requirements?*
- *Or do you dare to show bravery and vulnerability, revealing your authentic self and standing up for what you believe in, even if it may meet resistance from the leadership team?*

How strong is your integrity?
- *Are you prepared to be honest and make difficult choices to uphold your moral principles and values?*
- *Or do you compromise to achieve goals or fit in certain situations where your principles and values are challenged?*

In the following two pages, you will find ten differences between values-based and results-based leadership. Review each point and reflect insightfully on how you conduct your leadership. On pages 93-96, you will have the opportunity to write down your insights and reflections.

Values-Based Leadership	Results-Based Leadership
Definition The focus is on maintaining and communicating the organisation's values and culture.	**Definition** The focus is on achieving specific results and goals.
Leadership Style Emphasises the importance of leading by example and creating a positive work environment where team members feel motivated and engaged.	**Leadership Style** Emphasises the importance of achieving results and performance, and may be more inclined to use incentives and rewards to achieve these outcomes.
Communication Clearly and consistently communicates the entity's values and culture.	**Communication** Communicates specific goals and expectations to achieve desired results.
Decision-Making Considers the entity's culture and values, often prioritising team members' well-being and engagement.	**Decision-Making** Focuses on achieving results and may be more likely to make decisions that lead to increased performance, even if this may have negative consequences for team members.
Long-Term Focus Concentrates on building a strong corporate culture and creating a positive work environment that promotes employees' well-being and engagement in the long term.	**Long-Term Focus** The focus is both short- and long-term on achieving results and performance, even if this may have negative long-term consequences for the entity.

Values-Based Leadership	Results-Based Leadership
Priorities Building relationships and creating a culture of trust and openness within the entity.	**Priorities** Achieving specific goals and making decisions that lead to increased performance.
Feedback Style Primarily focuses on providing the more challenging form of feedback with the aim of changing behaviours and attitudes that promote values and culture.	**Feedback Style** Primarily focuses on providing the easier form of feedback aimed at achieving efficiency and performance that promotes specific results.
Conflict Management Works to resolve conflicts in a manner that is fair and respectful to all parties involved.	**Conflict Management** Tends to adopt an authoritarian stance (control, hierarchy, lack of participation) to resolve conflicts quickly and efficiently.
Development Style Emphasises the importance of individual development openly and transparently to create a positive, safe, and innovative work environment.	**Development Style** Prioritises development with an emphasis on achieving specific results and performance to meet short-term goals.
Encouragement and Creativity Encourages creativity and initiative by fostering a culture where the entity feels secure in taking risks and isn't afraid to fail. (Builds trust.)	**Encouragement and Creativity** Desires control over processes and is therefore often inclined to focus on proven methods. (Risk of micromanagement.)

Here are all the competencies. For each aspect, write down your genuine answers on a scale of 1 to 4 for self-reflection and personal development.

1. This is how I am mostly today, values-driven/results-driven.
2. Why am I like this (I am shaped by e.g., experiences, previous/current managers, decisions, past employments, education, I have not reflected on this, etc.)?
3. This is my clear vision of the future.
4. This is how I will get there (strategies, thoughts, ideas, milestones).

Definition

1. _____
2. _____
3. _____
4. _____

_____
_____

Leadership Style

1. _____
2. _____
3. _____
4. _____

_____
_____

Communication

1. _____
2. _____
3. _____
4. _____

_____
_____

Decision-Making

1. _____
2. _____
3. _____
4. _____

_____
_____

Long-Term Focus

1. _____
2. _____
3. _____
4. _____

_____
_____

Priorities

1. _____
2. _____
3. _____
4. _____

_____
_____

Feedback Style

1. _____
2. _____
3. _____
4. _____

_____
_____

Conflict Management

1. _____
2. _____
3. _____
4. _____

_____
_____

Development style

1. _____
2. _____
3. _____
4. _____

_____
_____

Encouragement and creativity.

1. _____
2. _____
3. _____
4. _____

_____
_____

I deliberately started this section in a clear and direct manner to provoke thoughts and feelings within you.

At the conclusion of this section, you will find a tool that I have personally used in my leadership for the past fifteen years; I call it quarterly reflection, which is a form of self-reflection.

What are your deepest values as a person?

It is important to periodically consider our values in life, as our deepest values largely determine who we are. Your values are a significant part of your identity as a person.

Your identity is the image you have of yourself.

I will not go into too much detail about this in this book, but it is very important for you as a person to become fully aware of your *self-concept* and the psychological factors that create the perceptions, thoughts, and feelings you have about yourself. *I can guarantee that this gives life a new dimension of self-awareness and self-perception.*

We do not compromise on our deepest values; We say *"no!"* , We say *"stop!"* , We say: *"I won't do that."*

Or rather, we <u>should</u> not compromise on our values.

Unfortunately, the reality is that many people compromise their values in life. *Perhaps it is to please others, to be liked, to fit in, because we are a man or a woman and certain things are then expected of us, perhaps playing a role to belong to one group while adopting a different role in another group? Perhaps cultural shifts also influence us more than we think?* We all need to compromise in

"When you change the way you see yourself, you change your identity in that very moment.

So, what image do you want to see?"
- Niclas Timmerby, on the importance of nurturing your self-concept.

situations and phases of life, but do not compromise who you are. It is as if you are psychologically committing violence against yourself.

When we compromise our own values, it reflects back on us in various ways; we simply feel unwell when we violate a deeply rooted value. In my coaching conversations with people, almost everyone, independent of one another, has said something similar: *"I feel a sense of discomfort within me," "it feels in my stomach," "I feel nauseous," "I experience feelings akin to anxiety," "I feel stressed inside and almost ashamed."* Perhaps that is why the stomach is sometimes referred to as **our inner compass**, or because of the term "gut feeling" in English, which denotes a sense, instinct, or intuition. Similarly, we can experience a good feeling in our stomach when we have followed our inner compass.

I now remember back to my younger self as an adult, how I repeatedly committed violence against myself. What I specifically recall is when people teased and bullied me during my school years, and even up until the age of 35, when people joked at my expense, and I allowed it.

I did not say "stop!" or "cut it out!" or walk away. I often laughed along to escape the situation or because I wanted to be liked.

Precisely in that moment when I joked along, I was committing psychological violence against myself.

I have since learned that this in psychology is referred to as **self-deprecating humour**. That is, when a person jokes about themselves or diminishes their own worth, as if making fun of their own flaws, mistakes, or weaknesses.

A study published in the Journal of Personality and Social Psychology found that "individuals who used self-deprecating humour had lower self-esteem and self-confidence than those who did not."
Another study published in the Personality and Social Psychology Bulletin found that "self-deprecating humour can diminish others' perceptions of a person's competence and status."
A third study published in the Journal of Personality and Social Psychology showed that "individuals who use self-deprecating humour to be liked by others are perceived as less competent and less attractive. Furthermore, it can lead to a negative self-image and decreased self-esteem in the long term."

This means that if a person frequently jokes about themselves and/or diminishes their worth, the thoughts can internalise these negative views and develop a negative self-image.
What we think creates what we feel inside, and what we feel determines whether we choose to act or simply react to our feelings. This natural process that everyone goes through countless times each day results in a positive or negative consequence for us, manifested in our wellbeing or achieved goals.

Self-deprecating humour can also influence how others perceive and treat the individual. This is because the impression others get may suggest that the person is not worthy of respect or appreciation.
This can be a very dangerous path that can lead others to exploit this perceived weakness to "gain power over the person who appears weak"

and consequently treat and shape the individual in an undesirable or
disrespectful manner.

It is important to differentiate between self-distance and self-deprecating humour, as these are two entirely different ways of relating to oneself.

Having self-distance is very healthy; it is a positive trait that helps individuals cope with stress and difficulties in life.
Self-distance means that a person can view themselves and their own flaws, mistakes, or weaknesses from an outside perspective in an objective manner and joke about them without undermining their self-worth or negatively affecting their self-esteem. For example, being able to laugh at oneself in a healthy way and having a relaxed attitude towards one's own shortcomings.

Self-deprecating humour, on the other hand, involves joking about oneself in a way that belittles or diminishes one's worth. The danger is that self-deprecating humour strikes directly at a person's self-esteem. If someone makes jokes that confirm their own negative thoughts about themselves or attempts to make others laugh at their expense, it directly impacts their self-worth.

The difference between self-distance and self-deprecating humour lies in the intention and effects of the jokes. Self-distance is healthier and more positive, while self-deprecating humour can be harmful to self-esteem and relationships.

As a person or leader, you have a significant responsibility.
Towards yourself and your surroundings. If you or someone you encounter on your journey through life uses self-deprecating humour: clearly communicate to yourself or the person you meet that you do not see them in that way. Clearly state that you dislike it when the individual

(or you yourself) speaks in those terms. Instead, praise their personality, attitude, drive, how they handle certain situations, or something else that shows *your belief in them*. This could be the most important thing you do in your role as a leader and as a person. <u>You can help someone change their perception of themselves</u> (their identity).

Everyone's values change over time, although some remain constant. It is crucial to continuously ref ect on this as our values can impact our well-being and, consequently, significantly influence how we experience our lives.

Several studies have explored the relationship between values and well-being, including:

Schwartz, S. H. Basic human values: Their content and structure across countries. In this study, Schwartz examined various values and their correlation with individual well-being. The results indicated that "people who live in accordance with their values tend to experience higher well-being."

Deci, E. L., & Ryan, R. M. The "what" and "why" of goal pursuits: Human needs and the self-determination of behaviour. This study focused on how individuals' values and goals impact their motivation and well-being. The results showed that "when people pursue goals that align with their values, they experience greater self-determination and well-being."

Kasser, T., & Ryan, R. M. Further examining the American dream: Differential correlates of intrinsic and extrinsic goals. In this study, Kasser and Ryan explored how different types of goals, tied to varying values, affect well-being. The results showed that "the pursuit of intrinsic goals, linked to personal growth and relationships, was positively correlated with well-being, while the pursuit of extrinsic goals, such as material success and status, was negatively correlated with well-being."

What Are My Deepest Values?

Yes, it can be difficult to just know or "come up with" your deepest values. Here's how I present it in my training and lectures:

1. Take a moment to reflect quietly on the things you never want to compromise in your life. Think about what you say no to. Or the best question: *What would you <u>never</u> do?*

2. Now comes the important part: *why*? Why do you not want to compromise on certain things in life? There is always a reason. You may have been influenced by external factors (which is not good, as it means you are living someone else's truth/life), but most likely, there is a situation or event in your life that has touched you very deeply within. It could be some form of trauma from your childhood that has left deep scars inside you, or an event in your adult life that has influenced you, often because you chose to act, not act, or remain silent in some context (i.e., *action bias* or *inaction bias*, which you can read more about in my books on self-leadership).

3. Once you identify that important *"why,"* it will impact you, as it becomes an insight that something you *may* have carried in your subconscious has influenced your identity, who you are, how you are, how you feel, how you speak to yourself, and the behaviour and attitude you present to those closest to you.

4. Every time you consciously or unconsciously think about a deep value you hold, it affects and touches you.

5. When you have articulated your deepest values, you can create an action plan for how to manage your insights.

My Deepest Values.
I will share my three deepest values to illustrate how important it is to reflect on this. I do not share this to gain sympathy or empathy, but to underscore its importance.

I really need to understand myself (who am I and why am I the way I am?) to be able to navigate through life towards well-being and the goals and ambitions I wish to achieve. If I can manage this, I am better equipped to understand and lead others.

My heartfelt recommendation to you is to share your deepest values with those closest to you so they know. This allows them to gain greater insight into who you are and what has shaped and continues to shape you. Because who knows, as time goes on, if your loved ones are unaware and one day you express how you feel or that you want to make changes to improve your life, it may come as a shock to them. The usual reaction is that they want to help, ask questions, and "solve your problem." If they are informed earlier, it is likely there will be no shock.

What I realised in my reflections during my thirties is that I have never compromised on the following three things: (1) I have always worked incredibly hard, (2) I have never become intoxicated to the point of losing control, and (3) I have never been unfaithful.

Now we come to the important part: asking _why_.

When I reflected, I quickly discerned my reasons:

1. Why have I always worked incredibly hard and sometimes held multiple jobs at once?

Answer: When I was growing up, we were poor; my father died when I was seven, and my mother was alone with a part-time job, raising my two brothers and me. In recent years, it has become clear to me why I never want to be acknowledged on my birthday; for example, I turned 50 a few years ago and asked my managers not to recognise it at all. Growing up, the situation meant I could not invite anyone to my birthday party, and when I was invited, I would say I was "sick" because it was too expensive to buy a gift. The same applied to school trips or any other events that might incur costs; I would again say I was "sick."

I was relatively good at soccer and loved playing and doing tricks (and still do). I remember wishing for an official European Championship football and knowing that a genuine one was incredibly expensive. It took two years, but my mother eventually found one at a clearance sale, and I finally got my ball. To this day, I remember crying with joy. I played for hours every day, in sunshine and pouring rain. I would bring the ball inside each time and polish it. It had the best spot in my childhood room. The ball lasted two years, but eventually, it broke. I still remember how much that hurt and how much I cried. It was undoubtedly the most precious thing I had ever owned in my life up to that point. This taught me gratitude and humility.

_So, the answer to _why_ is that I subconsciously do not want to end up in poverty._

2. Why have I always wanted to maintain control regarding alcohol?

Answer: As a teenager, I saw a drunken man hit my mother in the face with his fist in our living room. I remember how I (small and thin) jumped on the man's back to protect my mother, and how he threw me against the wall. Something good came from my "action bias," as my mother took us three children that night, and we slept on mattresses at her workplace.

The answer to <u>why</u> is that I see alcohol as something dangerous, something that can hurt people.

3. Why Has Infidelity Never Crossed My Mind?

Answer: Because I have been betrayed. I felt incredibly awful when I found out. Of course, I was furious and separated the same day, but what hurt the most was losing my identity and my self-concept *(Self-concept = self-esteem + self-awareness + self-worth + self-efficacy + self-understanding + self-image + self-ideal)* in that moment. I often describe it as seeing my life being flushed down the toilet; I felt so worthless. This left deep scars within me, and for fifteen years from that day, I was afraid to fully trust people. This affected not only me but also my closest relationships in a very negative way. I become more secure in myself every day, understanding that I have value and am a good person. I know that, like everyone, I go through phases in life when I do not believe in myself or feel unwell. It is very important to discover why, in order to move forward.

The answer to <u>why</u> I would never inflict that feeling and these lasting negative effects on another person is that I know how badly I felt.

Do you want to see your entity's true potential?

To see a fraction of your own potential, you need to *challenge* yourself in the areas where you feel comfortable. The comfort zone, the box, your established habits and routines, the habitual zone, the zone of security - the concept truly has many different names.

"Life begins at the end of your comfort zone."
- Neale Donald Walsch

I consider "comfort zone" to be the most applicable since the term describes exactly what it is. It is a zone in which you feel mentally and emotionally comfortable moving. You know what exists in your zone; you are aware of the situation there, and you know the routines and habits that are present.

This makes your zone safe, secure, and cosy, as routines *are patterns of your daily behaviour, while habits are when your* patterns *of various behaviours have become automated over time.*

This provides you with control and stability.
It is simply very comfortable inside the zone, and it is not particularly challenging or strenuous to be in that zone.

We prefer not to be outside the zone because there may be new things and behaviours we are unfamiliar with; thus, the expression "status quo" is very fitting in this context.

Holding on to the status quo means avoiding change and instead maintaining the current state, which is familiar and comfortable.

If you want to see your entity's true potential, you need to challenge your team members in their "zones."

As you may have noticed, I have italic sed "*challenge*"." This is because *challenging* is the keyword for change.

You cannot change a situation you find yourself in that does not feel good unless you challenge yourself. If I refer back to self-leadership (2) , you will remember that you have a current state, you have a clear vision of your goals, and what you need to achieve that vision is to lay out clear strategies for yourself on how to get there. Then there is just one small detail remaining: to challenge yourself; otherwise, the risk is high that you will not progress far from your current state.

As *Thomas Jefferson (1743-1826), the third President of the United States said: "If you want something you have never had, you must be willing to do something you have never done."*

"Great things never come from comfort zones."
- Roy T. Bennett

When you reach the section later on regarding *tailored coaching*, I will return to the word challenge. *If you do not challenge the recipient in coaching, it is not coaching; it is merely a regular conversation.*

In Old Norse (circa 800-1300 AD), the word "útmana" was used to describe the act of urging someone to overcome obstacles, test their limits, or face a difficulty. In Latin, the word "provocare" has several meanings depending on the context. In this context, "provocare" can describe a person being challenged on an intellectual or verbal level.

If I go back to your choices so far to demonstrate where you can connect "potential" and "challenge," I can show it like this:

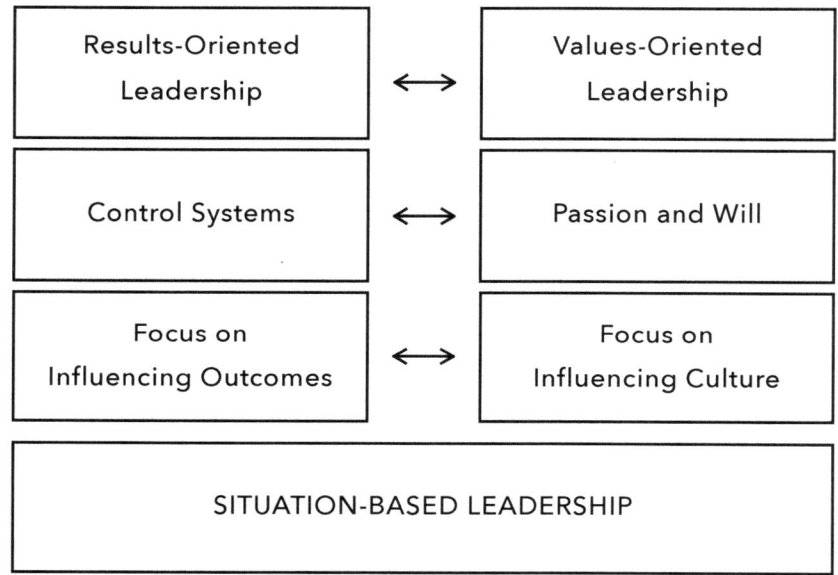

Situational leadership is the foundation where, through the workshop in section A, you can identify where your entity and team members are.
Choice 1 is whether you choose to lead by focusing on results or culture.
Choice 2 is the choice between using control systems or pursuing a leadership style that fosters passion and will.
Choice 3 is this section; the answers you wrote down for point 3 *(This is my clear vision)* on pages 93-96 will indicate whether you are inclined to choose the left or right side in the model above.

The left side does not challenge the entity's potential, whereas the right side challenges the entity's potential.
To realise your potential as a human being and in your professional life, you need to challenge yourself; you need to challenge your old truths/paradigms or make a paradigm shift, i.e., to replace or add a new perspective to an old truth, problem, or theory.

If you go back to the difference between leading through control systems or passion and will, you will see it directly.
Control systems keep team members within the zone and therefore do not challenge their potential. For some of them, it is a comfort zone, and if I go back to cultural shifts, it is likely comfortable for most who have operated during the industrial revolution.

I do not claim that it is self-evident for everyone; however, this way of leading is something that feels familiar and structured, and control systems can be directly linked to the concept of line organization.

For those who have not operated in the industrial revolution, that is, those who began working after 1980. the likelihood is higher that they wish to be more involved, to feel more trust, and to seek ways to achieve intrinsic motivation.

The later a person begins their career, the higher this probability becomes.

The left side can be related to the concept of line organisation, which is driven by control systems and is closely associated with job security, performance targets, and responsibility for a specific role or task.

The right side can be associated with the concept of a flat organisation that is driven by passion and will, and is closely related to participation, trust, open communication, self-determination, development opportunities, coaching, feedback, engagement, and intrinsic motivation.

Values-oriented leadership is a crucial factor in creating a strong and sustainable culture that promotes a positive work environment by considering values and ethical standards in your leadership.
You also take into account the individual values of your team members and work to ensure these are respected, for you it is a given that everyone should feel included.

> *"A results-oriented leader leads with performance targets.*
> *A values-oriented leader leads with engagement."*
> *- Niclas Timmerby*

You lead with values to consciously create passion and will, which fosters engagement, shapes your entity's culture, the atmosphere in which you work, and future results.

Here are three studies demonstrating the economic benefits of values-oriented leadership:

A study by Earley, P. C. and Mosakowski published in the Harvard Business Review found that "companies with high cultural intelligence (including values-oriented leadership) had an average revenue increase of 15-30% and an average increase in market value of 20-40%."
A study published in the Journal of Business Ethics found that "companies with a strong focus on values-oriented leadership had an average increase in sales revenue of 5% and an average increase in

operating margin of 1.7%." Source: Waldman, D. A., Siegel, D. S., &
Javidan, M.

    A third study by Orlitzky, Schmidt, and Rynes published in the
Journal of Business Ethics found that companies with a strong emphasis
on values-oriented leadership had an average increase in shareholder
returns of 5-7% and an average increase in market value of 2-4%.

A Real-Life Example.

An entity I had the trust and privilege to lead through a change process
was used to being led in a strictly results-oriented manner. There was a
vision and there were admirable values within the organisation, which
consisted of national units, but when these were mentioned, there was
no genuine response. To put it simply, there was no passion; people
were just there for the paycheck. A year later, with the same opening
hours, the same products, and virtually the same staff, our team had
increased revenue by 73%.

How was this possible? In any large team, there are positive and
negative cultural carriers. When you implement a change initiative, you
know after a few months who they really are. I gave everyone the
opportunity to be part of the culture I wanted to create, based on joy,
confidence/optimism, and the feeling that we are doing things
together.

My focus was not to seek right or wrong in people; that is not a
leadership quality. Most of them had worked in the old culture for many
years and were, of course, heavily influenced by it. What I focused on
was, with all my being and body language, showing that there was
another way to be together and achieve common goals. I arrived early
and personally rearranged the store before anyone else arrived to

demonstrate that it was okay to take initiative. I was as present as I could be in the daily work, got to know the people, and took the opportunity to make the staff room and kitchen a bit cozier.

Especially at the beginning, I concentrated on creating a culture characterised by the ability to have fun together. There is no "boss" in me; I am just as valuable. There is no one here who is more or less valuable than anyone else because we are a team. After a few months, it became obvious who did not like the change and who did. It is usually a few strong individuals who dislike the change, and it was the case here as well. Instead of reprimanding or trying to convince them, I simply continued to focus on the culture, and after a while, the staff began to change naturally; some left, and I was able to hire new employees who shared the same soft values of the culture in which the team thrived and who saw the entity's vision as something inspiring.

I did this with great care; I ensured I found individuals who were teachable. I talked about our culture and focused on the positives of our culture right in the recruitment interviews. I also focused on the vision, demonstrating where we should go together as a team. *Of course, you should join us in our pursuit of achieving the vision!*

My management team shared my values and moral principles, which allowed us to achieve incredible results (and have a fantastic time together) in a very short time. **The focus was on influencing culture, on creating passion and will, and ultimately it was profoundly values-oriented.** Participation and a good working environment created an atmosphere in which employees thrived, and they dared to take more and more initiatives, which I enjoyed seeing (you can read more about how to create *a culture of development* in the next section). *We almost* *stopped "selling," and instead, we had a culture that automatically generated excellent sales.*

And the customers loved the atmosphere. I remember several times customers asking, *"Have you changed the lighting?", "Have you changed uniforms?", "What have you done? It feels different coming here - in a good way?", "It's great to see you all having so much fun together."* Once, I heard a customer tell an employee, *"I wish it could be like this at my job!"* It made me tear up with pride for us as a team and what we had been able to create together in such an incredibly short time. Passion, genuine community, participation, the willingness to take initiative, joy, humour, the feeling that together we can achieve and overcome anything, pride, and much more.

> *"When you, as a leader, focus on changing the culture instead*
> *of changing people, magic happens right before your eyes."*
> *- Niclas Timmerby*

Customers began to laugh with us, spend more on larger purchases, buy more expensive items, and they returned more frequently. Before, we sometimes had customers who would become irritated or upset because their items might be delayed; even here, customer behaviour changed. It felt like as soon as they entered our culture, they became included in our culture.

Above all, my entity changed; what they radiated when I arrived and when I left a year later for a new role within the organisation was truly like night and day. I still meet several of them in my free time, and it feels like time has stood still.

It's truly magical to focus on culture, daring to let go of control tools to instead create passion and will, and lead with values.

When the culture creates the feeling that "together, we can accomplish what we previously said was impossible," then you have succeeded in your leadership, for you have enabled people to grow. They will <u>never</u> forget you.

Quarterly Reflection

As a conclusion to this section, you will find a tool I have used in my leadership over the last fifteen years; I call it quarterly reflection, which is a form of self-reflection.

This has helped me tremendously in my leadership (and also on a personal level, to understand myself better), and I hope it can be of great benefit to you as well. Expect it to take 2-3 hours in a quiet environment. If you find it difficult to see how each quarter works in your current routine, do it every semester, preferably before the holiday period and before Christmas.

If you have a management team, also emphasise the importance *for them* to take the time for this, as it will likely help them get to know themselves better.

When you have a self-sufficient, mature, and secure entity, it is very beneficial to spread the importance of self-reflection among them, as it is important for you as a leader that they reflect on their work, culture, and well-being.

Self-reflection is a concrete tool that cultivates a values-based culture.

1. Self-reflection on yourself as a person:

- *How have I handled stress and challenges over the past quarter?*
- *What personal progress have I made in the past quarter?*
- *What personal challenges have I faced in the past quarter?*

2. Self-reflection on yourse f as a leader:

- *How have I dealt with challenges and difficulties as a leader over the past quarter?*
- *What progress have I made as a leader in the past quarter?*
- *In which areas do I need to improve as a leader?*

3. Self-reflection on your role:

- *How have I managed my role as the leader of my entity over the past quarter?*
- *What successes has my entity had over the past quarter, and how have I shown my appreciation?*
- *What challenges has my entity faced over the past quarter, and how have I helped them overcome these?*

4. Self-reflection on recovery:

- *How have I taken care of my own health and well-being over the past quarter?*
- *What activities have I done to relax and recover over the past quarter?*
- *What changes do I need to make to improve my recovery in the next quarter?*

5. Self-reflection on communication and collaboration:

- *How have I communicated with my entity over the past quarter? Have I been clear and effective in my communication?*
- *What successes has my entity had regarding collaboration in the past quarter, and how did I acknowledge them?*
- *What challenges have arisen in communication or collaboration, and how have I worked to resolve them?*

6. Self-reflection on my self-leadership:

- *Have I kept my vision in focus in my way of leading myself?*
- *What situations have there been where I felt I led myself the way I want and where I did not fully succeed?*
- *How has this reflected in my behaviour and actions?*

7. Self-reflection on professional development:

- *What new knowledge or skills have I developed over the past quarter?*
- *Have I participated in any training, seminars, mentorships, or workshops to enhance my leadership skills?*
- *What areas do I want to continue developing in the next quarter?*

8. Self-reflection on goals and progress:

- *Have I achieved the goals I set for myself and my entity over the past quarter?*
- *What progress have I and my entity made toward our overall goals, and have I acknowledged them?*
- *Are there any adjustments or improvements that need to be made to increase the likelihood of reaching our goals?*

9. Self-reflection on leadership and feedback:

- *How have I given feedback and supported my team members over the past quarter?*
- *Have I created an environment where appreciative and developmental feedback is welcomed and encouraged?*
- *What improvements can I make regarding my leadership and my ability to give feedback?*

10. Self-reflection on time management and priorities:

- *How have I managed my time and priorities over the past quarter?*
- *Have I been effective in focusing on the most important tasks and avoiding distractions?*
- *Are there any improvements I can make in organizing my time and prioritizing tasks?*

11. Self-reflection on work-life balance:

- *How have I maintained a balance between my work life and family life over the past quarter?*
- *Have I spent enough time with my family and taken care of my personal relationships?*
- *Are there any adjustments or improvements I can make to better integrate work and family life?*

12. Self-reflection on innovation and change:

- *Have I and my entity identified new opportunities over the past quarter?*
- *Have we implemented any changes or improvements to increase efficiency and productivity?*
- *What challenges have we encountered regarding driving change and innovation, and how have we handled them?*

13. Self-reflection on my communication style:

- *How actively do I listen to opinions, ideas, and concerns?*
    - *Do I show genuine interest and empathy?*
    - *Can I listen more attentively?*
- *Do I create a safe environment?*
    - *How have I handled conflicts and difficult conversations?*
    - *Do I give my team members space to express their opinions and feelings?*
    - *Do I listen openly to different perspectives and try to understand others' viewpoints?*
- *Do I create conditions for participation and open communication?*
    - *How have I promoted a culture of open communication and listening within my entity?*
    - *Have there been situations where I needed to stand up for diversity and equality, and how have I handled these situations?*
    - *Have I created space for regular meetings and discussions where everyone can share their thoughts and ideas to promote a values-based culture with open communication?*
    - *Do I actively encourage attentive listening and mutual respect?*
    - *What additional actions can I take to promote a strong communication culture?*

Self-reflection: Values-based Leadership

A. Reflect on the past three months and identify which situations have been particularly challenging or successful. Consider how you acted in these situations and if there is anything you would have done differently based on your moral principles and values.

B. Reflect on the challenges that your entity has faced over the past quarter. Consider whether you have acted in accordance with your values, been authentic, and if there are areas for your development.

C. Reflect on the actions you have taken to strengthen the values-based culture over the past quarter. Think about whether there are actions you can take to promote and reinforce the values-based culture within your entity.

Self-reflection: Situational Leadership

A. Reflect on the different situations that have arisen over the past quarter where you needed to use your situational leadership. Identify specific situations where you have employed different leadership styles. Reflect on whether you chose the right leadership style for each specific situation.

B. Consider how you have used the supportive leadership style. Have you actively supported and encouraged your team members? Have you created a safe and positive work environment? Reflect on whether there are situations where you can improve being more supportive at both the individual and entity level.

C. Reflect on how you have used the coaching leadership style. Have you helped your team members develop their skills and reach their personal and collective goals? Have you provided feedback and supported them in their development? Consider whether there are occasions where you can improve in being more coaching-oriented and if you can challenge them in other ways that better suit their individual needs to help them develop and grow.

D. Reflect on how you have used the directive leadership style. Have you clearly communicated expectations and goals for your entity and in one-on-one conversations? Have you made decisions and provided guidelines to guide your entity? Consider whether there are situations that require you to be more clear and directive.

E. Reflect on how you have used the delegating leadership style. Have you delegated tasks and responsibilities to your team members to promote their development and engagement? Have you shown trust in their ability to perform their tasks? Are there occasions when you micromanaged after you clearly delegated a task with a deadline? Ask yourself why this happened. Consider instances where this occurred. Is there a pattern in your delegation style that is not fully effective in a values-based, trust-based environment?

Reflection, Section D

1. Pause if you have a bad feeling in your gut and reflect; have you violated your values, your moral principles, your moral compass? Is the answer found in your responses on page 90; in morality/ethics/whether you are authentic/do you stand up for your integrity?

2. Reflect on your deepest values. *What would you never do?*

3. Do you compromise your innermost values, and how does it manifest internally and to your surroundings?

4. Reflect on your identity, the image you have of yourself. Is it the image you want to have of yourself? Can you use self-leadership as support, where you make visible your current state, the image you want to have/where you want to go/feel/see, and establish your strategies on how to get there?

5. How about your comfort zone? Do you continuously challenge yourself by trying new things so you can uncover your true potential?

6. Do you primarily lead with metrics or by creating engagement in your entity?

7. Have you laid out a strategy for values-based leadership?

8. You can change the culture; do you have a plan for how?

You have reached the final section of what I see as fundamental. Leading situationally in the 2020s takes into account cultural shifts, people's needs, and the necessary adjustments in leadership to create intrinsic motivation regardless of background or culture. We have reached the final choice.

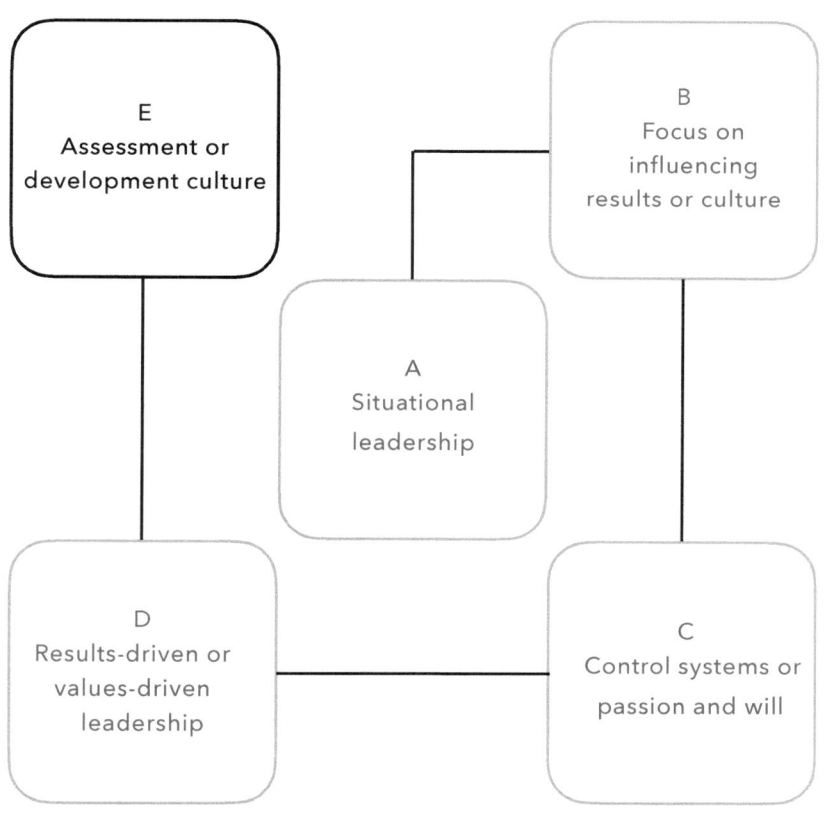

E

Assessment or development culture

A business can never thrive better than its leadership.
Niclas Timmerby

This section, like Section C, represents a choice where the organization you are part of is governed and led in a specific way. It may be based on traditions, old values, or new principles that characterize the entire entity. However, you might feel alone because you are deeply loyal but driven by inner moral aspects and values to lead in a different way.

There is an almost indescribable difference between leading in a judgment culture versus a development culture. This is yet another important choice for you in your leadership. I want to emphasize _your leadership_. You can read about various leadership styles everywhere, but in the end, it is you who faces a comprehensive choice:

1. Are you leading authentically? Have you found your unique and genuine way to lead that makes you feel secure and comfortable?

2. Or are you leading "automatically" based on other people's truths, other people's leadership, experiences, viewpoints, principles, old cultures, policies, or even values?

I deeply value your uniqueness, which is why I describe Sections B-E as choices. If you do not choose the path you should walk yourself, you are living by someone else's truth. I present different choices; then it is up to you.
Be gentle in your leadership towards yourself, choose the paths that you feel align securely with your moral principles and values, but lead in your way. Find your paths and dare to fail so that it comes from you; when it's genuine, your entity will sense that it is authentic and honest. Only when you show vulnerability, are genuine, and authentic can you change people's perspectives, and consequently, the culture.

"A business can never thrive better than its leadership."
I return to my earlier quote. Leadership is the fastest way to achieve a good work environment, to get an entity to strive towards the vision, to foster a willingness to contribute, which leads to loyal customers, profitability, productivity, and efficiency.

Leadership sets the pace for everything in an entity; hence my quote that a business never performs better than its leadership. If the leadership is motivating, the team members are motivated, and vice versa.

> *"A leader in a development culture is a visionary who can see the potential in their employees and help them grow and develop.*
>
> *Creating a culture where learning and development are part of daily life is essential, and where employees feel supported and encouraged to take their own initiatives."*
> *- Ken Blanchard*

If we take motivation as an example:
When a leader motivates, inspires, and supports their team members, it creates engagement over time, which positively affects the work environment. With a motivating culture and a positive work environment, the likelihood of the entity achieving successful results is higher. It is logical.

If the leader is not motivating, inspiring, and supportive, the team members will reflect this factor over time, influencing the culture, work environment, atmosphere, passion, will, and everything else that creates the entity's future results. This is also completely logical.

This applies to everything you as a leader communicate to your entity. You as a leader are extremely important and significant. As the very old quote from the philosopher, speaker, and politician from ancient Rome, Marcus Tullius Cicero, who lived from 106 BC to 43 BC states: *"What you sow, you will reap."* So much time has passed, and so many historically have used this quote. Notable figures like Mahatma Gandhi in his autobiography in 1927, Martin Luther King Jr. in several speeches and writings during the 1950s and 1960s, and more recently, figures like Oprah Winfrey, Steve Jobs, and Michelle Obama have employed this incredibly insightful quote. It should be framed in every home and workplace as a humble reminder from the beginning of our calendar (AD 1 according to the Christian tradition) to us and to future generations.

"It's not what you have said, done, or achieved that demonstrates how effective you have been as a leader.

It's about how many people have grown from your leadership.

Leadership is not about numbers; it's about people."
- Niclas Timmerby

Be Mindful, Think of Your Superpower.
In your leadership, whatever team you have the great privilege to work with as a leader; at home, in your potential parenthood, in the workplace, in an association, or among relatives and friends. Take time to periodically reflect: *"Am I a role model?" "Am I an exemplary figure?" "Am I a leader?"*

Visualize yourself in your superhero costume and consider your incredible superpower: the ability and power to influence people.
So, what are you continuously sending out to yourself and to your surroundings? What do you want to reap from what you sow? You are shaped by what you put out, and it becomes part of your identity. Your

identity is characterized by paradigms. Your surroundings are influenced by what you project, and as a leader, this creates your reputation. Be thoughtful. *What you sow, you will reap.*

Self-awareness.

I wrote this quote nine years ago:

"If the world were to turn in your favor for a day and observe your behavior and attitude; what would you teach the world?"

This came when I studied the incredible benefits of self-awareness as a leader. My truth in life until then was that self-awareness is: being aware of my strengths and weaknesses as a person.

Soon, I became aware that many factors together create good self-awareness. Here, I have distilled good self-awareness into six main components:

1. I am aware of my strengths and weaknesses, values, and beliefs.
2. I can identify and understand my own thoughts, feelings, behaviors, and motivations.
3. I have the ability to see how my behavior, attitude (my signals), and actions affect others.
4. I have the ability to have a realistic and clear understanding of myself.
5. I can see myself objectively without distorting reality.
6. I am aware of what I communicate to the outside world.

- *The only one who can take responsibility for your self-awareness is you.*
- *The only one who can understand, reflect, influence, and change the degree of your self-awareness is you.*

A Wonderful Tool for You.

When I was giving a lecture, a participant asked me, *"How can I easily achieve good self-awareness, because it's hard when life is just rushing by with all the musts?"*

Without thinking at all, I answered immediately in that moment, and it may have been the wisest insight I have ever gained:

"If you approach every situation in life with humility, whether in private life, professional life, or any other situation, you will automatically achieve the highest level of self-awareness."

This is indeed true. If you decide to be mindful, the next time you interact with a person, whether they are in the same room or you are communicating through phone, text, email, or any other medium - do so with humility. *To be humble means to fully recognize that you are not worth more or better than anyone else on the planet. It is also about being empathetic; listening actively and having the ability to place yourself in another person's feelings, perspectives, and experiences while being receptive and showing respect for their opinions and viewpoints.*

I heard a beautiful story about humility and self-awareness. I don't know if it is true, but authenticity matters less in this context: A question was posed to a group of adults: *"If you could have an extra pair of eyes, where would you place them?"* The most common answer from the adults was: *"On the back of my head."*

The same question was posed to a child who replied, *"What would I need them for? I already have eyes; I would give them to someone who is blind."*

Being humble can also mean giving up something for the sake of another person who needs it more, having the ability to see, perceive, and be aware of others' needs and being willing to sacrifice or forgo something to help or support someone else. For instance, giving up a spot in a queue, sharing, or relinquishing an opportunity so someone else who benefits more from that opportunity can take advantage of it.

If, hypothetically, you are humble in a store, you might notice a person who seems stressed, holding two items, hurriedly trying to reach the checkout. With humility, you see that person and, with a smile, willingly let them take your place in line. Later, as you exit the store, you see a crowd gathered around an elderly person lying on the pavement. You walk closer and see that the stressed individual in the store bought two bottles of water for the elderly person to help them hydrate because they are not feeling well. You notice many people are helping, and you hear that an ambulance is on the way, so you continue on your way. As you nearly pass the crowd, the stressed individual notices you and nods kindly in your direction.

Self-awareness and humility = Identity and character.
One of the seven factors that together create your self-concept is self-awareness. *It is interesting that both humility and self-awareness are part of that.*

(Self-awareness, as you learned earlier, is included in your self-concept. This theory was developed by psychologist Carl Rogers and published in 1951. In his book, "Client-Centered Therapy", Rogers describes self-concept as the image and perception an individual has of themselves, including their attributes, skills, and values. Carl Rogers' work has

greatly impacted psychology and therapy and contributed to understanding people's self-perception and self-esteem.)

In addition to these two wonderful tools in life, self-awareness and humility, the following aspects are also briefly included in self-awareness:
- Being aware of your values,
- Being aware of your patterns (behaviors/attitudes) that you unconsciously and consciously follow in life, and
- Being aware of the traits that create your character.

The image you currently see of yourself, the "truth" or paradigm you think of yourself right now, is your <u>identity</u>.

All the little traits you possess create your <u>character</u>. Your character is what others perceive and see as you.

Think about how changing your self-image can alter your identity and truth. I recall playing soccer just two days ago with a grandchild who only used his right foot. I encouraged him to try using his left foot, and he said, "I can't do that." I told him to give it a shot, and a few minutes later, I saw him smiling because he could do it. He changed his truth; a small part of his identity and self-concept transformed within minutes. He accomplished something he didn't believe he could do; he shifted his paradigm.

Another grandchild recently started sleeping in his own room. It resulted in several chaotic nights during which the parent patiently carried the child back. Then, all of a sudden, it worked, and the child could sleep in his own room. One truth shifted to another, and you could see the pride in the child when he happily announced that he could sleep alone. His identity and self-concept changed, and he grew in his own eyes, a significant step toward independence.

I wrote in "Show Your Gold": *"The meaning of life is not to try to change yourself. The meaning of life is to change your view of yourself."* *There is a crucial distinction; when we strive to change ourselves, we often do so for others' sake. We want to fit in and please others; we simply want to be liked and loved. When you work on changing your perception of yourself, you simultaneously change your self-concept (your identity, how you see yourself). When we change how we view ourselves, our abilities, and how others perceive us, it reshapes our perspective. This requires insights and courage. Without change, no development can occur.* **The more you challenge yourself and your learned truths, the more you grow.**

> *"We know that our development is progressing when our self-awareness no longer comes afterward."*
> *- Niclas Timmerby*

So with this insight, do you have self-awareness?
Humility and self-awareness are indeed best friends.
They constantly and cumulatively influence each other, which is fantastic because the effect becomes significantly greater than if you only think about or focus on one aspect. *If you focus on humility, you automatically gain self-awareness. If you have self-awareness, you are humble.*

Self-awareness is the most important tool for you as a human being and a leader. It takes you where you want to be and towards your goals.

*You remember the steps in (2) self-leadership: you have a **current state** and a **crystal-clear vision** of your leadership (or anything else in life, for your health, finances, relationships, or your own development), as well as **strategies** for how you progressively move towards your vision.*

I believe Martina Navratilova, at the height of her career, demonstrated incredible self-awareness when she said, *"The better I get, the more I realize how much better I can be."*

That's why I include self-reflection for you after each section and chapter, to create insight and self-awareness. For you to continually develop, self-awareness is required for you to consciously step out of your comfort zone and see yourself, your behavior, attitudes, and actions from a helicopter perspective.

> *"Self-awareness is the beginning of all wisdom."*
> *- Aristotle, Greek philosopher (384-322 BC)*

Reflection is an excellent way to create self-awareness and a deeper understanding of yourself as a person.

What is my leadership style in this context? Do I lead in relation to an assessment or development culture?
On the following two pages, you have a self-assessment questionnaire with eighteen statements where you can reflect in peace.

If you answer "yes," you are currently leading in relation to a development culture. Take the time to reflect on how you could act differently in future situations when you answer "no" to the statements.

Statements

1. I provide regular feedback to my team members.

Yes   No

2. I take the time to get to know my team members and their needs, interests, and goals.

Yes   No

3. I communicate clearly and effectively with my team members and actively listen to their views and opinions.

Yes   No

4. I encourage my team members to take initiative and try new ideas.

Yes   No

5. I focus on identifying and developing my team members' strengths and positive qualities.

Yes   No

6. I give my team members the opportunity to learn from their mistakes and grow through them.

Yes   No

7. I promote open and honest communication where my team members feel safe to express their views and thoughts.

Yes   No

8. I give my team members the opportunity to participate in decision-making and influence their own working environment.

Yes   No

9. I ensure that my team members feel appreciated and recognised for their contributions.

Yes   No

10. I encourage and support my team members' professional development and learning, and I also encourage them to take personal responsibility for their own development and careers.

Yes   No

11. I show respect and empathy towards my team members and treat them with dignity and integrity.

Yes   No

12. I strive to promptly resolve conflicts and misunderstandings in a constructive manner and avoid creating a negative working environment.

Yes   No

13. I promote a culture where mistakes are seen as opportunities for learning and improvement.

Yes   No

14. I offer support and guidance to my team members when needed.

Yes   No

15. I create an environment where my team members feel safe to challenge existing processes and suggest changes.

Yes   No

16. I try to give my team members the opportunity to develop and utilise their unique talents and competencies.

Yes   No

17. I am open to receiving honest feedback and regularly reflect on my own leadership style.

Yes   No

18. I take personal responsibility for creating a positive and inclusive work culture where everyone feels welcomed and respected.

Yes   No

As you could see, there was room to make mistakes in two statements. This is because creating a culture that promotes initiative within your entity and allows for failures and mistakes benefits:

- *Inner motivation,*
- *Participation, and*
- *Having trust in the leadership*

Three incredibly fundamental aspects of leadership that create the conditions for effective leadership today.

A development culture benefits the overall work environment, the reputation of the organization as a whole, and contributes to pride and the desire of team members to stay with their workplace.

Creating an accepted feedback culture.

The reason I wrote about feedback as statement number one is because feedback is linked to the word development. *If you can create an accepted feedback culture in your entity, it will foster development. It is like having the right key for the right lock, or like a bird having wings to be able to fly, or finding the missing puzzle piece.*

The greatest advantage of an accepted feedback culture.

It allows your entity to truly have high ceilings, meaning that everyone accepts feedback because they want to grow in their respective roles.

I want to start by highlighting ten differences between a performance culture and a development culture. Reflect to gain further substance around this important topic. Of course, there is always a combination of these when you encounter different situations and contexts in your leadership. The question is: what is your primary choice?

Development Culture	Assessment Culture
Feedback Given continuously and constructively to support individual development. Naturally viewed as an opportunity for learning and improvement.	Feedback Given frequently in the form of evaluations and scoring. Formal and more focused on assessing performance and results rather than promoting development.
Tolerance Level and Trust A high tolerance for mistakes and errors creates high trust in leadership. Mistakes are seen as part of the learning process and are used as an opportunity to grow and improve.	Tolerance Level and Trust Lower tolerance for mistakes and errors. Mistakes may be viewed negatively and can affect the assessment of an individual's performance, resulting in low trust in leadership.
Communication Open and transparent communication to facilitate collaboration.	Communication Communication can be more hierarchical and focused on reporting results.
Leadership Leaders act more as mentors and support individual development.	Leadership Leaders act more as evaluators and assess individual performance.
Self-reflection Encourages team members and managers to engage in self-reflection to promote personal growth, as well as to communicate with their immediate supervisor after self-reflection.	Self-reflection/Assessment Team members and managers are offered the opportunity to share their thoughts anonymously; external digital assessments and evaluations are also common.

Development Culture	Assessment Culture
Focus Concentrates on promoting and supporting individual growth and learning. Emphasis is placed on identifying and harnessing the potential of each individual.	**Focus** Focuses on assessing and evaluating individual performance and results. There is an emphasis on measuring and comparing performance against standards or norms.
Reward System Rewards are based on individual progress, initiative, and development.	**Reward System** Rewards are based on the individual's measured performance and results.
Work Environment An environment that fosters learning, creativity, and innovation. Flexibility is pursued to enable individual development and learning.	**Work Environment** An environment aimed at maintaining standards and achieving results. The focus may be more on following predetermined processes and procedures.
Career Development Offers opportunities for career development by promoting learning, growth, and the broadening of skills.	**Career Development** The focus may be more on assessing the individual's performance and experiences to make decisions regarding career opportunities.
Long-term Perspective Focuses on the individual's long-term development and growth. Emphasis is placed on investing in individual potential and creating an environment that promotes continuous development.	**Long-term Perspective** Focuses more on short-term results and performance. It may be more oriented towards evaluating performance based on specific goals or requirements.

Summary. In a development culture, personal and professional growth, as well as initiative and intentions, are encouraged, while an assessment culture is more focused on evaluating and assessing individual performance and results.

The process of creating a feedback culture.

1. Feedback is development through care.
2. Why a feedback culture?
3. The core of feedback.
4. Which feedback model is preferred?
5. The four levels of feedback and insight into the reaction ladder.
6. Process description/workshop to implement an accepted feedback culture.

(1) Feedback is development through care

You give feedback out of care because you want to see the person grow. If you lead by focusing on developing people rather than assessing them, you allow team members to fail when delegating a task, which they automatically feel in the development culture you have created.

You praise intentions and provide support for development through feedback, which means that the entity dares to take initiative and try things again = resulting in your team members and your entity developing and growing at a much faster pace than in an assessment culture.

When your focus as a leader is on development, you are already well on your way to creating a development culture. An entity that is secure in this culture is ready to take the next step: an accepted feedback culture.

(2) Why a feedback culture?

As a leader, you want to use feedback naturally and acceptably in everyday life to get the best out of your team members. You want to honestly express what you observe in daily life that can help develop the person.

All feedback models are essentially change models.

The foundation of appreciative and developmental feedback is that you want to:

- Build trust and strengthen relationships by recognizing and appreciating performances, intentions, and contributions.
- Create a positive work culture where appreciation and positive reinforcement foster intrinsic motivation, engagement, collaboration, and an objective perspective among employees.
- Promote learning and personal development by identifying areas for improvement and providing concrete action suggestions.
- Support growth and progress through constructive criticism and guidance to achieve goals and improve skills.

(3) The core of feedback

There are several key elements in a methodology that are important to establish for successful feedback. Feedback follows a clear pattern that is recognized. *My recommendation regarding feedback is to keep it simple. From my experience, having too many things to "think about" can detract from the naturalness of giving and receiving feedback. If it is easy and natural to give feedback, it is easy and natural to receive feedback. Feedback is given out of care, not because it is stated in a job description. Leadership is about helping people grow, including in feedback. It is also important for you to ask for feedback from people around you for your own development.*

Here are the four most important things to consider <u>when giving feedback</u>:

1. Have the conversation as soon as possible after the situation/behavior.

You cannot come a week after the situation/event and expect to achieve a successful result; feedback should be given as soon as possible, keeping in mind that it is likely the recipient has not thought about their behavior or attitude.

2. The conversation should be private.

Feedback should be given to the person concerned, without anyone else present. Your focus is on developing the individual in front of you, to increase their awareness, develop their skills, or perhaps improve their work. If you provide feedback in front of others, there is a significant risk that (1) the recipient will focus on what others might hear, and (2) it may create a lack of trust towards you as a leader, both from the recipient and those who are listening.

3. Use "I" and "You" in the conversation.

To gain trust from the recipient, do not discuss what others may have done or not done, or what they may have seen or not seen. It is about two individuals, no more. Use "I" and "you" to clarify perspectives and responsibilities. This indicates that it is <u>your</u> personal opinion, creating a constructive dialogue that can move the recipient forward. Saying "<u>you</u>" emphasizes that the focus is on the recipient and their personal development.

4. Connect the situation with the behavior you noticed.

A. You want to clearly highlight the event or situation you observed and directly link it to the behavior.

You do this to (1) separate the person from the event/situation to objectively avoid the recipient feeling attacked and taking a defensive position.

And (2) when you clearly connect the factors, the recipient can quickly gain a clear understanding of their own behavior/attitude.

B. After highlighting, ask how the recipient feels.

C. Focus on suggestions for how the behavior or attitude can be improved and what the benefits could be for the person's development.

D. Conclude by asking for confirmation that your feedback has been received, and thank the person for listening.

The four most important things to consider for the recipient of feedback:

1. Active listening.
Focus on listening and looking for the "gold." It is very easy to find faults in a conversation; if we look for faults, we will certainly find them. (In communication, I therefore talk about the "Gold in Every Conversation," as an "anchor" or "standard" I want to maintain in communication to show respect for the giver and for my own development.) If I look for faults, I do not develop; if I look for "gold," I do.

2. Openness to development.

When a giver indicates they want to provide feedback, it is a genuine gift for the recipient. If you, as a recipient, view it as a gift in the form of free development, which is simply fantastic, it creates receptiveness to what is to be shared in terms of attentiveness and anticipation.

Listen for "gold" without interrupting; when you find the "gold," you will understand. If you do not understand, show interest and ask follow-up questions.

3. Ask questions for necessary clarifications.

Your focus as a recipient is to understand. If you do not understand, the conversation will not yield anything valuable for you or the giver.

Ask for clarity: "Can you explain in more detail?", "Can you provide more examples?", "Can you suggest specific steps I can take to improve?", "Can you give a clearer picture of what you expect from me?"

By asking questions to understand, you show that you, as a recipient, are open to feedback in a constructive way.

4. Gratitude.

The person giving feedback has taken the time to reflect and then, with care, wanted to help develop another person. This is something to be very grateful for. Thanking for the feedback creates a positive atmosphere and encourages the giver to continue providing natural feedback.

(4) Which feedback model is preferred?

There are many different good models for feedback; my recommendation is to explore the competencies and previous experiences within your entity or, if you can choose, select one that you feel best fits your development. There are several good options, such as the Pendulum Model, Sandwich Model, SBI (Situation, Behavior, Impact), 360-Degree Feedback, and Strengths Model.

The model I have become fond of is Appreciative Inquiry (AI), created by researchers David Cooperrider and Suresh Srivastva in the 1980s. This model has over the years received significant attention and support from researchers and practitioners in areas such as organizational theory, change management, positive psychology, as well as in developmental leadership, education, social work, and healthcare.

The model can be described as follows:
"AI" focuses on identifying and amplifying positive aspects and strengths of individuals and organizations rather than concentrating on problems and deficiencies.

Several well-known entities around the world have utilized this model, including Apple, Google, NASA, The Coca-Cola Company, General Electric, Royal Dutch Shell, Microsoft, BM, Boeing, Marriott International, Procter & Gamble, Ford Motor Company, Unilever, Zappos, Johnson & Johnson, IKEA, Volvo Group, H&M, Equinor and Southwest Airlines.

The AI model emphasises focusing on the positive and identifying and building upon successes and strengths. By creating a positive and appreciative atmosphere, this can lead to increased motivation, engagement, and creativity among employees and within organisations.

The model follows a 4-D process, which stands for Discover, Dream, Design, and Deliver. This process aims to identify what works well, visualise a desired future, create an action plan, and implement changes. The model can be applied in areas such as organisational development, change management, team development, conflict resolution, and individual development. It can be used by companies, organisations, teams, and individuals and has proven effective in promoting engagement, motivation, and positive work environments.

The model has been further developed, one form of which is called "*The Four Feedback Types*," developed by researcher and author Anna Carroll (she has also created several models, including the well-known COIN model). Anna Carroll focuses on developing and improving performance in all four levels of "The Four Feedback Types."

I have adapted the model slightly and added the factors that create passion and will (section C) and am opening up for moral principles and values when I am involved in change work. I call this "*the four levels of feedback for all generations and cultures.*"

(5) The four levels of feedback and insights into the reaction ladder.
The higher level at which you provide feedback, the more is required of you as a leader in terms of training and preparation.

Level 1:
Appreciative feedback based on a good performance/a well-executed task. Something related to WHAT.
"What has the team member done that makes you want to give praise?"

I am sure you provide this form of feedback to your entity every workday; it can be praising and appreciating, for example:
- *A well-executed performance.*
- *Good collaboration, camaraderie, good leadership.*
- *Exceeding expectations.*
- *Significant progress or improvements.*
- *Managing a high workload.*
- *Demonstrating creativity, being solution-oriented.*
- *A high degree of accountability, having taken initiative.*
- *Meeting deadlines.*
- *The ability to prioritise.*
- *Consistency of good quality in work.*

Level 1 strengthens relationships, creates job satisfaction, and fosters a good working environment.
Saying, *"May I give you feedback?"* and after you have highlighted the situation saying, *"I think that was well done by you."* creates so many positive synergies: motivation, engagement, pride, courage to try things outside of one's comfort zone. The team member feels seen, appreciated, recognised, and valued. Take every unique opportunity that arises to give appreciative feedback at Level 1.

Do you remember the survey on page 50 regarding what employees feel is most important in the workplace? The most important was: "to be seen." Every time you give feedback at Level 1, your team members feel seen and acknowledged.

Level 2:
Developmental feedback based on a performance/a completed task. Something related to WHAT.
"*What* can the team member *improve* in order to develop?"

With training and a methodology presented in your own genuine way, this level is only marginally more difficult to provide than Level 1.

Take, for example, the ten points I mentioned at Level 1, and think of an opposite scenario. For example: the team member does not meet deadlines, does not take responsibility, or has difficulty prioritising.

At Level 2, you highlight that there is potential for improvement.
(1) Use "I" and "you."
(2) Clearly highlight the specific situation/event that has occurred.
(3) Suggest a solution.
(4) Ask for confirmation.

Examples of what feedback conversations might look like in the three situations:
- A team member does not meet deadlines.
- A team member does not take responsibility.
- A team member has difficulty prioritising.

"May I give you feedback? I find it disappointing when you do not meet deadlines; this morning you were 10 minutes late to work. I would appreciate it if you could arrive on time in the future. Does that feel acceptable to you?"

"May I give you feedback? When you spoke with the customer just now, I heard that you did not offer a complementary product or upgrade. I would like you to develop this for your own sake, for the customers' sake, and for our company's sake. I would be grateful if you could keep this in mind during the sales process."

"May I give you feedback? When you unpacked the goods earlier, I noticed that you placed the newest items at the front, which risks items needing to be discarded due to expiration dates. Would you like me to go through the procedures with you again, or is this conversation sufficient?"

Now I have gone through the two levels that provide **feedback on what.** *A behaviour or attitude related to a performance or completed task. When you give the gift of feedback at Level 1 and Level 2, you do not need to prepare in any special way; just be natural. The only thing needed is that you prepare your entity for a shared and accepted feedback culture.*

Now to Levels 3 and 4 regarding HOW, these require more from you as a leader. These levels are not something you do in passing; you need to prepare and you need to create space for reflection for the team member in the form of appropriate location and time.

Feedback on how at Level 3 is appreciative feedback and is a positive conversation that your team member will never forget.

Feedback on how at Level 4 refers to developmental feedback when there is no positive example. There is no what you can "sandwich" in, as in sandwich feedback, where you can frame your developmental feedback between appreciative feedback or positive comments.

As a leader, you always need to protect the culture and your team. Therefore, you emphasise that negative behaviour or a negative attitude on a deeper level is not acceptable and must therefore be improved or ceased promptly.

I recommend that you wait to use Level 4 until you feel completely comfortable giving feedback naturally and your entity has successfully worked in a feedback culture for at least six months.

The benefit of starting a feedback culture is that when you have had to give feedback at Level 4 and it is successful, you can provide the same team member feedback at the other three levels.

Level 1 = Appreciation for performance.
Level 2 = Minor adjustments to create improvement and development.
Level 3 = Appreciation for the person, sincere pride.
Level 4 = Insights and significant change, or possibly reassignment or termination.

Actively working towards an accepted feedback culture will create time, respect, and trust for you as a leader.

Level 3:

Appreciative feedback based on one's own drive, motivation, and enthusiasm to strengthen the culture as a role model through personality and character. Something related to HOW.

"<u>How</u>" has the team member acted to strengthen the culture?"

This level is something truly exceptional; it is here that you can really change people's lives. It is here that you can help a person truly believe in themselves and their abilities, ignite even more passion, and pursue their goals with greater enthusiasm. This feedback conversation will be one that your team member will never forget.

This feedback level, like Level 4, requires your preparation in terms of time and a place where the team member has the opportunity for reflection if they need it after the conversation. Also prepare time for your own reflection. Both Level 3 and Level 4 can be energy-consuming, even though they are two completely different forms of conversation.

What you should praise the individual for is <u>not what</u> the team member does in terms of performance, but <u>how</u> the team member strengthens the culture, which means that the team member reinforces/cultivates one or more of the following incredibly important factors: job satisfaction, working environment, engagement, communication, motivation, creativity, well-being, and team spirit.

Each of these elements positively affects efficiency, productivity, and focus, leading to positive results. So take the time to truly convey how incredibly significant your team member is through feedback at Level 3.

<u>Here are two examples of feedback at Level 3:</u>

"May <u>I</u> give <u>you</u> feedback? <u>I</u> saw how <u>you</u> praised and encouraged X to do a fantastic job and told X that you believe in him/her.

<u>I</u> appreciate <u>you</u> very much; <u>you</u> are so important to our team and take great responsibility in a humble way. Thank you!"

"May <u>I</u> give <u>you</u> feedback? <u>I</u> see every day how <u>you</u> share yourself with our customers. <u>You</u> genuinely offer your own personality to others, and <u>I</u> also see how they truly appreciate <u>you</u>. <u>You</u> do the same with your colleagues.

<u>I</u> wanted to let <u>you</u> know here in private how amazing <u>I</u> think <u>you</u> are; thank you!"

Be prepared for your team member to display a lot of emotions after receiving what you feel in private; allow the reaction to take the time it needs, and do not be afraid to show your own emotions.

At Level 3, you can express appreciation for all the soft values the person contributes within your entity, e.g., behaviour, attitude, passion, vision, mission, values, culture, and team spirit.

(You can later in the book connect Level 3 to Maslow's hierarchy of needs and how I have reinterpreted it from human needs to the needs a team member needs to feel internally in order to progressively want to "climb" higher up the ladder.)

Level 4:

Developmental feedback based on a behaviour or attitude that demoralises the culture. Something related to HOW.

"How has the team member acted to weaken the culture?"

Do you remember what I wrote briefly about negative culture carriers in an entity? I will address this clearly later in the book. Level 4 is about addressing this through feedback, at the highest and most challenging level, and getting the team member to gain insight into what they are causing, with the aim of creating improvement.

One person (1) can demoralise the culture and thereby negatively affect the mood and atmosphere and the working environment.

"It is easy to focus attention on those who are loud and take up space.

But do not forget the quiet, steady, and loyal ones. For in the end, they will leave – while those who are loud and take up space remain."

- Niclas Timmerby

If you, as a leader, do not provide feedback at Level 4, there is a very high risk that the team member will continue to display undesirable behaviour or a poor attitude, lack of engagement, or behave in a way that undermines trust and cooperation.

Based on my experience after working with many teams, it is common for this team member to also try to undermine you as a leader.

One person is enough to bring down the entire team. The greatest risk is that the best, most development-ready team members you have may leave if nothing is done about those who *are slowly dismantling the culture and job satisfaction.*

In every conversation I have had with managers and leaders (and there are many), 100 percent of them have answered the same thing when I asked the question, _"Which employees do you spend the most time, energy, focus, and engagement on?"_ They have all responded, _"Those who do not really want to be in the workplace."_ When I ask follow-up questions, it becomes clear that this is because these individuals are negative culture carriers who, through their behaviour and attitude, negatively affect their colleagues and the culture.

This is where feedback at Level 4 comes into play. I have previously stated that feedback is the tool that allows you to genuinely have an open environment in the workplace. _Feedback may not be the ultimate solution, as perhaps the team member and the entity simply need to part ways. The significant thing you have done as a leader is to clearly demonstrate what is not working; you have listened, and you have proposed a solution. If the employment is eventually terminated, you have acted as a role model and clearly strived to create a change/ improvement so that the team member could continue their employment._

At Level 4, you use the same four basic steps as at Level 2. The most important thing is that you can elicit what people feel inside in order to discuss potential solutions and achieve improvement.

Here are some fundamental suggestions on how to handle four different situations through feedback at Level 4. You will receive:
(A) Example of hypothetical situation.
(B) A start-up where you highlight the situation.
(C) Suggestions for solutions.
(D) A conclusion where you ask for confirmation.

(A) Lack of engagement.

(B) *"May I give you feedback? I have observed that you seem to have lost your engagement in your work. I want to understand what might have caused this and how we can work together to increase your engagement. Is there anything specific that has happened that has affected your engagement? Is there anything I can do to help you feel more engaged?"*

(C) *"Thank you for sharing; I understand that you have found it difficult to feel motivated and engaged in your work when you feel like you are standing still. If you'd like, we can schedule a meeting where you and I can discuss your tasks and see if there's a possibility to delegate differently or assign more challenging tasks to you?"*

(D) *"Thank you for opening up about what has affected your engagement. I am here to support you and help create a more engaging and productive work environment for all of us. I think it's very good that you and I can have open communication. Do you feel we have made progress?"*

(A) Difficulties in collaboration.

(B) *"May I give you feedback? I have noticed that you have been having difficulties collaborating effectively with your colleagues lately. I see how this clearly creates tension within the team. It is important that we all work together to strive towards the vision and achieve our common goals. Can you share what challenges you are experiencing regarding collaboration?"*

(C) *"Thank you for sharing your challenges so that I can understand what you are feeling. We are all different, and we need to tackle that with* respect and understanding. _I_ think this is very important, and _you_ are vital to the team. Would _you_ like us to schedule a lunch together so we can talk further?"

(D) _"I think it's so important that we can talk about everything; thank you again for sharing how you feel. Reflect on this calmly, and we can meet for lunch the day after tomorrow. Does it feel good for you that we had this conversation?"_

(A) Negative behaviour.
(B) _"May I give you feedback? I have personally heard on three separate occasions that you tend to speak poorly of your colleagues about their contributions and who they are as people. I cannot accept this form of behaviour; it creates a negative work environment, and it affects our culture and job satisfaction. For me, it is super important that we all respect each other and create a positive and supportive workplace. Can you tell me why you speak poorly of your colleagues?"_

(C) _"Thank you for understanding my perspective and sharing your thoughts. I want you and I to meet for five minutes once a week starting next week so we can talk openly about how you can be a role model for our team through your demeanour and how you can express your opinions in a respectful way directly to the person concerned through feedback. I will support you in this."_

(D) _"I ask you to reflect on our conversation and focus on the positive aspects of your colleagues and that you actively work on building a positive work environment. Does it feel clear to you that I want us to move forward together?"_

(A) Poor attitude.

(B) *"May I give you feedback? I have noticed that you are displaying a poor attitude towards our customers, most recently just five minutes ago. Rolling your eyes at customers and not saying a genuine thank you when they have made a purchase creates a negative experience for them and can affect our company's reputation and customer relationships. It is important for me that we all show respect and appreciation towards our customers. For me, this is not acceptable; can you tell me why you have this poor attitude?"*

(C) *"Thank you for sharing your feelings. Having a positive attitude towards customers is crucial in creating a good customer experience, building strong customer relationships, and maintaining our company's reputation. I suggest that you and I have a meeting this afternoon where we can discuss strategies for handling stress and workload in a more constructive way."*

(D) *"I am here to support you and help you. Do you understand my concerns and why I wanted to share this feedback with you directly?"*

I mention this again out of concern.
Feedback at Level 4 is the most challenging and tough to provide.
Enter the conversation with the understanding that you are offering a gift, which requires great courage from you as a leader, and that the conversation can evoke strong emotions in both the giver and receiver. Prepare the timing for the conversation so that the recipient does not need to go to work or is off the following day, even if they clearly state that it is not a problem.

To receive the clear message as a person that one needs to change in order to function within the entity is tough. The four examples I provided are ideal scenarios. *You do not know if the person will storm out of the room or raise their voice at you, or, as I am most accustomed to, the person may become upset. What you see in the room at that moment may not be the final reaction. In a way, it is a type of trauma that the recipient begins to process in that moment. The recipient will likely never forget the conversation; it is of utmost importance that you base the discussion on facts and prepare the meeting so that you are as secure as possible for various scenarios that may arise. Emphasise in the conversation that a change <u>will</u> create a positive development. Highlight that you are there as support, that you do not wish to harm but to help. Schedule time in your calendar for a one-on-one meeting with the recipient in the near future to follow up on their well-being, feelings, and thoughts.*

Reflection or rumination.

This is an important aspect to be knowledgeable about as a leader and, not least, as a person. *Self-reflection is a healthy and constructive process* where an individual actively and consciously thinks about a specific event or situation in order to learn, grow, and handle similar events and situations better in the future. *Rumination*, on the other hand, *is a negative and repetitive process* that does not lead to any solutions or changes. The individual creates an internal, repetitive process where the focus is on negative thoughts, feelings, worries, mistakes, situations, and events. It can be likened to reflecting excessively, which can be harmful to well-being and mental health over time. Getting caught in this negative thought cycle, where repetition and analysis do not cease, can lead to anxiety, stress, and depression. What creates a negative double effect is that rumination can also prevent the individual from focusing on solutions and handling problems constructively, as they remain trapped in their cycle.

Feedback at Level 4 can create either reflection or rumination.
Thus, it is important that you place great emphasis on getting the recipient's acceptance that a change will help them move forward in their career. You need to convey that you are in the room to help by expressing what you see, and that it comes from genuine concern. It is vital that you schedule follow-up meetings in the near future to monitor the recipient's development and well-being. (At Level 4, more than the other levels, it is a sign of progress when the recipient can speak openly and honestly about their feelings with you.) In your follow-up work, praise small progress and intentions through feedback at Level 1 and larger achievements at Level 3. You may also need to assist the individual in setting short-term goals during your discussions, and it is beneficial to communicate with your entity's HR department should additional support and interventions be needed.

On Rumination.
The American psychologist Susan Nolen-Hoeksema introduced the concept of "ruminative thinking" (over-analyzing or getting stuck in negative thought patterns) in the 1980s, and since then, she has explored its connection to depression, anxiety, and other psychological issues. She emphasizes in her research that rumination is not just about thinking a lot but rather about getting stuck in negative thought patterns and being unable to break that cycle.

Her work has made significant contributions to understanding rumination and its effects on mental health. Research has shown a link between ruminative thinking and an increased risk of depression, anxiety, sleep problems, impaired problem-solving abilities, and poorer recovery from stress and traumatic events.

Researchers like Susan Nolen-Hoeksema, Katharina Kircanski, Stefan G. Hofmann, Alice Sawyer, and Edward Watkins have also conducted studies demonstrating how individuals can break free from ruminative thinking. This is something that should be addressed by therapists or psychologists, as anyone who is in a ruminative state requires individually tailored professional support. A therapist or psychologist can help identify and manage rumination through various therapeutic methods and techniques.

However, I find it essential that you, as a leader providing feedback, have insight at a fundamental level *to more easily interpret signals from your team members. To mention some approaches that research has suggested for breaking the cycle of rumination: CBT (Cognitive Behavioral Therapy), ACT (Acceptance and Commitment Therapy), and MBCT (Mindfulness-Based Cognitive Therapy). Very briefly, these approaches focus on increasing awareness of rumination, challenging negative thought patterns, and learning to let go of negative thoughts through various strategies.*

Introduction: Insight into the Reaction Ladder.

As a wise, unnamed person once said: ***"Feedback is someone caring about you so deeply that they tell you*** <u>***what you need to hear,***</u> ***instead of what you want to hear..."***

Of course, your feedback will create a feeling that leads to a reaction within the recipient. This may be why this "ladder" has so many different names; I have heard of the "aggression ladder," "conflict ladder," "feedback steps," and "escalation and de-escalation model." Altogether, it is a combination of research and theories. The foundation is considered to have been laid in 1994 by the Austrian conflict researcher and author Friedrich Glasl when he published the book

"Konfliktmanagement: Ein Handbuch für Führungskräfte, Beraterinnen und Berater" (Conflict Management: A Handbook for Executives, Consultants, and Mediators). It focused on how a conflict slowly escalates, *ideally not reaching all the stages.*

Very briefly, these are the six steps:

1. Latent conflict.
There is a fundamental disagreement or tension between the parties. The conflict is not yet expressed or visible.
2. Escalation.
The parties begin to show clear signs of an escalating conflict, for example, by expressing dissatisfaction or frustration.
3. Open conflict.
The parties can now engage in open confrontations and exchange arguments, criticism, or even threats. The conflict becomes increasingly visible to those around them.
4. Dehumanisation.
The parties see each other as enemies or as less worthy as human beings. This can lead to prejudice, hatred, and even violence.
5. Damage limitation.
The parties have realised, either on their own or after the involvement of others, that things have gone too far. This is the last step to prevent a breakdown. The parties may here (if they have the courage) attempt to find concrete solutions or compromises.
6. Breakdown.
It becomes clear that the conflict cannot be resolved or managed satisfactorily. A breakdown is a fact, and the parties end the relationship and/or collaboration.

If I go back to what I wrote on page 70 about self-leadership (1), I want to demonstrate the connection: *The better you understand and lead yourself, the better you can understand and lead others.*

Now I am being a bit tough and perhaps challenging you? Your way of _communicating_ and _handling conflicts_ as a leader has a direct symbiosis with your _self-leadership_. The better you understand and lead yourself, the quicker you will notice latent conflicts. You can be more honest, straightforward, and effective, which increases the likelihood of smothering conflicts and disagreements in their infancy. A concrete way for you as a leader is feedback at Level 4.

Never forget that giving feedback is a gift.

This insight makes it easier and more natural to use feedback. I love the following quote by Patricio Telman Chincocolo.

"Feedback is the fruit of courageous people who wish to help others grow."
- Patricio Telman Chincocolo

The Reaction Ladder.

The basic premise of the ladder is to better understand and manage reactions in a conflict. It is perfectly suitable to also use the ladder for feedback. I prefer the term "reaction ladder" because it explains what feedback creates. _A reaction -> how it may manifest -> how you can manage the reaction._

Feedback will _always_ create some form of reaction and some form of change/improvement.

There are many ways to describe the reaction ladder. In the following pages, I will describe one of the most common models. (I have developed the description to facilitate for you as a leader to easily apply the steps to a practical reality.)

Step 1: Ignorance.

In this first step, the recipient does not understand or chooses to ignore your feedback. The reaction may manifest as the person not listening, not taking the feedback seriously, or dismissing it as irrelevant. To manage this reaction, you need to be clear and repeat the feedback in a constructive manner. It is important that you communicate the importance of listening to the recipient and that it is vital to be open in order to develop.

Step 2: Defence.

In the second step, the recipient reacts defensively to the feedback. He or she may argue against, deny, or try to explain away the feedback. To manage this reaction, you need to show empathy and listen actively. This is necessary because you need to understand why, and you will not know unless the recipient shares how they feel. If you can create a safe and permissive environment where the recipient feels comfortable sharing their thoughts and feelings, the conditions for progressing in your conversation are greatly enhanced.

Step 3: Denial.

Here, the recipient very clearly denies your feedback and refuses to accept it. The reaction may be that the recipient does not want to acknowledge their potential shortcomings or believes that what you are saying is outright incorrect. To manage this reaction, you need to be patient and provide specific examples that clearly support your feedback. If you already know that the recipient has difficulties accepting feedback, deliver the feedback right after a specific situation/

event so that it is clear and cannot be denied. What you want with your feedback is to promote positive development.

Step 4: Reflection.
In the fourth step, the recipient begins to reflect on the feedback and its implications. (This is why it is so important to allow for reflection at Level 3 and Level 4.) The reaction may be that the person begins to question their own behaviour and attitude or their own performances and choices. Here, the recipient is very mature, results-oriented, and unpretentious. To manage this reaction, encourage self-reflection and offer your support through follow-up conversations. Inform them that, should they wish, you can also provide support through more frequent feedback for their personal development. Here, the recipient can truly understand and analyse your feedback on a deeper level.

Step 5: Acceptance.
In the final step, the recipient accepts the feedback and takes responsibility for improvement. The reaction may be that the recipient, during the conversation, demonstrates understanding, engagement, and offers suggestions for their own initiatives to develop in their professional role and grow as a person. To support this reaction, you provide positive reinforcement and acknowledge the recipient's efforts and contributions (ideally by openly expressing genuine feelings). The recipient in front of you is an important piece of the puzzle in your long-term work to create a development culture where feedback is seen as an opportunity for growth and learning. The individual you are engaging with is likely a positive cultural bearer for your entire entity and the results you create together.

Process description/workshop for implementing an accepted feedback culture.

I have now gone through appreciative and developmental feedback at all four levels, demonstrated examples, provided concrete suggestions, described the difference between reflection and rumination, and discussed the reaction ladder.

I hope you see the immense benefits of implementing an accepted feedback culture in your entity, which means: *a genuinely open environment by choosing a development culture over an assessment culture.*

If you focus internally on developing rather than judging in every situation in your workplace, you are already on your way to creating a development culture. This allows your team members to grow, fail, and dare to try again - leading to their development. You give appreciative feedback to show appreciation for what is good for the individual and the entity. You provide developmental feedback to highlight factors that can enhance both the individual and the entity.

It is now time for you to establish a plan for when and how you will gather your entity to initiate an accepted feedback culture.

My suggestion is through a workshop, and you should individually follow up with all team members in the weeks following the launch to energise, create engagement, and of course, take the opportunity to provide feedback at levels 1 or 3.

Proposal for Workshop: Implementation and acceptance of the four levels of feedback for all generations and cultures.

Plan for a half-day for this workshop. Prepare yourself by thinking through each point of the agenda, what discussions may arise, and which specific examples you can use to illustrate the points.

Agenda
Feedback Culture

1. Introduction: Why feedback?
2. Benefits for you and the workplace.
3. Joint exercises.
4. How it will work in practice.
5. Acceptance.
6. Reflection and discussion.

---

1. Introduction: Why feedback?

- Present and go through the agenda (see above suggestions).
- Start by explaining that *you want to implement a feedback culture* to promote development, communication, learning, collaboration, motivation, and engagement. Feel free to mention some of the companies I referred to on page 143 to demonstrate that the use of feedback exists in many companies and organisations.
- Explain that the word feedback can sound negative and therefore be misinterpreted. *Feedback is not about finding faults but about supporting development and success.* Clarify that the purpose of feedback is that you genuinely want to help them grow and develop in their roles.
- Use yourself as an example, *stating that you also want feedback because you wish to grow and develop.* By clearly positioning

yourself in the introduction as highly participatory in a culture where feedback is viewed as positive anc constructive, you contribute to changing any existing misconceptions that feedback is negative. Reinforce that feedback is an opportunity to identify strengths and areas for improvement, and that it does not involve criticizing or finding faults.

- *Highlight the importance of viewing feedback as a chance for progress, learning, improvement, and development*, which in turn can lead to increased competence anc success for everyone in the entity.
- Say, for example: *"Today we are starting a feedback culture, and I want it to develop and endure."*
- Clarify that you will only give feedback *to the person it concerns* and that you will ask, *"May I give you feedback?"* This allows the individual the opportunity to say: *"No thank you, this is not a good time"*, and you will then ask at a later time.
- Emphasise the importance of creating *a safe and permissive environment* where all team members feel comfortable receiving feedback.

Allocate time after the introduction fcr discussion and questions.

2. Benefits for you and the workplace.
- *Describe how an accepted feedback culture can benefit each team member individually.* Please outline or display the following examples of opportunities that feedback creates: personal development and growth, building on strengths and improving skills, increasing self-awareness and understanding of one's behaviour and performance, receiving recognition and validation, creating engagement and motivation, building a higher degree of trust and confidence with colleagues and leaders, the opportunity to take

responsibility for one's own development and success, providing clarity and direction regarding expectations and goals, the opportunity to identify and improve areas, the opportunity to learn from mistakes and avoid repeating them.

- *Describe the benefits of a feedback culture for the workplace and the entity*, and please prepare these suggestions for opportunities: promoting a culture of learning, continuous improvement and development, improving the quality of work and decisions, the opportunity to reduce conflicts and misunderstandings by clarifying expectations and providing feedback, maintaining a positive and constructive work environment, the opportunity to identify and develop the potential of team members to meet the future needs of the entity, identifying and addressing problems and deficiencies in work processes or systems earlier, strengthening relationships and promoting open and honest communication.

3. Joint exercise 1 - Reflection/Insight.

- Ask your team members to individually *reflect on their own goals they have or have had in life and write these down*. There can be as many goals as they wish, and they can be goals from both personal or professional life. It is important to convey that this is not something they need to share with anyone else.
- After about 10-15 minutes: Ask them to now look at their goals and, regardless of whether they have achieved their goals or not, reflect *on how feedback from another person could have helped them reach their goals faster, better, or more effectively, and what that feedback might have sounded like? ("May I give you feedback...?")*

Allocate time for discussion and insights.

3B. Joint exercise 2 - Awareness/Understanding.

- Divide your entity into smaller groups, ideally no more than four per group. *They should spend 15 minutes identifying at least ten benefits of using feedback in the workplace*, ideally as many as possible. They write down the benefits on post-it notes and then place them in a designated area in your group room.
- They should then read out what they have come up with while you write it live in the presentation in bullet points so that it is easy to follow in real-time and is also documented.
- After everyone has presented, thank them for their engagement and openly discuss in the room what the groups have discovered.

Ask follow-up questions to each group regarding the benefits and inquire how they reached these conclusions.

4. How it will work in practice.

It is now time for you to tell your entity how you will practically work to promote an accepted feedback culture. Explain that you will establish regular feedback conversations, that you will use clear and constructive discussions, and that you will create structures to follow up and evaluate the feedback process so that everyone feels secure.

I wrote on pages 141-142 about the four most important things to consider for the recipient of feedback. Find your own genuine way to explain this so that it resonates well in your entity.

Here are a few suggestions:

- *Explain that feedback relies on collaboration; for you to give feedback that will help a team member develop, the recipient needs to be open to feedback and understand that feedback is given out of care. The person receiving feedback needs to be open to receiving feedback; it is a form of a gift.*

- *Emphasise the importance of being receptive in order to develop.*
- *It is a continuous process for development and not just something done once a year.*
- *It is important that after receiving feedback, time is taken for self-reflection:* <u>*"This person said this to me out of goodwill and care; how can I take this information on board and use it as a tool for my development?"*</u>

5. Acceptance.

(Commitment, engagement, obligation. There are many expressions to describe acceptance.) Now is the time to request acceptance. This is an important step in all change initiatives; *if you do not gain acceptance from your entity, you will not have the right conditions to work successfully on your change efforts.*

- Emphasise the importance of doing this together.
- Emphasise that the purpose is for everyone to have the opportunity to grow in this entity.
- Emphasise the benefits they identified in Exercise 3 A and 3B.
- Emphasise that you are there as support and that you are open to feedback even now.
- Conclude by saying, for example: *"Can I have everyone's acceptance in the room to proceed with this now?"* Make sure to try to make quick eye contact with everyone in the room.

6. Reflection and discussion.

Conclude the workshop with 10-20 minutes for discussion and reflection in a large group, in smaller groups, or if team members prefer to discuss one-on-one. You may wish to display a final text in your presentation. *"What have I learned and how can feedback help me in my development and career as well as in our work environment?"*

Why have I allocated so much space to feedback in this section on assessment or development culture?

Because feedback is a concrete and practical tool that can be used in all industries and entities to promote personal development and success for the entire entity. If you refer back to page 50 and the survey on what employees consider most important in a workplace, number four was: *personal development*; a development culture has a direct connection to several factors in the survey. Later in the book, you will read about trust, delegation, and participation. These three important concepts can be directly linked to a development culture that works with an accepted feedback culture. (

(Below: "The Trust Wheel.")

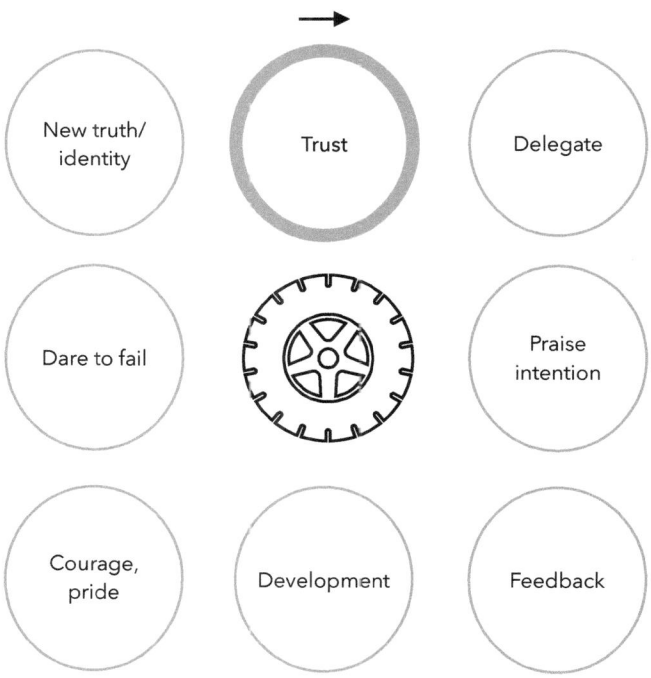

Reflection, section E

1. How do you reflect on whether you have a good self-awareness in relation to the six main aspects I describe in the section?

2. Are you currently leading in relation to an assessment or development culture, and how do you reflect upon this after the section?

3. How do you assess that an accepted feedback culture can develop you as a leader and your team members?

4. Reflecting on Exercise 3B, how could an implemented and accepted feedback culture have changed how and when your entity has achieved previous individual and collective goals and ambitions?

5. Do you have positive cultural carriers in your entity today, and how can you prepare for a level 3 feedback conversation after implementing an accepted feedback culture?

6. And if you have negative cultural carriers today, how can you prepare for a level 4 feedback conversation?

7. Do you feel confident in the difference between reflection and rumination so that a level 4 conversation takes place insightfully?

8. The next time you hire a new team member, do you have a strategy in place for how you can prepare the person for your feedback culture already in the onboarding process?

CHAPTER 1

What, why, and how

What you want to achieve and accomplish determines your actions.
Niclas Timmerby

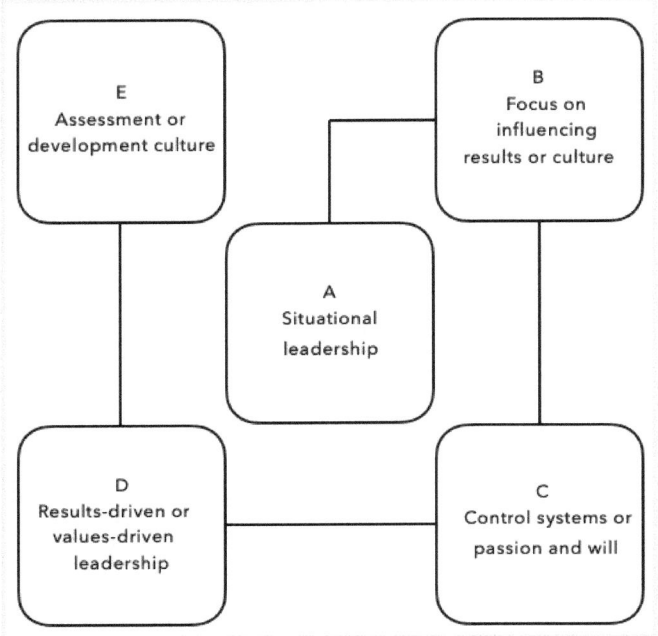

The necessary **foundation** has been laid, and as you can see, all parts of the model are now interconnected. My ambition with Sections A-E has been to break down very large and complex areas, add my own experiences from reality after more than 20 years as a leader and consultant, and thereby provide you with the most essential tools to navigate yourself and your entity with confidence during ongoing and upcoming significant cultural shifts.

Your concrete tool in daily life is the courage to (A) lead with a situational leadership style. As a leader, you genuinely and flexibly adapt to the individual's current situation, focusing on helping the team member grow and develop by supporting, directing, coaching, or delegating in various situations.

In this secure leadership, you have implemented *an* accepted feedback culture, maintaining everyore's focus on development and creating an open environment to address natural challenges within the entity.

Summary of Synergistic Effects from Sections B-E:

B: *Choosing to focus on influencing culture* *means that your focus is on creating an atmosphere where those operating within the culture achieve good results.* *Culture is so incredibly powerful that it drives everything else in the workplace and is a significant factor in the long-term results that are created. People shape the culture, and you, as a leader, have the greatest opportunity of all to shape it through your understanding of cultural shifts, your way of leading, and the amount of trust you have built with each of your team members. A focus on results creates a culture based on achieving results, while a focus on culture creates an environment that reaches good results. Understanding the power of culture means you will not want to lead in any other way.*

C: *Choosing to lead people with passion and willingness* *creates intrinsic motivation.* *Control systems developed in line organisations over 100 years ago were necessary at that time as they created extrinsic motivation, i.e., "I receive a salary if I follow the control tools." The question is whether you want your team members to come to work and look up to you as a leader for the sake of the salary or because you instil passion and willingness. If you create passion and willingness, you will have an entity that is self-sufficient and secure, willing to take responsibility and initiative for the overall development of the entity, and feeling included, which in turn encourages contribution. By approximately 2038, the last individuals who have worked in line organisations will have retired. The flat organisation that has naturally emerged in parallel is aligned with the cultural shifts that have occurred to date, promoting open communication, participation, personal responsibility for outcomes, independence, personal development, adaptability, equality, creativity, and decision-making at all levels.*

D: <u>Choosing a value-driven leadership</u> creates future leaders who want to be active in improving the workplace and work environment. When you, as a leader, take into account your own personal values and ethical standards as a human being and allow them to influence your leadership, you promote a positive and open work environment where people dare to show who they really are. This naturally encourages them to share with you why they may not be performing as usual, why they feel downcast, or why they wish to be a little more reserved. Genuinely leading in a value-driven manner brings you closer to your team members in a way that allows you to challenge them (read more about this in coaching later on). This enables you to unlock their full potential because they feel seen and can go above and beyond for you and their colleagues. If the entire organisation adopts this approach to leading "from the top down," it creates incredible synergistic effects. Regardless, you have created an environment where everyone feels respected for who they are as individuals rather than what they do in terms of performance. This fosters engagement and shapes your entity's culture, the atmosphere in which you work, and your individual and collective future results.

E: <u>Choosing a development culture</u> encourages people to dare to fail and take their own initiatives. When everyone in your entity views problems and challenges as opportunities to grow and develop, you have created a constructive work environment where people are better *mentally equipped to face and handle the future. It also strengthens collaboration, motivation, communication, and adaptability.*

The structure in Sections B-E is not only intended to understand the logical differences but also to connect these to understand people's needs and *"why people do what they do,"* which aids you in your situational leadership and when giving feedback. **Everything in <u>the foundation</u> is interconnected.**

Later in the book, I will provide you, as a leader, with the final decisive factor for the foundation.

If you view the foundation as a house consisting of everything that creates culture, the house needs a roof that holds the other sections together when it is cold outside, when change shakes things up inside the house, or when there is turbulence and storm outside affecting the

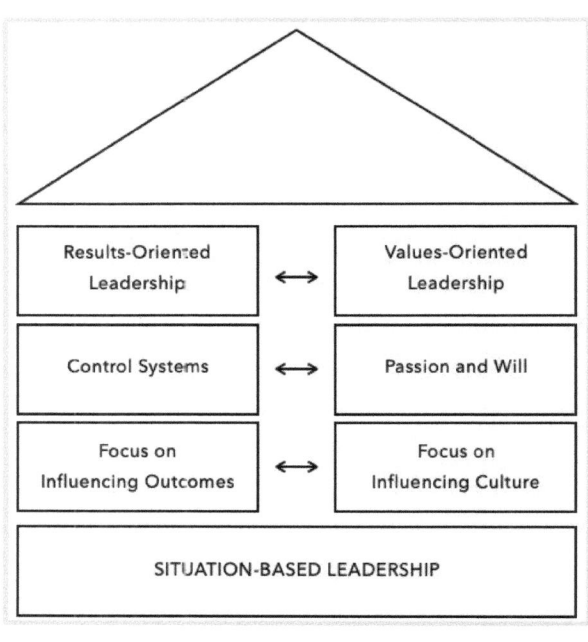

*house. <u>**The final decisive factor is what keeps your house in place regardless of challenges inside or outside**</u>.*

What I mean by my quote on page 171 is that all the goals and ambitions you have in life influence how you act through actions and decisions. All the goals and ambitions impact your drive, some more than others in your professional (and personal) life.

All your goals and ambitions that you have or have had are the fruits of something else, something much larger and more powerful: Your Vision. The vision is a clear, crystal-clear, and inspiring picture of the future that you strive to achieve together with your entity. A picture within you, a mental image of how you want things to be in the future or the purpose you aim to achieve.

Your vision is your visionary, your guide, like a star in the sky that you can navigate by, helping you to head in the right direction for decisions and actions. It should be challenging, engaging, and inclusive to involve and motivate people to want to realise the vision through its words.

A vision must be organisational and aspirational.
Aspirational means that the vision demonstrates a very high aspiration to achieve something incredibly significant. The aspirational part of the vision should challenge the current state so that it almost feels entirely impossible yet still attainable.

Organisational within visions means that the organisation/entity is structured and operates well enough to fulfil what the aspirational part expresses. All team members must feel significant because they know that their respective roles are a piece of the puzzle in fulfilling the vision. **It is essential that the vision is visible to all team members in their daily work and actively communicated within the organisation,**

especially during meetings and collaborations between departments. It is crucial to clearly highlight and regularly reflect on the question, _"Are we on our way to the vision?"_ This influences the culture towards achieving the vision.

Of course, it may be that your entity has a vision created by your organisation or an external consultancy. As a leader, you need to understand why, embrace the vision, and get your entity to feel engagement and motivation.

Examples of four companies that clearly embody both aspirational and organisational elements in their vision:

Amazon: _To be Earth's most customer-centric company where customers can find and purchase everything they need. Amazon aspires to offer a wide range of products, fast delivery, and a simple and convenient shopping experience._

Tesla: _To accelerate the world's transition to sustainable energy by offering innovative and attractive electric vehicles and renewable energy solutions. Tesla's vision is to reduce dependence on fossil fuels and promote a sustainable future for transport and energy._

Apple: _To create the best products in the world that change people's lives. Apple aims to be a company that combines technology, design, and user experience to create innovative and user-friendly products._

Google: _To organise the world's information and make it universally accessible and useful. Google's vision is to provide users with fast and easy access to information through search engines and other digital tools._

Vision, goals, ambitions, and strategies (What, why, and how).

The clearer, more precise, and inspiring your vision is, the more motivated you are, and the more focused your actions and decisions become, which creates the degree of your determination and focus in your pursuit of fulfilling your vision.

Your vision represents your WHY, which drives your motivation and dictates what you strive to achieve in the short term (goals) and accomplish in the long term (ambitions). A crystal-clear and inspiring vision provides you with specific goals and ambitions (your WHAT) and shapes your strategies (your HOW) to reach your vision.

Think of it as a map.
If you know where you want to go, you will choose a direction and follow it as carefully and accurately as you can to reach your destination within the timeframe you have set in your plan. During the journey, you will make choices and take decisions that help you reach your goal, and you will need to plan before and during the journey for, for example, when and where to eat, sleep, refuel, or buy tickets.

You need a crystal-clear vision (WHY). You need concrete short-term goals (WHAT you want to achieve in the short term) and long-term ambitions (WHAT you want to accomplish in the long term). You need clear, time-bound strategies (HOW). These are all hard values.

"A vision without action is merely a dream.

Action without vision is just passing time.

But vision with action can change the world"
- Nelson Mandela

Hospitality, Reputation, and Culture. (What, why, and how.)

There are two elements that you as a leader can use to motivate your entity to strive towards the vision: as above, with <u>hard, concrete values</u>. Goals, strategies, efficiency levels, gross profit margins, and other measurable and quantifiable parameters. *You need to use hard values in your leadership to create the necessary structure and know where to allocate your resources. You need to measure concrete values to ensure your entity's survival and competitiveness.*

<u>However, you need the second element.</u> *For leading with too much focus on hard values risks that your team members lose motivation, engagement, and passion as they experience the work environment and culture as pressured, where safety and compassion do not have a natural place.* As you have read, salary, in light of the rapid cultural shifts in recent years, is no longer as strong a motivator. Since 1980, when the information society made its entrance, the need has increased to balance hard values with soft values (gradually year after year and cultural shift after cultural shift). *Soft values that focus on the well-being of team members, building sustainable relationships and a good work environment. Soft values that create a culture containing trust, safety, open communication, respect, compassion, and a natural balance between work and personal life.*

The WHAT, WHY, and HOW of Soft Values.

During my journey as a leader, consultant, speaker, and educator, soft values have crystallised for me. I see *WHAT as hospitality*, *WHY as reputation*, and *HOW as culture*.

We now begin the journey to the formula for profitability.

CHAPTER 2

IH ⇢ C ⇢ EH : (E = potential$^{\wedge\infty}$) ⇢ R = P

Words without action are like sunbathing indoors.
The intention is certainly good, but it yields no results.
Niclas Timmerby

The first part of the formula is IH: Internal Hospitality.

I had a young man as an employee about ten years ago, and it was not until a little over a year after I left that assignment that I understood what had made such an immense impression on me.

He was beloved by everyone.

Colleagues always spoke highly of him. All customers; elderly couples, young couples, families with children, men, women, and even the children adored him. He could sell anything to anyone. How was that possible?

He had a very calm, relaxed, and even peaceful body language. He spoke in a low, soft voice that created trust in everyone. When I observe some Asian cultures and particularly Tibetan monks who walk slowly in their kasaya or sangha robes (their characteristic attire), I think of him.

Then it struck me how he could be loved and respected by all.

> *"The humble person does not know it themselves."*
> *- Martin Luther King Jr*

He was unconsciously humble, which gave him unconscious self-awareness at the highest possible level. He was surely aware of the fine signals he sent out to his surroundings and took full responsibility for these since he received so many positive signals in return *(You reap what you sow…)*.

The young man did his best for his surroundings with his superpower, sharing it with everyone he came into contact with. He was an exceptionally positive cultural ambassador.

You remember what I wrote about the superpower we all have within us, that we walk around this earth with our superhero outfits under our ordinary clothes. Every day, several times, we reveal our tremendous superpower: the ability to influence other people. People use their superpower, consciously and/or unconsciously, to create positive influences, and unfortunately also negative ones. Both types have consequences for the recipient.

The moment you are affected by another person's superpower, you are imprinted whether you want to be or not. In that very moment, the imprinting reaches you, it influences your thoughts, leading to increased production of hormones and neurotransmitters. This combination of other functions in your brain creates emotions and reactions within you that govern your choices, decisions, and actions.

Sometimes you might read or hear people say, "Be positive, and most things will work out." I do not believe in that because life is not that simple. Life will always involve minor problems every day and, unfortunately, also greater challenges and tragedies. Our human brains need considerable training so that we do not feel at least a little stressed over the unpleasant situations that arise. It is possible to train and build resilience against the minor issues in life so that we do not let these affect us too greatly, understanding that minor problems are part of life.

If a person expects life to be positive, they will likely struggle to live their life in balance and harmony. When I lecture, I often emphasise that it is much more important to strive for an optimistic outlook on life and a belief in the future than to focus on trying to be positive.

This enables a person to better handle setbacks and feel gratitude on a deeper level, such as the fact that we can even walk around on this planet that orbits our star, the sun, at over 107,000 km per hour.

Tragedies, problems, boulders, little stones, and *no problema*.
To continuously adjust internal hospitality requires an optimistic outlook on the future, which means being able to distinguish between the above headings. When I lecture, I describe *tragedies* as *boulders* that will always have a significant impact on our lives and relationships. These are experiences we all face in life. Hard experiences, tough experiences, personal tragedies like deaths and serious illnesses. Events that require you to be there for your loved ones and find time for yourself. You need time to be by yourself to process, to be sad, to receive comfort, and to take time to comfort others. You need to dedicate time to this so that when you feel mentally ready, you can return to your work.

Problems, or as I call it: *little stones*.
I discussed the historical significance of the word with my dear friend Markus Senften. The word "problem" comes from the Greek compound word "*problema*." If we divide the word into its two parts, we get the Greek prefix "pro-", which means "in front of," "against," or "before," and (ballein) "blema," which means "to throw or to place." Therefore, the word "problema" can literally be translated to *"something (an item or task) that is thrown in front of someone to be examined."* The Latin meaning can be interpreted as *"something that needs to be examined and evaluated to determine its truthfulness."* The reason I mention this is to demystify problems. <u>We humans expend so much energy, emotions, engagement, focus, and time on little stones.</u> With a good portion of self-awareness, we understand that *if we are imprinted in our thoughts by a little stone, it affects our feelings and actions.*

If we share our little stone with others, it is like a bad magic trick. Ta-da! And we have immediately imprinted another person's thoughts, feelings, focus, energy state, engagement, and actions with that little stone. *We immediately influence the recipient's emotional state.*

If I imagine how it might have been in ancient Greece when people encountered a problem, they might have said, "*Aha! We have a task to solve!*" *For that is the meaning of a problem*, <u>*a temporary state before a solution*</u>. A problem is *a temporary condition*. A tragedy is *not a temporary condition* but a state that will, in some way, always live on within a person. It is essential for you as a leader to talk about and possibly provide necessary support long after a tragedy has affected a team member. Often, the solution is simply to listen and be a genuine human being.

> *A valuable insight: The importance of training oneself to adopt a different perspective on problems should not be underestimated. Training activates different parts of the brain that promote cognitive flexibility and mental sharpness. By actively engaging in one's problem-solving abilities, neural connections are strengthened, creating new patterns of activity in the brain.*

When we focus on a problem, we automatically increase our stress levels, which results in our brains ceasing to think in terms of solutions. Simply put, the stress response is activated in the amygdala while the capacity to think clearly diminishes in your prefrontal cortex, inhibiting your creativity and ability to think of solutions. Negative thoughts and stress also affect the hippocampus, making it difficult for you to remember past experiences and knowledge that could help you manage, resolve, or even let go of the problem. I refer to this as "*the negative veil*" in my books on self-leadership.

For example, if you go out for a walk and see that it is starting to rain, focusing on the little stones (the rain) instead of immediately focusing on a solution (which might be putting on rain gear, walking a little later, or jogging in place indoors for ten minutes) affects your feelings, well-being, and actions. You can likely relate directly to various concrete

"A problem is only a problem when you perceive it as one.

The solution is to focus on the solution until all you see is the solution."
- Niclas Timmerby

situations in your personal and professional life.

Every time you, as a leader, consciously focus on solutions when small stones arise in your entity, you develop yourself, your entity, and your culture. You are now collectively shaping a culture that focuses on solutions.

"Locus of control" and "Need for control."

Like everyone else, I experience phases in life when I don't feel well or doubt my abilities. Everyone goes through minor crises at regular intervals. It does not matter how much money a person has, where they come from, or their gender. Everyone, weighted against their situation in life, goes through minor crises related to relationships, health, finances, and professional life. Deliberately working on self-awareness and self-leadership is a good tool for managing these minor crises.

When you listen to your team members' feelings and when you coach, it is important to understand two significant differences that will help you as a leader better understand and strengthen relationships with your team members. *Understanding the difference between locus of control and need for control, as well as the earlier distinction between reflection and rumination, allows you to make natural and thoughtful decisions in your situational leadership.*

185

Internal, external, or powerlessness <u>locus of control</u>.

Locus of control, or control orientation, describes a person's belief regarding where control over their life lies. A person can have several different types of locus simultaneously, known as a "spectrum of locus of control." For example, one for health, one for work, one for private life, one for finances, one for relationships, etc.

Internal means that a person feels they have control over their own life and therefore their actions and future. They believe that their efforts and actions determine the outcome *("you reap what you sow"). The individual is driven by the belief that they can influence their own life.*

External means that a person feels that external factors, other people, or even luck control their life and results. They believe that the outcomes in their life depend on factors they cannot control. *The individual is driven by the belief that they cannot influence their own life,* which may lead to feelings of helplessness and depression.

Powerlessness (also called "fatalism") means that a person feels pure powerlessness, believing that neither they, others, nor luck influences the outcomes in their life. *They perceive that the events that have happened and are occurring in their life are beyond their control, and their belief is a sense that everything is predetermined.* This can create a feeling of meaninglessness, potentially leading the person to become passive and give up easily, which results in negative thoughts, anxiety, and stress.

Cognitive, control over others, or situational <u>need for control</u>.

There are three major components that are good for you as a leader to be fundamentally aware of regarding what we often read and hear about the concept of the need for control. The psychological term describes a person's desire to have control over their environment, situations, and other people. In many cases, it is an instinct that is normal and healthy to want control over important aspects of life. However, when it becomes excessive, it can lead to significant challenges for the person themselves and their surroundings, both privately and professionally. This is because an exaggerated need for control affects the person's behavior and actions in various ways.

Cognitive control means that a person wants to experience control over their thoughts and emotions to such an extent that their behaviour can create anxiety and stress. Within psychology, there is the term *adaptive self-regulation*, which refers to a person's healthy ability to balance the need for control by being flexible, open to others' perspectives, and able to relinquish control when necessary. *Maladaptive self-regulation* is characterised by excessive control, difficulties in adapting to change, and being closed to others' perspectives. This can lead to significant challenges, particularly in relationships.

Control over others means that a person has difficulty trusting others and may attempt to manipulate or dominate them, a form of martyr behaviour. It involves getting others to behave in the way that the person with the need for control desires.

Situational control refers to a person's desire to have control over the circumstances and situations in their environment. People with a high degree of situational control need can experience considerable worry and stress, which can lead to anxiety and depression.

What should you be aware of in your behaviour as a leader?

It is human and very easy to see the faults and shortcomings of others. It is significant to have the capability to want to develop your own. So, with control orientation and need for control fresh in your mind, do you exhibit any signs of this? How might this manifest to your surroundings through your behaviour, the signals you send out, and your actions? Does this even negatively affect your entity regarding essential factors such as trust, energy levels, and development? **How do you, *as a leader*, impact the internal hospitality?**

Micromanagement.

Your team members feel that you are involved in every detail, controlling every aspect of their work, requiring constant detailed reporting, or continuously demanding that they report where they are and what they are doing.

Risk: Your entity may experience a lack of trust, feel monitored, feel that they cannot take initiative or make decisions, and feel unable to implement pragmatic solutions in pressured situations.

Overall, this can affect motivation and performance.

Lack of trust:

Your team members feel that you double-check their work or frequently question their completed tasks or work abilities, such as effectiveness, productivity, or prioritisation.

Risk: Your entity may feel that you do not recognise their good intentions for the entity or trust their professional abilities to perform their tasks.

Overall, this can undermine their confidence and motivation.

Lack of delegation:

Your team members feel that you do not fully relinquish control to them to perform and complete tasks or projects, despite having knowledge and experience. That you retain all responsibility and decision-making for yourself.

Risk: Your entity may feel limited and undervalued.

Overall, this can lead to your entity feeling that they are not allowed to participate, show, and be recognised for their professional knowledge and competence.

Difficulty in receiving and accepting feedback:

Your team members feel that you dismiss, ignore, or reject their suggestions or opinions when they provide you with feedback.

Risk: This directly affects the culture, as your team members may lose motivation and courage, and therefore no longer want or dare to provide feedback in good faith for your development as a leader or of the entity. There is a significant risk that good ideas will not reach you in the future, as team members do not feel appreciated and recognised.

"Control is just another word for fear."
- Joyce Meyer

Overall, this can lead to decreased engagement, confidence, passion, willingness, and motivation.

Excessive emphasis on results:

Your team members feel that your focus on targets and achieving goals puts pressure on them. They feel that they must perform quickly and efficiently without you considering their well-being or work environment.

Risk: This can lead to stress-related absences, burnout, or team members actively resigning on their own initiative.
Overall, this can lead to decreased performance and long-term motivation.

Lack of space for mistakes and failures:
Your team members feel that you have difficulty tolerating mistakes and failures, even if you do not say anything, they sense your signals, body language, and tone of voice.
Risk: This can lead to them not daring to take risks, challenge old ways of working, and experiment, which poses a significant risk for an organisation.
Overall, this can hinder the development of your entity and the entire organisation. Team members may feel reduced responsibility and engagement regarding their tasks.

G-I-F-T
Generosity, humility, thankfulness, responsibility
All the examples I have mentioned influence the internal hospitality, which in turn affects the culture.

Everything you do as a leader and the signals you send with your superpower has a concrete and direct impact on your entity and the internal hospitality, and the emotions that arise from this contribute to the culture.

*I use my own methodology (G-I-F-T), which I have described in other books, to move out of a phase or feeling that does not benefit me or my surroundings. Getting out of a phase or feeling we do not want is about one thing: **changing focus**. In psychology, concepts such as self-*

awareness, self-reflection, positive reframing, and self-care are mentioned. Many aspects are encompassed in what I have previously written about our self-concept. Gaining insight into our self-concept and our "identity" is a significant step forward. For when we begin to view ourselves differently with self-insight, humility, and self-reflection, it becomes easier to change focus. To move out of a phase that does not benefit us, we need to understand ourselves, our thoughts and feelings, find meaning, and see our purpose.

Here is the meaning of G-I-F-T that I share with you:
Generosity.
To show generosity in words and actions.
Humility.
To approach all situations with humility.
Thankfulness.
To feel deep gratitude for the good things in my life, for my relationships, and for what I have in life.
Responsibility.
To take full personal responsibility for my life, choices, decisions, time, relationships, and actions

In section F, I develop this theory.

Hospitality and what it can offer your entity.
The concept of hospitality comes from the fundamental human trait that has been described since ancient times (circa 3000 BC to circa 500 AD), when hospitality in Roman and Greek civilization was a central part of societal structure and moral values.

The best expression I have heard that explains worthy leadership is: **The art of making people feel welcome**. The foundation of the expression is said to come from the wonderful Maya Angelou and her incredible quote below.

The quote should certainly be displayed on the wall in every home and in all professional entities in a golden frame, as it encapsulates everything that hospitality stands for in just three simple sentences.

"People will forget what you said.

They will forget what you did.

But they will never forget how you made them feel."
- Maya Angelou

Life is about authentically touching people from the heart.
Every time you are authentic in your personal and professional life, you touch people because they feel that you are genuine, that you are not playing a game or fitting into a suitable role. You dare to show emotions, which creates deeper and more meaningful relationships.

You have come so far in your personal development and in your self-leadership that you are true to yourself. This makes you more independent, and you are perceived by your surroundings as relaxed and confident in a humble way.

You dare to show empathy and compassion for other people, and you do this automatically, without thinking. This creates trust and respect in your surroundings. You feel that you have a purpose and meaning. You dare to be yourself.

The Internal Hospitality IH).

The internal hospitality is reflected in <u>how team members feel, treat each other, and collaborate</u>.

- That they genuinely care for and look after each other.

- That they have insight into how they collectively <u>are</u> their work environment and, consequently, co-creators of the shared culture.

- The degree of trust and confidence they have in you as a leader and the overall leadership.

- The degree of trust and confidence they have in each other.

- How equally and fairly tasks are distributed among them.

- The extent to which they take personal responsibility for their working time, their personal goals, and their tasks.

- That they strive towards the vision.

- That they accept their role and have insight into how each of them is a significant puzzle piece for the entity's well-being and success.

- Their level of attentiveness and acceptance towards each other regarding differences, cultures, well-being, perspectives, opinions, and ideas.

- Their degree of self-awareness and humility when communicating.

- That they accept development through feedback.

- The courage to speak their mind to the person concerned with the intention of helping their teammate or you to develop.

- That they strive to achieve common goals.

- The degree of respect they show one another.

- How open and honest they are with each other.

- How they handle tensions and conflicts with your assistance.

- The extent to which they genuinely praise and encourage each other.

- Their adaptability and how much they genuinely care for and take responsibility for each other and the entity's results.

- That they share knowledge and experiences with one another.

The foundation of the entire formula is the internal hospitality.
It is the starting point that creates the basic conditions. The culture is influenced by the internal hospitality, as well as the external hospitality, and everything that follows in the formula towards profitability.

As you may have already noticed, the internal hospitality is rooted in sections B-E; that is why I have placed a significant focus on *the foundation.*

How do you work as a leader with the points on the previous page that influence how your team members feel, treat each other, and collaborate? You, as a leader, are the person who primarily creates the degree of the internal hospitality. Your leadership is the foundation of the internal hospitality. The internal hospitality, in turn, affects:

- *Work environment* (physical and psychosocial conditions).
- *Work climate* (the atmosphere and mood created based on your relationships, collaboration, and communication).
- *Culture* (what is created by how you interact based on your shared values, norms, and behaviours).

Your tools for the positive development of the internal hospitality are your __situational leadership__ and __an accepted feedback culture__. What will be added as the third concrete tool later in the book is __tailored coaching__.

So everything begins with something that is not measurable, that is not visible or audible; you cannot buy it for money, and you cannot purchase a machine that creates good hospitality. __Your internal hospitality is invaluable.__

That is why I have previously written that those who begin to lead with a focus on the immense power that culture has will not want to lead in any other way. Focusing on culture brings long-term positive synergetic effects for people and results.

A look back at the vision; the leader's task is to connect the vision to the internal hospitality so that a symbiosis emerges.
You know the significance of the vision; it is the organisation's and your entity's direction, why the organisation exists, where your entity strives, your why: why you go to work. When I have held leadership roles in entities, I have used the vision as my guiding star.

Especially in challenging and tough times, focusing on the vision is what directs you and your entity to, or back to, the right direction.

My three steps to make the vision visible:
1. Start each day and meeting with the vision visible.
Reminding yourself and your team members of the overarching purpose at the beginning of the workday and when meetings start helps to focus on what is important and to avoid distractions that do not contribute to achieving the vision. It is also a way to inspire and motivate your entity by reminding them of what you all collectively strive to achieve.

2. Link all strategies and actions to the vision (does this lead us to our aspirations?).
Consciously linking all strategies and actions to the vision means that you, as a leader, openly ensure that all decisions and actions taken are in line with the vision. This shows that you are a leader who strives forward and clearly indicates that the vision is your guiding star. This helps to ensure that all work done is meaningful and contributes to

achieving the overarching purpose. It is also a way to avoid wasting time
and resources on projects that are not relevant to the vision.

3. Make difficult and significant decisions with the vision as your guiding star.

As a leader, you inevitably need to make significant decisions or have
difficult conversations; this is part of the job. Here, the vision is your
anchor to hold onto. By using the vision as your guiding star, it becomes
your filter of truth when assessing various options and choosing what
you know is best to achieve the vision. Avoiding decisions that go
against the vision is a concrete tool that positively affects the
organisation and the entity in the long term. It is also a way to ensure
that decisions made align with your leadership values and moral
principles.

Three very valuable tools for you that are in symbiosis with the vision and a positive internal hospitality.

You will now receive three tools that you can concretely link to the
vision, your and your entity's values, and to your personal moral
principles and values. These three tools also create positive synergies
for the internal hospitality, for the culture, and for the external
hospitality.

Tool 1: The Leader's Mission.

Typically, the vision is set by owners or a management team, sometimes
in collaboration with an external firm whose proposals are modified
and then approved by owners and/or the board.

You, as a leader in a larger organisation, fully support the vision
and strive towards it in everything you do in your work. However, it is

unlikely that your own personal words are included in the vision. There is a possibility that it does not fully reflect your perspective.

This means that your personal values, feelings, passion, will, or collective reflections are not visible. When you read or present the vision to your entity, which is the reason for your why, why you go to work, you are reading or showcasing someone else's wise words. <u>You need to use your own words.</u>

Create your mission.
The word <u>vision</u> comes from the Greek word "horama," which means "sight" or "to see."

The word <u>mission</u> also comes from Greek, from the word "missio," which means "to send forth." The original meaning was to describe a journey, a mission.

*I often describe the vision as a clear guiding star, to which we should all aspire within the entity and organisation. To give your entity a clearer, more distinct, and sharper picture of the vision, you need to show the path or map. And this is your mission. Your mission is your way of standing before your entity and clearly pointing out the direction where you, with your words, say, "**This is our path to the vision.**"*

If I were to think of a fictional, short, and clear vision for a sales organisation that should remain strong in tough times, it might look like this: "Our vision is to have the best customer service in the industry. We achieve this by, in every encounter, seeing and addressing our customers in a human, professional, and genuine manner."
If I were to have my own entity in the organisation with that vision, a mission in my words could look like this:

"My mission is to create an outstanding customer experience by uniting our strong corporate culture, our way of seeing one another, and our genuine hospitality.

I believe in a work environment where each of you feels significant and inspired to contribute to your colleagues and to our common goals.

By promoting open communication and respectful collaboration within our team, we create together an atmosphere of trust and engagement that permeates every single customer interaction.

We strive to understand our customers' unique needs and wishes, and by exercising genuine hospitality and care, we deliver personalised and tailored solutions.

Our focus is always on exceeding expectations and creating long-lasting relationships based on trust and loyalty.

With our culture, collaboration, and hospitality, we strive to be the industry's best in taking care of our customers in a human and genuine way."

Your mission is informal, intended solely for your entity.

*Its purpose is to foster clarity, motivation, engagement, drive, and pride. The mission should delineate what your entity does on a daily basis and provide answers to the following three questions: **What do we do? How do we do it? For whom do we do it?***

Why?

The wonderful Bengt and Lotta Wiström, with whom I have had the privilege of attending an extended coaching programme, have taught me something incredibly important. You have seen that I mentioned it earlier in the book: the significance of "why."

If a person does not understand "why" or another person's perspective, they are sadly, by default, negative or fearful, and are likely to look for faults. A team member who does not understand "why" is not motivated to their full potential.

"The greatest waste, and at the same time the greatest potential in the workplace, is when employees go about their daily tasks without knowing why."
- Niclas Timmerby

<u>*This can be one of your greatest tasks as a leader: to ensure that everyone in your entity fully understands "why."*</u>

Why do we have a vision, why do we have policies and checklists, why do we have training, why is it important to arrive on time, why do we have a feedback culture, etc.

Your mission is the map to the vision. The clearer your map is, the better your team members can navigate towards the vision.

Tool 2: Provide emotional information.

- *This tool fosters involvement, gives all team members direction, and makes them feel seen.*

- *This tool shows that you genuinely care about them, that you care about the organisation, your entity, and that you clearly strive towards your mission and your common vision.*

- *This tool creates clarity in daily work by making mutual expectations visible.*

To change cultures and people, you need to speak without filters and without pride, from your heart. Having the courage to show your vulnerability by sharing your moral principles and values demonstrates to your entity that you are honest, genuine, and secure in yourself. A secure leadership creates secure team members.

Providing emotional information means that you honestly and openly share your feelings, reflections, experiences, and wishes. This builds trust, which is fundamental for long-term motivation. It shows that you truly care about your team members, and it also shows that you care about the organisation and that you want to achieve the vision through your mission. You set the direction and demonstrate that you are leading them forward.

I have four key points for your emotional speech to your team members, and I have also included an open suggestion under each point that you may use for inspiration. The important thing is that you use your own words and express it in a way that is "you."

Prepare yourself and then gather your entity to:

1. *Share your driving force.*
2. *Share what your entity can expect from you.*
3. *Share your expectations of your entity.*
4. *Share how you envision the future.*

1. Share your driving force.

"My driving force is to see you grow and take responsibility for one another. This is what brings me joy when I come to our workplace each day. I am extremely proud and grateful to be part of our team, and I want this feeling to persist and grow."

2. Share what your entity can expect from you.

"What you can expect from me is that I am well-prepared and bring energy to each workday to provide you with the best possible conditions to thrive and develop. What you can expect from me is that I treat you all equally and that I will intervene if someone is not treated fairly. What you can expect from me is that I will provide feedback because I truly want to see you grow as individuals and in your professional roles; remember that when I give feedback, it is always with good intentions."

3. Share your expectations of your entity.

"What I expect from you is that you always keep the vision in focus and are well-prepared when you come to our workplace. What I expect from you is that you always give our customers, suppliers, and contractors the best genuine reception possible. This builds our reputation as a team and the brand of our organisation. What I expect from you is that you treat each other kindly and with respect, and that you all step in *appropriately if you see someone who is not doing well or is treated unfairly. Then we are a real team today and in the future."*

4. Share how you envision the future.
"How I envision the future is that we thrive as a team and have a great time together. That we continue to develop as team players and as a team, and that we are proud of each other in both good times and bad. The courage to challenge each other to reach goals brings us all joy as we can witness a fellow human grow and develop."

Tool 3: The shared foundations of values of the team.
The third tool for you that interacts in symbiosis with the vision and positive internal hospitality.
Creating a shared foundations of values is another valuable way to establish direction, collaboration, and focus. My recommendation is that every larger entity/department within the organisation has its own developed shared foundations of values.

The reason is simple; people are unique, and everyone has unique values. The larger the entity, the more difficult it becomes to feel an emotional connection to the value foundation.

To stand behind a shared foundations of values that a person has not been involved in creating can hardly serve as the same motivational factor. A shared foundations of values should not be developed as a PR strategy or marketing strategy; I do not consider it respectful to take values lightly, as values over time have shaped and influenced people.

A shared foundations of values takes its starting point in the present and shapes the future internal hospitality and culture.

As a leader, you bring forth tool number 1 (The Leader's mission) and tool number 2 (Provide emotional information); now you give your entity a blank sheet of paper to create common guidelines and principles.

The purpose.

The reason for creating a shared foundations of values, in which all your team members can participate, has both psychological and motivational benefits that strengthen the bonds between team members and the entity as a whole.

Being involved in the development of the shared foundations of values provides a lasting sense that everyone's opinions and values are taken seriously, which fosters security and engagement.

Your team members feel that they can contribute to something meaningful and valuable, which increases motivation.

Opening up for participation in the shared foundations of values gives each team member the opportunity to reflect on their own values, ethics, and moral principles. Questions such as "What values are important to me and drive me? What values do I appreciate and want to live by?" create increased awareness and provide an opportunity for growth through personal development.

Being part of shaping something unique and lasting creates a sense of ownership and personal responsibility.

Collaborating, discussing, and sharing what is important for each individual as a person opens up for open communication among team members, which fosters stronger cohesion, understanding, and community.

Being involved makes team members feel more connected to the entire organisation's identity, which can strengthen feelings of belonging and pride.

Here is a proposal for a workshop to develop a shared foundations of values for your entity. (Approximately 3 hours of effective time.)

If your entity is large, prepare breakout rooms or a way for smaller groups to have privacy during the group exercise. If your entity has fewer than 25 people, you can do the exercise in a larger group room.

1. Introduction. Suggestion: 10 minutes:

Explain the purpose of the workshop and the significance of having a shared value foundation.

Example: To create a consolidated document where everyone is involved in defining and highlighting what is important to us as individuals and in our work. A shared value foundation creates a clear direction where our common values are reflected in how we act in our workplace and how we approach our tasks.

- Create a positive, safe, and open atmosphere where everyone feels comfortable and prepared to share their opinions and ideas.
- Prepare A4 papers with the following 40 examples of value words and feel free to add more that are important to you. This is to create inspiration for the group exercise more effectively.

1. Honesty, 2. Accountability, 3. Respect, 4. Trust, 5. Collaboration, 6. Creativity, 7. Attentiveness, 8. Equality, 9. Ethics, 10. Thoughtfulness, 11. Sustainability, 12. Quality, 13. Creativity, 14. Openness, 15. Learning, 16. Passion, 17. Courage, 18. Reliability, 19. Empathy, 20. Feedback, 21. Solutions-focused, 22. Joy, 23. Innovation, 24. Professionalism, 25. Honesty, 26. Inclusion, 27. Customer focus, 28. Humility, 29. Environmental consideration, 30. Growth, 31. Safety, 32. Credibility, 33. Innovation, 34. Drive, 35. Optimism, 36. Tolerance, 37. Mutual respect, 38. Open communication, 39. Strategic thinking, 40. Unity.

2. Brainstorming value words. Suggestion: 30 minutes:

- Now divide your entity into groups of about five people. In the group exercise, within 30 minutes, they should write down the ten value words they agree are the most important for each group on an A3 sheet (they are welcome to be creative and come up with their own suggestions).
- When thinking individually and as a group, it could be words that are important to them in their personal or professional lives; these could be values, traits, principles, or ideals.
- It is important that everyone is involved and that everyone gets a chance to speak.
- Encourage them to discuss when they have different opinions and feel free to share why they may have strong views.
- They write down the ten value words they collectively feel best reflect them on the A3 they have been given.

3. Prioritisation. Suggestion: 45-60 minutes:

- While the group exercise is underway, prepare to post all A3 sheets so that everyone can clearly see and refer to them when you reconvene. Allow team members to openly discuss and analyse the various suggestions that the groups have come up with.
- Instruct them to now agree on ten value words that together can symbolise all the suggestions. Start by writing down the values that appear the most frequently, then create an open discussion to have your team members collectively discuss which value words should complete the list to ten: Which do they feel reflect the people, the spirit of the entity, which are the most significant and relevant, and which propel them forward in their pursuit of the vision?
- It is important to encourage those who may be more reserved to share their thoughts; their voice is just as valuable as anyone else's. This is all to create participation. You do not want anyone from your entity to

come to you after the exercise and say that they cannot support the value foundation because they did not have a say. Check in individually with everyone before concluding the exercise.

4. Formulate the shared foundations of values. Suggestion: 30 minutes:
- Write down the ten jointly selected value words physically or via PowerPoint/Keynote/another tool.
Divide your entity into two, five, or ten groups, depending on your size, and let each group take responsibility for five, two, or one value word per group. Each group is tasked with formulating one or two sentences per value word that incorporate their individual values and moral principles. Each value word must be included in its respective sentence. Encourage them to make their sentences powerful and highly motivating. (A good strategy I often use in this type of workshop is to ask them to consider that two new team members will start tomorrow, and these two individuals should feel engagement and passion from what they read.) Also, use the role distribution per group as you see on pages 78-79 to maintain structure and ensure everyone is alert and has the opportunity to participate.
- Distribute note-taking materials and an A3 sheet per group where they can write their final sentences, highlighting or underlining the value words.
- Once again, I emphasize the importance of everyone having the opportunity to participate and contribute personally.

5. Commitment and implementation. Suggestion: 45 minutes:
- Prepare again while the group exercise is taking place so that you can post all A3 sheets where everyone can clearly see them when you reconvene.

- Thank everyone for their efforts, read through all the sentences slowly, and invite reactions after each one. If any sentence is incomplete when you regroup, brainstorm together to create a complete sentence so that everything is finalized when everyone is in the room.

- Discuss openly, sentence by sentence, which situations and prompts might arise in daily work where the shared foundations of values can be a guide, a support, and even a solution.

- Communicate that the work they have done is valuable, which you as a leader can use in contexts such as hiring interviews. You can say: *"This is what the team members have created, this is what they feel and think. These are their guidelines for how work should be conducted and how they treat one another."*

- Also, inform them that you will print out the value foundation and then ask everyone to sign it, which creates personal loyalty to the shared value foundation. After everyone has signed, you will display it, for instance, in a common room or staff room. Your entity's value foundation is unofficial.

Be prepared to revisit the three tools roughly every three years or when a significant portion of your entity has left and been replaced by new team members. Your three valuable tools, which are in symbiosis with the vision and a positive internal hospitality, are:
1. The Leader's Mission.
2. Provide Emotional Information.
3. Your shared foundations of values.

Why is hospitality more important than ever today?

Hospitality has been with us since before our calendar began; it is in our human nature to make others feel welcome. It has never been clearer than now how significant hospitality is. The competition is fiercer than ever, the world has just gone through a multi-year pandemic, a terrible war in Ukraine is ongoing and the President of the United States is currently initiating a pointless global trade war. All of this has resulted in increased energy prices, market anxiety, a rising number of bankruptcies per year, and high inflationary pressures that drive up interest rates and prices, affecting currencies. This negatively impacts investments, economic growth, and trade.

Hospitality in the context of sales.

If you sell to customers, you can know everything about your products or services. You can answer any question your customers ask.

Fantastic! But that is probably not the factor that makes customers keep coming back to you repeatedly and recommend you and your business to everyone they meet. <u>Somewhere, they expect</u> that if they take the time and energy to visit your establishment and are willing to pay for your products or services, they will receive answers to their questions. **<u>(People will forget what you said.)</u>**

You nearly run yourself ragged when selling to customers to meet their wishes. Customers have never encountered anyone so incredibly service-oriented who immediately arranges what they need.

Incredible! But that is probably not the factor that makes customers keep coming back to you repeatedly and recommend you and your business to everyone they meet. <u>Somewhere, they expect</u> that if they take the time and energy to visit your establishment and are willing to pay for your products or services, the seller will show engagement. **<u>(They will forget what you did.)</u>**

To create loyal customers who spend more than the average customer, who keep coming back again and again, who just want to do business with you, your team members, and your business, who speak highly of you and recommend you and your business to everyone they meet, something else is required. You need to make the customer **feel** something they do not experience with your competitors; you need to send genuine, authentic signals. *(Make them feel in a way they will never forget.)*

You need to exceed the customer's expectations.
- You need to create a warm, genuine atmosphere where people simply enjoy being. An environment that people want to be in.
- The atmosphere must make the customer feel genuinely welcome, relaxed, and comfortable.
- The customer needs to feel seen and acknowledged as soon as possible in a genuine and natural way.
- The customer should feel that they are the focus of your attention.
- When you begin your conversation, the customer should feel genuinely appreciated for choosing to come to you.

If you exceed the customer's expectations, they will feel that they've received a reception and an experience beyond the ordinary.
I often say that customers today can immediately sense when a salesperson smiles because "it's in the job description" to greet customers with a smile, versus when a salesperson genuinely smiles because they truly appreciate the person coming to them.

We all know how it feels when someone asks us to smile for a photograph, it feels a bit forced and contrived, doesn't it? Or when we smile in daily life because we see something joyful and a spontaneous photo is taken? There is a significant difference between the two photos: one is genuine and authentic, while the other is for appearances' sake.

That exact difference is what the customer picks up on when talking with a salesperson or sales assistant who smiles because it is expected, versus one who smiles genuinely from the heart.

Selling, Then and now.

Why hospitality is more important than ever today is that the way we sell is in constant flux, following the major cultural shifts that occur. *To understand cultures is to understand people's needs.* In sales, I believe it's a pure survival factor to understand cultures.

(In the next chapter, "Reputation," I will discuss the tremendous difference between striving for "satisfied customers" and striving for "loyal customers," which is the choice between survival and profitability.)

The old view of selling.

Today, as I write this in 2023, the year 1898 occurred 125 years ago.

Amid the industrial revolution that began about 260 years ago, the first written description of *the sales funnel* emerged. This article was written by E. St. Elmo Lewis and published in the magazine "The Inland Printer." This magazine was printed in the USA from 1883 to 1922.

Addressing objections and *empathy techniques* were clearly documented for the first time in 1936 in Dale Carnegie's book "How to Win Friends and Influence People" (also during the industrial revolution).

The AIDA model (Attention, Interest, Desire, Action), which guides a potential customer through the entire purchasing process, was first described in 1925 by E.K. Strong.

If we go even further back, _persuasion techniques_ were described by Aristotle in the book "Rhetoric" in the 4th century BC.

Authority techniques were outlined by Cicero in the book "Oratore" (meaning "On the Speaker") in 55 BC.

Needs analysis techniques were articulated by Benjamin Franklin in 1758 in his book "The Way to Wealth." These are just a few examples.

Many years have passed, generations have come and gone, societies have changed, and we have gone through several significant cultural shifts. With this, people's needs have naturally evolved.

The old view of selling can be seen as focusing on two primary factors:
- Service-based selling: The importance of which has been documented for centuries.

- Brand-based selling: The first documented advertisement was published in 1836 in France in the newspaper "La Presse," and this groundbreaking advertisement was the first not only to inform about a product or good but also used the brand "Dubonnet" as a central part of the advertisement. What was the product? A French soft drink.

The old view of selling focuses on informing and telling the customer why they should buy this particular brand through good service.

If you look in a bookstore or online bookstore today at the selection on selling, the titles overwhelmingly focus on _how_ to sell. Very few deal with the psychology behind _why the customer makes the final decision to buy_ (which is always based on some kind of feeling). This means that you can always influence a customer's purchasing decision if you understand their needs and the signals they are sending.

There have been several occasions when I have reflected on the messages that are sent out and whether they truly resonate with people's needs. One example is the laundry detergent advertisements that were frequently shown on television in the past. In all these commercials, dirty laundry was shown becoming clean, with children accidentally spilling things but the garment coming out clean after washing. That's impressively good. However, when I curiously asked people, "What's the first thing you do when the laundry is done and you open the washing machine door?" Everyone in some way responded, "I smell the first garment I can reach to see if the laundry smells good."
– "So you don't check if the garment is clean?" – "Only if it's a specific stain I want to get rid of; I expect it to be clean."
(I also smell the first garment…)

Only recently have I noticed laundry detergent companies focusing less on what customers expect, that the wash will be clean, and instead concentrating on value-enhancing factors that customers are willing to pay more for.

Today's necessary view of sales can be seen as focusing on these main factors (both of which were introduced in 1994):
<u>Mechanical Selling:</u> On August 11, 1994, the first product was purchased on the Internet. It was on a website created by Dan Kohn at Stanford University. The customer was Phil Brandenburger, and he bought a CD, "Ten Summoner's Tales" by Sting.

On October 27, 1994, the very first advertisement appeared on the Internet. It was global telecommunications company AT&T that, with a simple clickable banner ad on a website, allowed the user to click through to their site. This was a significant event that opened the door to digital marketing and developed technological platforms. From August 11 to October 27, 1994, mechanical selling was born.

Value-Based Selling: There has been discussion regarding this concept for some time. The first influential author to introduce this concept was Michael Bosworth in 1994 in his book "Solution Selling." In the book, Bosworth introduced the concept of value proposition (VP), which can be described as the importance of understanding and communicating the unique value that a product or service can offer a customer. It emphasizes the benefits and solutions that the product or service can provide to address the customer's needs or problems.

(Value proposition, abbreviated as VP, should not be confused with USP, "Unique Selling Proposition," a term coined in Rosser Reeves' book "Reality in Advertising," published in 1961. VP describes the value and benefit a product or service offers to a customer, while USP describes the unique advantages and characteristics a product or service has compared to others.)

- *USP = focus on the product or service.*
- *VP = focus on the value.*

Today's necessary view of selling focuses on mechanically and value-based evoking emotions within the customer that lead them to initiate contact, ask questions, or make purchasing decisions on their own.

"Stop selling on price - position your value."
- Victor Antonio

Reflections, Chapter 2

1. How do you handle *the little stones* today? How does it affect your emotions, and what signals do you send out to your surroundings or, how does your way of handling problems shape your environment? How does this affect your own development, and how can you practice thinking in everyday situations to shift your focus to solutions?

2. How can your concrete, direct focus on possible solutions positively impact your entity; their development, decision-making abilities, actions, motivation, energy levels, engagement, focus, efficiency, productivity, and results?

3. Do you have insight into the three components of *locus of control* and the three components of *need for control*, and how does this insight help you as a leader to better understand your team members as well as more confidently know which type of situational leadership to apply for the best long-term effect?

4. Have you reflected on your behavior and the signals you send out, and how they affect your entity? Is there any risk that you want one thing internally but send out different signals that your entity experiences or interprets differently?

5. How do you influence your entity in daily life to create a positive internal hospitality when you reflect on the points on page 193? Is there anything you can do differently?

6. How would a higher degree of genuine internal hospitality, in conjunction with the three tools, affect your entity and your work environment?

CHAPTER 3

$$IH \dashrightarrow C \dashrightarrow EH : (E = potential^{\wedge}\infty) \dashrightarrow R = P$$

It is sufficient for one person to enter a room to change the culture for the better.

Be that person.

Niclas Timmerby

The culture = The atmosphere = The human conditions that the people in the entity continuously create together.

The internal hospitality continuously shapes the atmosphere that the people in the entity experience.

The human conditions are that the individuals in the workplace, through their values, moral principles, behaviors, signals/attitudes, and norms, as well as how they act and interact with one another, collectively influence the atmosphere.

This is my interpretation of how culture is created, whether it is, for example, a team in a workplace, a school class, a sports team, family/relatives, a group of friends, a board or management team, a political organization, a religious congregation, an artistic association, a charity group, a student organization, a military unit, a music group, a healthcare organization, an environmental organization, a theatre ensemble, a housing cooperative, or a trade union. Or two individuals influencing each other, as they also have an atmosphere, a culture.

Even a highly temporary entity, such as those that meet at a party, a trip, a concert, or a cooking course, also creates a culture built from what the people together contribute to shaping the atmosphere.

The atmosphere/culture is constantly in motion; it never stands still.
Your task as a leader is to long-term nurture and maintain the internal hospitality with your mission (your map) focused on the vision, with the value foundation, by providing emotional information and other tools you have received in the book.

Structure, checklists, rules, and routines create very little development.

Building a culture enables people to grow.
The very word culture says it all; the Latin word "cultura" originally meant: to describe the cultivation and processing of land.

Building a healthy and developing culture ensures that people have the conditions for well-being in the workplace, that they simply feel they are in a good place in life. Here are four studies that demonstrate the psychological and mental benefits of a healthy culture in the workplace:

2005: "The Impact of Organizational Culture on Employee Well-being: Evidence from a Cross-sectional Study." This study showed that: "a positive and supportive corporate culture is linked to better mental well-being among employees."

2017: "Organizational Culture and Employee Mental Health: A Multilevel Model." The study showed that: "a positive and healthy corporate culture is associated with lower levels of stress and psychological distress among employees."

2019: "The Impact of Organizational Culture on Employee Engagement." This study examined the relationship between culture and employee engagement. The results showed that: "a positive and supportive corporate culture promotes higher engagement and better psychological well-being among employees."

2016: "The Relationship between Organizational Culture and Employee Job Satisfaction in the Public Sector." This study demonstrated that: "a positive and healthy corporate culture is linked to higher levels of job satisfaction and psychological well-being among employees."

When you nurture the internal hospitality, you influence the culture.

Leadership is very little about what "I" do; leadership is about what my leadership can do for the development of others.

The first to describe leadership was the Greek philosopher Plato in one of his most famous works, "The Republic," written around 380 BC. Plato believed that a good leader should, among other things, be just, wise, courageous, have received an education in philosophy and morality, possess the ability to make wise decisions, communicate effectively with people, inspire others to follow, and have the ability to see beyond the immediate consequences of their actions.

In line with the significant cultural shifts I have described in the book, the concept of leadership has been challenged and changed, which is entirely natural. Here is a brief insight.

Frederick Winslow Taylor (1856-1915) is considered a pioneer in the concept of leadership. He coined the term Taylorism in the late 1800s, and his methodology had a significant impact on work methods and leadership during the industrial revolution. The methodology focuses on maximizing profit, optimizing work processes, increasing productivity, performance-based reward systems, and precisely timed work tasks for maximum efficiency, all overseen by a clearly hierarchical model where managers were responsible for supervising and directing the work.

During the information society, the most prominent methodology in leadership was Transformational Leadership. This was developed by historian and researcher James MacGregor Burns. He described that leadership should focus on inspiring and motivating employees to achieve common goals. The methodology also emphasizes the importance of _creating a vision and communicating it in an inspiring way_, as well as _supporting employees' potential_. James MacGregor Burns highlighted the importance of adapting to rapid changes, fostering innovation and creativity, and creating an engaging work environment.

Our most recent significant cultural shift, prior to the ongoing AI revolution, was _the digital/social revolution_. The most prominent methodology was _agile leadership_, which has been developed by several researchers and experts, though no specific individual. Agile leadership is a flexible and responsive style that emphasizes _adaptation to rapid changes and collaboration_. The focus is on _creating a culture of trust, innovation, and learning_. It also emphasizes promoting faster decision-making processes. Agile leadership _encourages participation and a flat organization_.

The reason I advocate for _situational leadership_ is that it works regardless of the type of leadership style that has characterized the entity you operate in up until today. With the structure of this model, you can develop both the individuals and your entity, independent of team members' individual needs based on cultural shifts and age. The leadership style means that you, as a leader, adapt to each specific situation and the team member's level of maturity.

You develop yourself in your situational leadership through each unique situation and conversation. As you grow, you find a quicker balance between the demands of the task and the team member's abilities and inner motivation, and how you can challenge the team member to help them grow and develop.

Combining your <u>situational leadership</u> with <u>tailored coaching</u> within an accepted <u>feedback culture</u> allows you to make what you may have thought was impossible, possible.

What makes your culture visible in words is your shared foundation of values. The shared foundation of values is created by the team members themselves. Everyone has been able to participate and, in an adapted context, contribute their individual moral principles, feelings, and values. The value foundation provides a clear direction, in the team members' own words, on how they are expected to treat one another, how they are expected to act, and how they are expected to perform their work. It is, of course, of great importance that you, as a leader, have also signed and adhere to your entity's shared foundation of values.

"A strong culture is one based on shared values and norms, permeating all aspects of the organization, from recruitment to decision-making."
- Charles Handy

If the culture is healthy and the atmosphere is pleasant to be in, <u>the team members will adhere to the value foundation</u>.

If the culture feels uncomfortable and the atmosphere is tense, <u>one or more team members may violate the value foundation</u>.

Everyone senses your culture.
I promise. You, all your team members, and people who temporarily visit your entity *immediately* sense the atmosphere. The atmosphere directly reflects how you, as a leader, are feeling, how the team members are feeling, how they treat each other, and how they collaborate. How you feel collectively is the fundamental factor that shapes your shared contribution to the organization.

The leader must stand up for the culture.
In the book, you have been provided with the long-term tools that constantly work for you and your entity in the background.

But what do you do if you have negative culture bearers whose negative superpowers drain the atmosphere by:
- not understanding the consequences of their signals, behavior, or attitude,
- refusing to accept their role,
- failing to understand the "why," complaining and draining energy,
- not being team players, acting according to their own rules,
- openly showing that they do not care about their team members and/ or the goals and results,
- lacking humility and putting themselves at the center,
- lacking self-awareness and manipulating their team members to influence the culture in the direction they desire,
- challenging you as a person and your leadership in the corridors (for they rarely dare to do so face to face),
- understanding that they are in the wrong workplace but remaining and spreading negative energy?

If you do not protect the culture, your leadership is in a zone of danger.
You need to protect the culture; you must stand up for the atmosphere the entity has collectively built. Here you need to show decisiveness and clarity to demonstrate to everyone in the entity that you do not hesitate for a second to protect your entity and its values. By clearly taking a stand and demonstrating decisiveness, you create trust and confidence from that part of your entity that wishes to grow with the organization, and you show the negative culture bearers that their behavior and attitude are unacceptable.

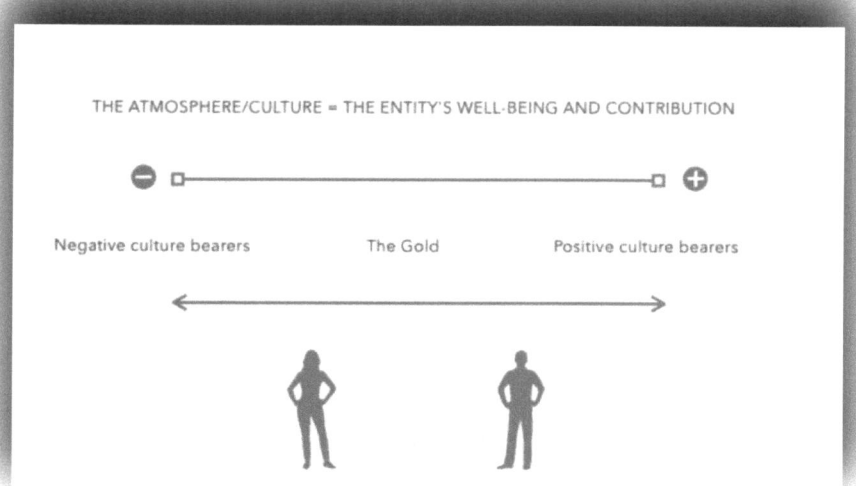

The atmosphere/culture = the entity's well-being and contribution.
The outcome of your atmosphere/culture directly influences the well-being of the team members and their contributions to results and success. A healthy, secure, and pleasant atmosphere fosters collaboration, productivity, and engagement. An unhealthy atmosphere filled with uncomfortable tensions negatively impacts communication, work environment, work climate, performance, and results.

If you reflect and then mark with a line on the top line, how is the atmosphere/culture right now? (At the far right is the goal: a healthy, secure, and pleasant atmosphere.)

Negative culture bearers, the Gold, and Positive culture bearers.
The two-way arrow symbolizes the constant movement within your entity, how your team members shape, influence, and maintain the upper line, which represents your culture and the atmosphere in which people operate. The culture never stands still. The culture/atmosphere, like the wind, is always in motion in some direction.

Positive culture bearers radiate genuine warmth to others. They dare to show emotions and openly care, encourage, and praise others. *They spread joy, optimism, and enthusiasm.* The feeling of being near a positive culture bearer is one of safety and trust, as they listen to others, take great responsibility, stand up when something is not equitable or just, and openly respect differences. It is evident that they want to be involved in creating an environment where everyone feels comfortable being themselves and can share opinions and ideas.

Imagine the image as if the positive culture bearers are physically using all their strength and a big smile to pull the culture in the right direction.

Negative culture bearers. Unfortunately, there is often the opposite in all entities. You may even be able to see their faces in the image, how they physically, decisively, and stubbornly do everything they can to pull the culture to the left side. *It must be done their way.*

It is important to understand that the negative culture bearer may not be aware of what they are doing, how they are influencing others, and how they undermine the entire entity's well-being and performance.

The undermining occurs when the team member, for example, has a lack of willingness to cooperate, spreads dissatisfaction, causes tensions and conflicts, creates an atmosphere of distrust and insecurity, exhibits a lack of accountability, shows low work morals, spreads negative comments, and creates misunderstandings between team members that you, as a leader, need to manage.

The Gold, which consists of those who are a bit in between. For various reasons, they lack the courage to follow the positive culture bearers who, with all their might, want to pull the engine (the culture) forward, and they find it intimidating to be near the negative culture bearers who with all their might grip the emergency brakes of the train.

How will you, as a leader, lead to protect, nurture, maintain, and advance the culture?
On page 152, before level 4 of feedback, I shared what managers and leaders have answered when I asked them which employees they overwhelmingly dedicate time, energy, focus, resources, and commitment to.

They responded: "Those who don't really want to be at the workplace." When I asked follow-up questions, it crystallized that this was due to the individuals being negative culture bearers who, through their behavior and attitude, negatively affect their colleagues and the culture.

So, if the image I have gathered from my professional life aligns with the general reality in workplaces, it is indeed sad. <u>There is a significant risk that the best will ultimately leave if the leader does not clearly stand up for a healthy and pleasant culture.</u>

Don't forget the positive culture bearers.
It can be human, as they are just racing ahead with energy and engagement, smiling all the way. They do what they are supposed to do, and they do so much more. They are co-creators of a positive culture and atmosphere. They uplift others and have a significant impact on well-being and results.

But, in the end, they may become weary because they pull the train without truly being recognized for the contributions they make. Number one in the survey you have on pages 49-50: what employees answered when asked the question, "<u>What is most important to you?</u>" was:

"To be seen."

The secret to guiding a culture in the right direction is 3+1.

1. Positive culture bearers <u>require little</u> = **Feedback and Signals**.
2. The Gold <u>requires clarity</u> = **Feedback**.
3. Negative culture bearers <u>require you to take action</u> = **Consequences**.

<u>A positive culture bearer</u> needs so little to continue running and contributing. Stop them when they are spreading their energy the fastest and say, "I think you're fantastic." When they are about to leave work for the day, stop them and say, "I appreciate you very much." Share whenever you have the opportunity that you value the person as a human being, their attitude, signals, qualities, and personality. Continue to give appreciative feedback and signals that show the person is important, valuable, and significant.

<u>The Gold.</u> These are the individuals you should <u>focus on the most to steer the culture in the right direction</u>. Reason (1) is that most team members are usually in this part of the entity, as negative and positive culture bearers often represent a much smaller proportion of the total number of people in the entity. Reason (2) is that these people are the most malleable: They usually follow the negative culture bearers because it is easier; <u>it requires no effort to be negative</u>. They very rarely follow the positive culture bearers, as <u>it requires courage and a significant mental effort to transition</u> from "The Gold" to becoming a positive culture bearer. This is where you can make a big difference.

The Gold, naturally, is those who need the most clarity and direction to gain the courage and mental strength to become a positive culture bearer. Engage in discussions with them about the long-term tools such as vision, your mission, and the shared foundation of values, and ask them to give you feedback about your emotional information.

The most straightforward tool is feedback; nothing can be clearer than feedback. Working with levels 1 and 2 allows you to consciously and positively steer them "to the right," encouraging them to occupy a more natural positive space in the entity.

Tell a malleable person: "You, just you, can change the atmosphere in our workplace. I believe in you. What is your dream scenario in terms of the feelings you want to have when you come to work on a typical day?" Giving feedback to The Gold is your most effective recipe for a healthy culture and the overall development of the entity.

Think back to the two-sided image on page 222, where negative culture bearers pull to the left, while positive ones pull to the right. It is in constant motion, with the malleable Gold in the middle. Your goal in protecting and nurturing the culture is to get Gold to move to the right with <u>small, small, small steps</u>. These tiny steps create a momentum that will soon influence both the negative and positive sides. Both sides will sense that something unstoppable is about to happen. And what you, as a leader, are essentially doing is consistently working with your feedback culture (which you have clearly stated you will do in the workshop) and telling them that you believe in them.

<u>A negative culture bearer.</u>
One of the leader's most important insights is that <u>everyone</u> can change. *All change involves development.*

A negative culture bearer <u>can change and become</u> a positive culture bearer.

An egotist <u>can change and become</u> your very best altruistic team member.

A pessimist <u>can change and become</u> an optimistic team member.

*Do you remember my quote from page 51? **"A true leader understands that it is not the people who are "wrong". It is the communication between them that is flawed."** Your task as a true leader is to first reflect, selflessly on your communication. How can <u>you</u> change your communication, <u>your</u> body language, <u>your</u> tone? Can <u>you</u> listen more attentively without judging to try to see the other person's perspective?*

Have <u>you</u> attempted to give feedback at all four levels? Do <u>you</u> show that you are the adult in the conversation, clearly moving the level of the conversation forward with your calmness, tone, and body language? How do <u>you</u> demonstrate this? Do <u>you</u> see how your communication lands with the recipient?

If none of this works, there is nothing left but to prepare yourself to give a consequence. A consequence is given to demonstrate that a behavior is not acceptable in the workplace. You need to begin clearly documenting the occasions when a team member undermines the culture with reasons, dates, and times.

This may include, for example, not keeping time, failing to follow established rules, policies, and checklists, doing things in their own way, treating their colleagues disrespectfully, or acting in ways that harm the entity, organization, or brand.

The consequence can be a verbal or written warning. Or, in the case of a serious incident, you might inform the team member that they will go home for the remainder of the day with full pay and that they are welcome to return the following day, while also informing them that you will be notifying their trade union about the incident and your actions.

It is advisable, in every instance you consider giving a consequence, to consult with your HR department.

3+1 = Tailored coaching

The fourth factor you can use is tailored coaching. The great thing about this tool is that coaching is suitable for everyone in your entity: negative and positive culture bearers as well as The Gold.

As a leader, you have two incredibly powerful tools to influence your team members' development both in the short and long term. You have previously received tool number 1: *"The four levels of feedback for all generations and cultures."*

Tool number two is *tailored coaching*. <u>Coaching means that you genuinely believe in the human capacity for development, with a positive perspective on people.</u>

Tool 1: Feedback = This enables you to have a genuinely open environment in your entity.

Tool 2: Tailored coaching = This allows you to avoid doing everything yourself while still ensuring the quality you strive for.

Feedback at all four levels develops your entity and helps individuals grow. Your intention with feedback is to demonstrate that a person is developing or improving in some respect if it leads to a change in behaviour or attitude.

With tailored coaching, you do not have to be a manager who controls people with directives. Your focus is on trusting people's ability to develop and, through coaching, developing the entity so that they do not need directives.

Your intention as a coach is to demonstrate that you believe in a person's or entity's capacity to reach a new state from the existing current state. You believe that the person or entity can become self-sufficient and that you are there as a coach to challenge them.

"A manager directs people through controls.

A leader develops people, teams, and organisations.

A mentor develops leaders."
- Niclas Timmerby

Risks of not using feedback and coaching.
Potential Risk 1: You will not be able to cope.
Potential Risk 2: You will spend more time putting out fires than leading, motivating, and developing.

Using feedback and coaching as tools in your daily leadership is beneficial for your well-being. It is easy to fall into the trap of using structural measures to almost automatically guide team members to do what is required for your business to function. *However, this means that you begin to take <u>too much responsibility for what others should do</u> when you should be following up to see if the measures have generated results, which will lead to time constraints and stress because your own tasks will be sidelined.*

There is also a significant risk that things will not turn out as you intended, despite very clear measures, and you might sometimes think, *"Oh, I will just do it myself and make it so incredibly clear that others understand how it should be done!"*

<u>Then you need to ask yourself two questions:</u>
1. What are your employees there for?
2. What is your role?

Certainly, you can take responsibility for things for several years that you could (or should) delegate, and then give feedback and coach the team member to the desired outcome. However, the truth is that if you do things yourself that you could teach others to do for too long, there are two potential risks. The ones you see on the previous page.

But what about you? What happens to your development, the vision you set in your self-leadership (page 70), and your personal goals and ambitions if you do not use coaching and feedback?

The risk is clear: without feedback and coaching, you will constantly be putting out fires and encountering challenges in meeting the expectations you have set for yourself. I urge you to be kind to yourself. Practice, use, and reflect on your self-leadership to make wise decisions in your life and career.

Your vision may be very high; you do not want to stop at being a leader.
You want to be a mentor who nurtures new leaders and shows them the way. This is fantastic; the world needs many new mentors who can guide managers to become leaders.

Master feedback and coaching, and you will create tools, trust in yourself, and the reputation required to be a mentor.

Differences between feedback and coaching.
There are two essential differences you should be aware of before you start to strategically coach and give feedback.

How many can I give feedback to/coach at the same time?
- Feedback is given to one person, the individual it concerns.
- You can coach one person or an entire group of people.

When should I give feedback, and when should I coach?
- Feedback highlights something that has happened.
- Coaching focuses on what is happening in the present or towards a goal.

Feedback:
- You provide feedback because you want to highlight a behaviour you have observed in the rec pient through appreciative or developmental feedback to help the team member grow.
- You give it to avoid misunderstancings and to clearly show the direction (where are we going? What standard should we have?).
- Feedback creates efficiency.
- Feedback clarifies why, what, how, and when.
- You provide appreciative feedback at *levels 1 and 3* to encourage more of a desired behaviour, attitude, or performance. When you give praise, it reinforces behaviours and moves the individual, entity, and organisation forward. You provide developmental feedback at *levels 2 and 4* to make the recipient aware of a behaviour, attitude, or performance that hinders them. Ycu demonstrate that you believe in the recipient and their potential for growth. This feedback helps reduce undesired behaviours, attitudes, or performances, moving the individual, entity, and organisation forward.

Coaching:
- You coach from the actual current state to a specific goal or in the present (more common in sports). Your focus is on the future.
- You challenge individuals with questions so that they can arrive at the answers themselves and thereby develop.
- As your entity develops through coaching, it will create more time for you as a leader.

Combining tailored coaching with feedback at all four levels enables team members and the entity to become self-sufficient.

Why can't everyone be like me?
I am sure you have thought somewhat like this at some point during your leadership journey: *"What if everyone worked as fast, as efficiently, was as good as I am with customers, sold as much, looked after contractors and subcontractors so well, or could write contracts with our suppliers as effectively?"*

    If I may challenge you. If you think this way, perhaps you should not be a leader. You might not even be suited to be a manager. Instead, you might specialise in what you do best and create a successful professional career that way

You are a leader because <u>you develop people</u>. I am me, you are you, and we are completely unique. <u>Every time you have a team member in front of you, think that they are saying to you: "*<u>Develop me, bring out the very best in me, show me how good I can become!</u>*"

That is your task as a leader: to develop people, teams, and organisations. What can an individual become? With feedback and coaching, you can reveal more and more of their hidden potential.

Being a leader who coaches involves constant development for you and everyone in your entity. Tailored coaching means that you consider the individual needs of all team members, and this cannot be rushed. If you focus on the quick solution, you focus on where the person is today, which often means you provide the answers quickly. That is not coaching.

Coaching focuses on the individual's development, what they can become. How can I develop the person in front of me so that they can perform this task independently next time, and perhaps even better than I would have done it?

You will need to train for a long time to become a confident coach; it does not happen overnight. To coach consciously through tailored coaching means that you, as a leader, have started working on yourself in your self-leadership. You have begun to gain insight into your own values (which subconsciously guide you and your choices), and your moral principles become clearer and sharper with each passing month.

What you see happening with and in yourself (your development) is that you, in real-time, create a responsible leadership perspective, making you very aware of how you affect others through the signals you emit/your attitude, how your behaviour influences others, and how you shape your team members. You now have a bird's eye view and possess the ability to see yourself from others' perspectives.

Every time you reflect on your own values, behaviour, and attitude, you gain not only a deeper understanding of how you function as a person and why you "are the way you are and act or react the way you do" but also insight into how other people function. As a bonus: you become more humble; as a second bonus, your self-awareness increases.

No one is like you; everyone is unique.

To be a successful coach, it is important to understand and keep two key factors in mind: the line of separation and your view of humanity.

<u>The line of separation</u> is the clear boundary that you always need to maintain between the recipient and yourself.

When you step into the coaching role, your focus is on two things: <u>the recipient's success and the organisation's results.</u>

Your role is not, let me reiterate, not to be a friend or companion. As a coach, you need to view the situation or obstacles to the goal from a neutral perspective.

<u>A good view of humanity</u> is that everyone wants and can develop if given the conditions to succeed.

Your fundamental values and how you see other people permeate your interactions with them. These signals are rarely easy to hide during times when people are very stressed or angry.

What is your fundamental view of humanity? Is it a positive one?

Your team members see you as the one who holds the responsibility and possesses all the answers and solutions. You are to show the way.

However, as you know, you cannot always be present in every situation to show the way or tell your team members what to do.

This is where coaching is the solution; <u>you develop people by challenging them</u>, which makes them self-sufficient.

<u>You can coach in two different scenarios:</u>

- Goal-oriented coaching:
When you set personal or joint goals. Or when you encourage your team members to set goals, either personally or for the entire entity during conversations or meetings.

- Problem-solving coaching:
When a team member comes to you with a problem. Then you are faced with a dilemma that likely happens to you in everyday life:
- *Either you provide the answer, and the team member receives the simple and short-term solution served on a silver platter = the person remains in their comfort zone where very little development occurs.*
- *Or you ask questions and challenge the team member = the person develops, takes more personal responsibility, and is given the opportunity to become self-sufficient in the long run.*

<u>Everyone working as a leader has a fantastic opportunity for development every time a team member presents a problem.</u>

The choice for you as a leader is simple: you can (1) develop and enhance your entity, or (2) solve the problem yourself with the potential risks that entails as I described on page 229:
- *In the long run, you will not be able to cope.*
- *You are spending more time putting out fires than leading, motivating, and developing.*

You remember how I described paradigms/truths.
As a coach, you want to change thinking patterns by challenging the old ingrained truths/paradigms. You do it because you want to see and

bring out the full potential of the individual. You do this naturally and genuinely out of 100 percent goodwill because you have a positive view of humanity and want to see people grow and thrive.

Do you remember the important "why" I described on page 199?
Coaching, which is your tool for bringing out your team members' "whys," is an insight that has helped me immensely as a leader: *There is always a why.* You have a "why" for why you behave in different situations. Everyone in your entity has different "whys" for why they behave in various ways in different situations.

- *It is precisely <u>here</u> you can turn a selfish person in your entity into an altruist.*
- *It is precisely <u>here</u> you can transform a pessimistic team member into an optimistic one.*
- *It is precisely <u>here</u> you can motivate a negative cultural bearer to reflect instead of ruminate. From criticizing to taking responsibility for behavior, attitude, time, tasks, and for their entity.*
- *It is precisely <u>here</u> you can encourage " the Gold" to dare to take small, small, steps to become positive cultural bearers in your entity.*

If you, as a coach, can get the recipient to articulate their "whys," you will, with a high probability, come closer to that person than most others have done before. This creates trust and deep confidence.

EVERYONE has an iceberg.
Every individual has an iceberg; you have an iceberg, all your team members have one, everyone in your family and relatives has one, etc.

I view the icebergs as people's "whys."

Sometimes you observe things that "annoy you." Behaviors and attitudes that are not good or acceptable, or you react to them because they do not align with <u>your</u> truth of how people "should be." *(Why can't everyone be like me!)*

The behaviors, attitudes, body language, and actions you see above the waterline tell you ***nothing*** about the 'why", absolutely nothing.

<u>*Your task as a coach is to discover what lies **beneath** the waterline, the person's "why."* </u> *Here are a few examples:*

- *Irregular attendance, increased sick leave.*
- *Is poor at completing checklists and finishing tasks, starts missing deadlines.*
- *Looks worried, has subdued body language and tone.*
- *May have dirty or torn clothing.*
- *Is not doing what they are supposed to do.*
- *Exhibits subdued body language and tone.*
- *Snaps at colleagues, gets angry, ends up in conflict situations.*
- *Does not want to socialize outside of work hours, withdraws from social interactions at work.*
- *Reduced productivity.*
- *Looks sad / has little facial expression.*
- *Feels a lack of experience.*
- *Health problems.*
- *Addiction issues.*
- *Wants more responsibility.*
- *Wants to be more involved.*
- *Dislikes themselves.*
- *Is not happy at work.*
- *Personality issues.*
- *Struggles in social situations.*
- *Feels unacknowledged.*
- *Worries about their family situation.*
- *Difficulties with social interactions.*
- *Feels excluded from the team.*
- *Inner stress regarding their finances, is facing personal difficulties.*

While feedback is your tool for adjusting and correcting towards development, coaching is your tool for going deeper and creating real change within the individual. Consider what a gift it is as a leader to have the opportunity to truly change people's perceptions of themselves and help them open up.

It is one-way.
People enable entities and entire organizations to grow and achieve success. It can only go in that direction. It is _people_ who create the conditions to achieve results. Then the fruits of that result can very well be reinvested into the people, and then it starts over, _people_ create new and better conditions for achieving better results.

Tailored coaching is a fantastic tool for an organization to invest in, as it not only yields results in numbers but also helps team members thrive and develop.

"Only things you are engaged in leave an impact on people and your legacy."
- Niclas Timmerby

Coaching is not something you can engage in half-heartedly and expect results. Building a rewarding coaching relationship takes time and must be allowed to take time, as all individuals have a starting point and different whys. The better prepared you are, the better you listen, the more you challenge, and the more energy and genuine engagement you bring to the coaching conversation, the greater impact those conversations will have.

In the journal "International Journal of Mentoring and Coaching" and the book "Coachology; Team Spirit, Joy, and Profitability," the following positive synergistic effects of coaching are demonstrated: a 24%

reduction in employee turnover over one year, a 4.5% decrease in sick leave over one year, and a 19% increase in productivity over one year.

Coaching or artificial respiration?

In coaching training, I explain that it is very common for people to think they are coaching when they are actually providing artificial respiration.

It's so easy to fall into a regular conversation because we are afraid to challenge people.

What is artificial respiration?

- You provide the answers to the recipient.
- You focus on where the recipient is today or their past.
- You do not challenge the recipient.
- You concentrate on a quick solution.

What is coaching?

- You ask questions and listen.
- You focus on the recipient's vision for the future.
- You get the recipient to identify the obstacles they see.
- You challenge by asking questions that push the recipient out of their comfort zone. Challenging a person is like giving a wonderful gift–the gift of development.
- Your focus is not on where the recipient is today but on what they can become, how far they can reach, what their potential is, and how to get there.

To coach successfully:

1. The better you understand the recipient's "why," the better you can coach, lead, and develop your team member.

2. You need to build confidence and, ideally, trust. Don't rush.

3. During conversations, you need to challenge the recipient's old ingrained truths.

4. Be mindful of your role; even when it feels tough, continue to challenge.

5. Take breaks if emotional issues or memories arise that the recipient needs to process.

6. Sincerely thank the recipient after each coaching conversation.

<u>A</u>. In your initial coaching conversations, ask <u>questions related to the professional role</u> to make it easier for the recipient to respond. Here are some examples:

- *How are you challenged in your current professional role? Are there areas where you feel you can grow and develop? What obstacles do you see, and how can you overcome them?*

- *What specific goals or results do you want to achieve in your professional role, and how can you challenge yourself to reach these goals? What obstacles do you see, and how can you overcome them?*

- *What are your strengths, and how can you use them more effectively in your work?*

- *In which areas do you feel insecure or need more knowledge or skills? How can you challenge yourself to fill these knowledge gaps? What obstacles do you see, and how can you overcome them?*

- *How can you take more responsibility and initiative in your professional role? Are there areas where you can take on more challenging tasks or projects? What obstacles do you see, and how can you overcome them?*

- *How can you use your previous experiences to grow and develop further?*

- *How can you develop others and thereby grow yourself?*

<u>B</u>. Here, you delve deeper by asking <u>questions about the recipient's</u> <u>drive and motivation</u>. Here are some examples:

- Why do you go to work? What is your main motivation?
- What are your other motivating factors? Why do you have these
motivating factors? Are there other factors that could motivate you
more? What obstacles do you see, and how can you overcome them?
- Is there anything that prevents you from feeling motivated and
engaged in your work? How can you overcome these obstacles and find
new sources of motivation?
- What role does feedback, praise, and recognition play in your
motivation? How often would you like me to give you feedback to
enhance your drive and motivation?
- When do you feel the most driven or motivated at work? When are you
at your best? How can you challenge yourself to find new ways to
maintain and strengthen that motivation?
- Do you have any personal goals you have set for yourself, and how do
they relate to your inner drive? Can you challenge yourself to set even
more ambitious and inspiring goals?

<u>C</u>. After discussing A and B, it is time to delve into the deepest level: <u>the recipient's own values and moral principles</u>. You may have obtained certain insights from earlier conversations that both you and the recipient can rely on now.

This is where you can connect with your team member on a deeper
level. If they can share personal events or situations that have shaped
their identity today, challenging these can lead to remarkable
developments during these conversations. This is where the person can
challenge their conditioning and the identity they may have lived in for

a very long time. At C, the recipient needs to have a high level of trust or confidence in you.

Some examples:
- *What is important to you in life? Why do you think that is?*
- *What is important to you as a person? What has created this feeling within you?*
- *What do you never compromise on? What situations in your life have shaped these deep values within you?*
- *What do you want to change in your life? What obstacles do you see, and how can you overcome them?*
- *How can you use your values and moral principles to create greater meaning in your life and professional life? How can you challenge yourself to actively seek and create opportunities that align with your values and principles, even if it means making difficult choices?*
- *How do you handle dilemmas that arise in the workplace when there is a conflict between your own values and the organization's goals or in your relationships with your colleagues? What obstacles do you see, and how can you overcome them? Can you challenge yourself to find ways to resolve such dilemmas in a manner that is both morally right for you and sustainable in your relationships?*
- *How can you use your values and moral principles as a guide to create a positive, ethical work environment while living according to our shared values? How can you challenge yourself to be a role model and influence others to act in accordance with our shared values and wise moral principles?*

Share what you want.
I will give you my best tip that I use when coaching

The word "**Want**."

First, some background: Sometimes, perhaps often, people in your personal or professional life come to you and express how they feel. Overwhelmingly, they share how poorly they feel or how bad something is. In the next chapter, you will read more about "social identity," which may explain why people want to air negative things. As a coach, you occasionally need to break the pattern or shift the focus if the conversation is not progressing in a forward direction.

Everyone goes through tragedies such as the loss of a loved one, serious illnesses, lifelong injuries, or difficult traumatic events. However, this section is *not* about those matters.

This is about phases or temporary states in life that manifest as problems, setbacks, and concerns.

Everyone faces minor crises related to finances, relationships, work, or health. When people come to you to talk in your personal or professional life, or if you are in a coaching conversation, I can guarantee that if problems, setbacks, or concerns arise, they will be in one or more of these four areas.

To move past these crises in life, people sometimes need help. It takes great strength to ask others for assistance. However, to genuinely help the person in front of you, you need to challenge them.

If someone says to you, *"I don't feel well,"* what can you do? Internally, you may feel sorry for the person, and might respond, *"That's unfortunate. How terrible. How unfair. Poor you. You've had such bad luck. If it's not one thing, it's another. Keep fighting."*

This does <u>not</u> help the person at all to move out of their current state or phase. This is because it is incredibly difficult for you to challenge someone regardless of the situation when they express how they feel. When someone says something negative, it inevitably affects you and how you will respond.

Especially if it's a close loved one, we naturally care even more about the person's well-being.

If you receive such a comment, you can respond, *"How do you <u>want</u> to feel?"*

If you can get the person in a conversation or coaching session to answer that question, it will move them forward.

Something magical happens when a person shifts their focus from a current state to a desired state. When they express how they <u>want</u> to feel, functions are activated in both the recipient's and your brain.

You begin to think in solutions; the prefrontal cortex is activated, whose functions include problem-solving, decision-making, creativity, and planning. Other areas of the brain also activate, suddenly making it possible to draw new conclusions, see different perspectives, and adapt to new situations.

The word <u>want</u> is the fastest path to personal development.
When you are in a phase or state that you are not satisfied with, your dominant thoughts are about how you feel. You can use this at any time. Shift your focus to how you *<u>want</u>* to feel.

If you can't move out of the feeling, talk to someone you trust and ask for help. For example:

- *Can I talk to you about something?*

                                        - Absolutely.

- *I don't want you to feel sorry for me, okay?*

                                        - Okay, if that's what you want.

<u>*Then, share the phase you are in and that you want to move forward. Ask the person not to come up with solutions, but to challenge you instead.*</u>

(When there are two, the likelihood of getting out of the phase is greater than if you are alone. Don't underestimate the importance of asking to be challenged; otherwise, no lasting change can occur.)

Here are some examples of "<u>want</u>" questions in coaching conversations to break patterns and shift focus from the current state to the desired state:
- How do you want to feel?
- What do you want to achieve? (Vision.)
- What do you want to accomplish? (Ambitions.)
- How much do you want to sell per day, week, month, or year?
- How do you want the office/store/staff room to look?
- How do you want to complete your training?
- How many client visits do you want to make?
- How quickly do you want to finish "this part" of the work?

Reflection, Chapter 3

1. Reflect on the atmosphere within your entity. Who are the positive and negative cultural bearers? How can you use feedback and coaching to shape a better atmosphere?

2. Reflect on your team members. Do you know their human needs? What influences their behavior and effort?
    1. Why do they come to work?
    2. What do they need to stay?
    3. Do they feel loyalty to you?
    4. Do they feel safe with you and their entity?
    5. What do they need to grow and develop?
    6. Does everyone understand the important "why": vision, mission, values, and feedback culture?
    7. Do they feel pride and engagement? If not, why?

3. To coach successfully:
    1. Your most important ambition when coaching is to uncover what lies beneath the surface of the "iceberg," to understand the "why." What are the causes and background of each team member's unique behavior, signals/attitudes, and actions?
    2. Are you genuinely interested in each team member's life?
    3. Is your goal to develop a genuine, unique relationship with each team member?
    4. Do you continuously observe team members and the entity as a whole to see how you can improve collaboration and chemistry among them?

CHAPTER 4

IH ⇢ C ⇢ EH: $(E = \text{potential}^{\wedge}\infty)$ ⇢ R = P

Satisfied customers can make a business survive.
Loyal customers make it profitable.
Niclas Timmerby

Cultures are the strongest thing there is.

- Cultures influence and affect everyone who is part of the culture.
- Cultures shape people's identities, how people relate to each other within the culture and to the outside world (that which exists outside of each culture).
- The cultural shifts we have lived through are rooted in societies, which makes societal culture the "normal," what is expected of us.
- The daily cultures we live and work in are rooted, which makes the culture the "normal," what is expected of us.

When you travel to a country, there is a culture there; when you go to a neighbouring country, there is a different culture. You sense different cultures everywhere: Countries, communities, villages and cities, districts, blocks compared to other blocks, different professions have different cultures, etc.

You have your own atmosphere you "live in." Then, when you come into contact with a person, even if it is just for a minute, you together create a new shared culture. When a third person comes along, the dynamics change immediately. It affects how you speak to each other and how you behave towards one another.

If a newly hired employee starts at your workplace tomorrow, they will immediately sense your atmosphere. It is invisible, but it affects the new team member immediately; people don't even need to speak for them to feel it through the hormones and chemical signals you emit. That is why I describe culture as the atmosphere. And more impressions come for the new employee: they will sense how you treat each other, how you collaborate, the energy level, engagement level, general body language and tone of voice, which words you generally use, what pace you work at, etc.

The culture/Atmosphere automatically becomes the external hospitality.

I have described how the internal hospitality creates culture. The culture, which I liken to the atmosphere, is where people dwell and are shaped. The external hospitality is a mirror image of the culture.

Imagine that you knock on the door of a stranger's family to tell them that a cat is stuck in a tree in their garden and is meowing because it cannot get down. A few seconds after they open the door and you have managed to say what you want to say, you feel it: the external hospitality. How their internal hospitality has over time shaped their culture, the atmosphere that you now feel in their external hospitality. You feel very clearly if you want to say goodbye and leave immediately or if you automatically feel that you are somehow already part of their culture, that you are almost one of them. They have invited you in and welcomed you without saying it in words. Their external hospitality, the atmosphere they project to you, has done the job.

Imagine you are eager to buy a new piece of clothing and you walk into a store you have not visited before. A few seconds after you enter the store, you sense it, the external hospitality. No one has said anything, and it is not necessary. Their internal hospitality has over time shaped their culture, and you feel it, whether you like it or not. It is sent from them as an invisible signal, whether they want it to or not. The culture, which you feel after a few seconds, affects you. Their collective superpowers that created the external hospitality influence you, and it impacts your purchasing decision.

If you are positively influenced by a genuine signal that shows that people are happy in their workplace, it makes you more inclined to want to purchase. Or is it the opposite: do you receive a signal that is not positive? Our brains are incredibly advanced, but you can only sense a positive or negative hospitality; there is no in-between. As soon as the external hospitality affects your feelings, it affects you (in this case, your purchasing decision).

In the Store.

If you sense positive signals from a thriving culture.
Then the feeling you get within you will very likely trigger the release of **dopamine** (giving you a sense of satisfaction linked to reward and joy), which can increase your motivation to shop. **"Of course, I deserve a new shirt, or maybe two!"**

Likewise, it is likely that the so-called "love hormone" **oxytocin** is released. You like the atmosphere and feel comfortable in the atmosphere; that is enough to trigger oxytocin, which is linked to positive social interaction (it must be genuine) and closeness, making you feel genuinely welcome and cared for. This creates trust, and your likelihood of making a purchase increases. **"Goodness, what a lovely and fun atmosphere they have here; I could work here. I'll probably buy an extra shirt!"**

Then comes the wonderful hormone **serotonin**, which is triggered by the same signal/atmosphere that the other beneficial hormones thrive in. If you feel content and happy, this hormone is released, which fills you with a sense of well-being and positivity, likely influencing your mood to complete a purchase. **"I'm just walking around smiling here; hmm, there are some really nice trousers that match the shirts..."**

If you sense negative signals from an unhealthy culture.

The feeling you receive within a negative atmosphere triggers entirely different hormones. The stress hormone **cortisol**, which you have read about previously in the book, is released when you feel uncomfortable and/or stressed. So, if you sense that the atmosphere in the store is a bit oppressive and that you feel low levels of engagement and energy, it means that you do not like the feeling you get within the store; cortisol will most likely be released. Cortisol makes you aware of potential risks, and you begin to think about possible negative consequences. **"The shirt is nice, but the colour doesn't really match my red shoes; I can't buy that. Maybe I shouldn't shop at all today."**

Adrenaline, like the hormone cortisol, is linked to the fight-or-flight response that is activated in response to a perceived threatening or stressful situation. At the same moment, the sympathetic nervous system activates and releases this stress hormone, which increases your blood pressure, heart rate, and blood sugar levels. As adrenaline surges through your body, **noradrenaline** (norepinephrine) is also activated as a conversion. Adrenaline is released quickly as part of the initial stress response, while noradrenaline is more involved in regulating your blood pressure and mood. Naturally, you do not feel much urge to shop in this atmosphere. *"I don't feel good here; I feel a bit unwell, almost dizzy; I think I should leave."*

<u>The external hospitality is a signal that indicates how people feel, how content they are, how much passion and engagement they have, how much responsibility they take, and how they treat each other.</u>

The choices you have made as a leader in sections B-E, and how you work with the short- and long-term tools I have given you, are the recipe for counteracting long-lasting doses of cortisol, adrenaline, and noradrenaline.

You can never prevent negative hormones from affecting your entity's culture and consequently your results. However, the tools you have received and your strategic work allow you to counteract these hormones early on, which affect the external hospitality.

This is extremely important because the external hospitality naturally reflects the internal hospitality. It is inevitable. That is why the culture/atmosphere is stronger than anything else as everything is interconnected. <u>Your focus as a leader who understands the tremendous power of cultural shifts and cultures, how they affect people and their needs, which in turn impacts the internal hospitality, creates a culture that is the atmosphere others immediately sense.</u>

The leader's vision of what genuine hospitality provides is loyalty.
<u>The leader's goal is loyal customers and loyal team members.</u>
Your team members are the ones who create results because you cannot do everything yourself. A genuinely conscious effort for good hospitality gives back so much; here are a few examples:

125% less burnout (HBR), 51% higher turnover (Gallup), 43% higher productivity (HayGroup), 33% higher profitability (Gallup), "Workgroups that experienced a high level of hospitality had better collaboration, communication, and conflict resolution, which led to better results." (The Impact of Hospitality on Team Dynamics), "Workplaces that promoted hospitality helped their employees achieve a better work-life balance, leading to increased well-being and reduced stress." (The Effects of Hospitality on Work-Life Balance).

How do you create and maintain loyal team members and customers?
If I temporarily take a business perspective, it is evident that a person running a business needs to work operationally. *What I have noticed while working as a consultant within organisations are two factors that hinder the company's growth and profitability. (1) Too little time is spent on strategic work and planning. (2) The aspect of personal development and learning is rarely mentioned.* There is so much focus on the operational that the strategic and developmental are put on "hold."

These are the same three components that are needed in leadership. Many <u>operate</u> at full speed and are exceptionally good at it, but spend too little time on <u>strategic</u> leadership and <u>developmental</u> leadership.

Reflect for two minutes: If an employee asks you for time to reflect on planning, strategies, and personal development and learning in their work, it is a very healthy sign. You have a team member in front of you who sees the whole picture, who works with the vision in focus rather than salary, and who wishes to develop themselves to become better and thus contribute even more to the organisation.
How large a portion of your time do you, as a leader, spend operationally, strategically, and developmentally?

Otherwise, when should the "hold button" be released?
When it is logical that *what creates time is* to consciously plan well, establish clear and time-bound strategies, and develop what makes a person better, more secure, and efficient.

Is there a clear plan for how and when you, for example: follow up on team members' well-being and development, review results and balance sheets and compare them against the budget, conduct competitor and market analyses, and analyze your own operations?

Are there clear and time-bound strategies for, for example: how many meetings I will have per year that focus on culture and how many on results? This is how I will clarify and systematically work with the vision, values, and mission over the coming year. This is how often I will have coaching conversations to develop my entity, etc.

And what about personal development and learning? For instance: how much time and when each month should be allocated to it? What can I become better at, what do I want to improve, and what can most benefit my entity and results if I become better or more efficient in? (Labor law, coaching, feedback, meeting structure, Office/iWork/Google tools. Can I become more knowledgeable in business intelligence, business personnel, business systems, or staffing systems?

"Be aware in your leadership.
It is not habits and routines that develop people.

The foundation for all development and success is
continuous challenges to people's habits and routines.
- Niclas Timmerby

Let me summarize what you have received so far as your tools in your leadership for your strategic leadership. (You will receive more later in the book.)

These strategic tools are what help you as a leader to shape and nurture the culture. They develop you and your team members in your respective roles and move the entity forward.

Long-term:
- The vision.
- The mission (Your clear map to the vision).
- Shared foundation of values.
- Emotional information.
- The "why."
- Challenge yourself and your team members to reveal potential when a person is "forced" out of their comfort zone.
- Passion and will.

Short- and long-term:
- The four levels of feedback for all generations and cultures.
- Tailored coaching.
- Inner, genuine motivation (Competence, belonging, independence, personal responsibility).
- Acceptance of roles.

What you emit as a person:
- Human messengers and influencers in the form of hormones and chemical substances.
- Values.
- Moral principles.

For yourself:
- Self-leadership.
- Insights that create change and development.
- Ongoing reflections on your leadership style and humanity (that you dare to show yourself as human, considerate, and vulnerable) create the right kind of hormones and chemical signals that care for and guide the culture in a healthy direction.

- You are aware of the hormones that can cause customers, team members, and yourself to risk feeling bad in the atmosphere.

<u>Your superpower:</u>
Fortunately, the secure signals you constantly send out as a leader can create more of the "good" hormones that counteract the onset of cortisol, adrenaline, and noradrenaline.

Your superpower, how you influence everyone around you, is your most important daily tool as a leader in your daily leadership. When you influence the atmosphere, <u>everyone</u> who is in and belongs to the culture is affected.

Your superpower influences people, people who create results and profitability. What signals do you bring into a room and spread around you? What signals do you leave behind in the room for others to experience when you leave? At home, in your workplace, etc.? Even when you are off duty, the signals you send into the atmosphere continue to exist and influence the entity.

The more insight you have into this, the more you will reflect on it, and the more you can influence people in a way that benefits them, you, and the organization.

You remember my quote on page 128: "If you approach every situation in life with humility, whether in private life, professional life, or any other situation, you will automatically achieve the highest level of self-awareness." Use humility as a concrete, conscious tool to influence the culture.

Here are examples of a neurotransmitter that affects you, along with four hormones that contribute to counteracting cortisol, adrenaline, and noradrenaline:

- **Oxytocin** *helps reduce feelings of stress and anxiety as the hormone increases feelings of relaxation and well-being.* <u>How can you enhance the feeling of a pleasant working environment, reduce stress impact, and recognize your team members' good efforts and contributions in a humane and genuine way?</u>

- **Dopamine** *helps to reduce the feeling of stress as the hormone increases feelings of reward and motivation.* <u>How can you create motivation and goals that, by being clear, allow for praise through feedback at level 1 and 3?</u>

- **Serotonin** *counters stress responses and anxiety as the hormone (which is also involved in regulating mood, sleep, and appetite) increases feelings of well-being and calm.* <u>How can you create security, especially in stressful situations, through your way of being; the signals you send chemically, in your tone of voice, and in your body language? Is there an opportunity to invite people to talk about the importance of sleep and diet? Do you listen to people when they talk, or are you focused on others/other things at the same time? Do you turn off your phone when you have meetings or are in conversations with a person, or does it beep/tone and you pick up your phone? (Even having the phone visibly present at a meeting, "Phubbing," can consciously and unconsciously trigger a stress response that activates adrenaline, noradrenaline, and cortisol.)</u>
- **Endorphins** *counteract feelings of stress when endorphins increase feelings of well-being. The hormone is released in your body during*

physical activity, joy, and pleasure. <u>Do you experience that everyone can have fun and feel joy during working hours? How do you check in and encourage physical activity? Does everyone feel that they are and can be part of the team and that they are accepted as they are? Is there open communication? Does everyone feel they can talk to you if they have a need? Is feedback given at level 1 and 3? Are there attainable, relevant, and applicable personal goal images that you coach team members towards? Is there an opportunity to create a better balance between work and private life through hybrid work and flexible working hours? Do all feel that they are developing?</u>

- *Gamma-aminobutyric acid (GABA) is a neurotransmitter, a chemical substance that transmits signals between nerve cells in your brain, which reduces overactivity in your sympathetic nervous system and promotes feelings of relaxation and calm. This is crucial for you as a human and in your leadership. GABA is essential for all people (research is ongoing to try to understand to what extent GABA influences hormones and vice versa) since it is involved in hormone regulation. GABA influences, among other things, emotional processing and reactions to stress and fear in the amygdala, as well as learning and memory in the hippocampus. Motor control and movement in, usually five in number, the basal ganglia, which are clusters of nerve cells near the center of the brain. As a small note to understand the complexity of our bodies and functions, the human brain has about 100 billion nerve cells (neurons), and estimates show that your brain has up to 10 times more glial cells, which can be likened to cells that nourish, protect, and repair your neurons. The human body is estimated to have about 30-40 trillion cells.*

In all goodwill, I want to emphasize once again the power of your superpower. How it affects you and how your thoughts influence your feelings, which in turn affect your behavior, your attitude (what you project to others), and your actions. And how this impacts the people around you. The internal hospitality -> The atmosphere/culture -> The external hospitality. <u>You, as a leader, are the foundation that creates the well-being, performance, and results of your entity.</u>

Your leadership is <u>the most decisive factor</u> in creating and maintaining a culture of loyal employees.

The difference between a satisfied customer and a loyal customer.
In the quote at the beginning of this chapter, I stated that satisfied customers can make a business survive while loyal customers make it profitable. *Let me tell you a fictional story:*

You are really craving milk (or perhaps oat drink). So, you go to the store. You walk into the store, find <u>exactly</u> the product you were looking for, and there is no queue at the checkout. The clerk serves you <u>exactly</u> as you expected, and you head home. Once home, you take out a large glass and pour what you bought into the glass. The consistency and color match <u>exactly</u> what you expected. You take a big gulp, and it tastes <u>exactly</u> as you expect it to taste.

What are you then?   Answer: Satisfied.

But that does not mean you stand outside shouting so that all the neighbors in the nearby streets can hear: "YEEEEES, I GOT MILK!!!". It does not mean that the first thing you do when you arrive at work the next day is to say: "You can't guess what happened to me yesterday... I bought milk."

A satisfied customer does not tell anyone else about it. No one. *Unless they are directly asked, "- Did you buy milk last night? - Yes. - Are you satisfied? - Yes."*

<u>Getting what we expect is a normal state.</u>
We humans do **not** talk to others about being satisfied with a purchase unless we receive a direct question about the purchase, and the reason is that we received <u>exactly</u> what we expected. Nothing more, nothing less.

    If we are treated poorly or if the product/service does not meet our expectations, **we are likely to share** that information, even if we are not asked. This is due to a combination of various psychological and social mechanisms.

*We want to feel **social support** from others regarding our experiences, a form of affirmation that our reaction is reasonable. Complaining or sharing a negative experience can, through **an emotional outlet of feelings**, relieve a person's own internal negative tensions.*

All groups of people have their own form of culture or atmosphere. In psychology, this is referred to as **social identity**. A strong social identity makes a person feel a sense of belonging within the group; this belonging can create well-being and also contribute to a good self-esteem. Thus, sharing negative experiences becomes a social identity that creates feelings of community and belonging, and negative experiences become a topic of conversation that everyone can gather around to vent.

It creates a form of social cohesion and is something natural. If a team member in this social identity stops talking about negative experiences, the dynamics of the group would change in that very moment.

(Compare social identity with, for example, supporter cultures in sports and when people compare Apple and Samsung, how strong this identity is and the strong feelings of belonging this can create. Other social identities include nationalities, ethnicities, religions, gender identities, professions, etc.)

Many emotions can arise and spread further when a person does not get what they expect, which can impact *the reputation*.

<u>*Now, if I change a few things in the fictional story…:*</u>

You are really craving milk (or perhaps oat drink). So, you go to the store. When you enter the store, you are greeted by smiling staff holding out a small plate with pieces of freshly baked cinnamon buns; they cheerfully say "hello" and joke light-heartedly, "How nice that you came just when we baked cinnamon buns." As you walk through the store towards the dairy section, several staff members nod at you with a smile, and you feel a good feeling within you, relaxing because you enjoy the environment. You find <u>exactly</u> the product you were looking for; there is a bit of a queue at the checkout, and you hear the clerk cheerfully say to the customer in front of you, "Have a lovely day; you can save the receipt as a keepsake." The clerk asks you while the oat drink goes down the conveyor belt, "Is it sunny outside now? I can't see from here." "Yes, it's sunny outside now," you reply with an automatic smile because she is genuinely smiling at you. When you pay, she happily says, "Please enjoy the sun a little extra today for my sake, and have a nice day!" As you take your oat drink, you hear her say to the next customer, *"Are you here today? How lucky, then my day is complete now."* On your way out, the staff who gave you a taste on the way in smile and wish you a nice day.

<u>What was the difference?</u>

The difference was that the people in the store genuinely put themselves out there, which allowed them to share signals that influenced you. The likelihood that they all genuinely present themselves is almost zero unless the workplace has a healthy culture, which enables them to create an atmosphere in which people thrive together. They gifted you the following hormones:

- You received **oxytocin** multiple times as you sensed a pleasant environment and received genuine smiles.
- You received **dopamine** when you got a "reward" in the form of a small piece of a cinnamon bun, and when the clerk at the counter provided you with a personal, specific, and achievable goal: to enjoy the sun a little extra.
- You received **serotonin** because the clerk focused on you at the checkout and made you feel seen and acknowledged.
- You received **endorphins**, both from genuine smiles that created a sense of well-being and comfort, and from the staff and the clerk being personable and joking, which generated joy and a form of pleasure. (That you received more endorphins from walking inside the store, thus engaging in physical activity, is a small bonus.)
- Moreover, since you felt relaxed because you enjoyed the environment, it likely had a positive impact on your brain's production of **GABAA**, which can help reduce overactivity in the brain and even

improve sleep. (GABA is the neurotransmitter, while GABAA is a receptor that interacts with GABA and helps to regulate its effects.)

- *Culture creates the atmosphere.*
- *People in an unhealthy culture do not genuinely put themselves out there unless they are very, very strong internally.*
- *If the staff does not genuinely put themselves out there, they miss the opportunity to influence the customer and receive positive signals in return.*

When I shop and receive a poorer service than I expected, I think that it is not the person in front of me who is to blame; it is the culture and the leadership.

If a person is positively affected internally during a purchase, hormones and chemical signals are released into that person's bloodstream.

"It is not what we see or hear that leaves the greatest impression on our lives. It is what we feel inside."
- Niclas Timmerby

The fact that a person feels good can also stimulate increased production of other positive hormone-like substances such as prostaglandins and cytokines, which regulate inflammation, immune functions, blood pressure, digestion, pain, mood, and much more.

<u>Consider this thought, regardless of the type of entity you operate within, what fantastic outcomes a positive culture creates for people's well-being:</u> That a thriving, positive, developing, and healthy culture creates what others experience in the atmosphere and the external hospitality feels, is ***the greatest hidden potential within sales***.

What is a loyal and profitable customer?

The average loyal customer is repeat business, spends a higher average than the average customer, is less price-sensitive, and has a long-term positive attitude towards one or several of the following factors: your brand / your entity / your team members.

The global consulting firm Bain & Company has produced the following interesting figures regarding loyal customers in its studies:
- Loyal customers account for more than 60 percent of total sales.
- Loyal customers spend up to 67 percent more each time they shop.
- After ten purchases, a loyal customer has recommended you to seven potential customers.

Here are figures from 2023 regarding customer loyalty:

- 72% of global customers feel loyalty towards at least one brand or company. (Zendesk)
- 88% state that it takes three or more purchases to build brand loyalty. 37% say they need to make five or more purchases before committing to a brand, while only 12% say they are ready to commit after two. (Yotpo)
- 56% of global consumers say that customer service is "very important" when choosing a brand and loyalty. (Microsoft)
- 61% of global consumers have broken ties with a brand due to poor customer service. 48% ended relationships with a brand in the past year due to issues with customer service. (Microsoft)
- 36% of American consumers switched brands during the COVID-19 pandemic. (McKinsey)
- Brands that invest in customer loyalty aim for several positive outcomes. Attracting new customers is the most common goal, with

65% of brand managers mentioning it as a top goal. Other desired outcomes include building strong emotional connections to the brand (57%) and gaining insights into customer preferences (50%). (Harvard Business Review). 42% of brand managers reported that their customer loyalty strategies are effective.

What I directly associate with the potential of focusing on the external hospitality is the potential to create loyal customers if 88 percent say that it requires three or more purchases. Contact with some type of customer service is yet another potential because:

"Service," for me, is some type of active action towards the customer.

"Hospitality" for me is about creating a state of mind in which people feel comfortable.

If the hospitality is reflected in the customer's interaction with customer service, the likelihood that the customer experiences the conversation positively is higher.

On the last point above, brand managers in this study still strive more to attract new customers than to retain loyal customers, which I find somewhat remarkable. In the same study, 57 percent of brand managers stated that they want to build strong emotional connections to the brand, which I find very wise. Also in the same study; only 42 percent of the same brand managers believe their strategies are effective.

I summarize: The potential of a thriving external hospitality is still very, very significant within sales.

An example of how hospitality can create significant results.
On March 13, 1974, a shopping centre opened in southwestern Sweden that repeatedly ranks highly in surveys regarding which shopping centre is the best in Sweden.

Despite the fact that it still largely has a low ceiling, typical of shopping centers built in the past before elaborate glass facades and advanced construction techniques were employed to create a fashionable exterior, the shopping center has won the NCSC Sweden Awards for "Best Shopping Center" in 2000, 2012, 2018, and 2022. Furthermore, the shopping center was named "The Best Shopping Center in the Nordics" in 2013.

I am writing about Väla Centrum in Ödåkra, just outside Helsingborg. What makes Väla Centrum so special? How can an over 50-year-old shopping center win these awards in competition with newly built shopping centers? My answer, as someone who has visited many shopping centers in Sweden with my "hospitality eyes," is that the external hospitality at Väla Centrum truly resonates within and stimulates the release of many positive hormones as soon as people walk through the doors and experience the atmosphere.

Reaching both hemispheres of the brain to create even more loyal customers.
Of course, both hemispheres of the brain constantly collaborate. However, it might be very wise for an organization and its affiliated entities to pause at least once a year to reflect: *What do our customers experience and feel? Do we reach both hemispheres of the customer's brain? Do we understand the whole perspective of the customer? What can we do better strategically and mechanically? Do we dare to offer ourselves? Should we have more feedback and coaching sessions?"*

You are surely aware that the left hemisphere of the brain is more involved in logical thinking, critical thinking, and human analytical ability, while the right hemisphere is more involved in emotions, intuition, creativity, and human emotional ability. While the brain hemispheres cooperate, there is one half that is dominant depending on what the customer thinks in the moment and what thoughts and feelings they bring into the situation when visiting your business.

So, to create the maximum number of loyal customers, it is crucial to have strategies for reaching the dominant hemisphere of the visiting customers' brains. Here are some fictional examples:

If the left hemisphere dominates:
- The customer likely already knows exactly what product/service they are interested in.
- They are looking for super clear signs outside the store or equivalent online.
- They want order, tidiness and cleanliness; it should be neat and tidy, and clearly indicate where they should go.
- They want very clear price tags.
- Perhaps they have made a checklist at home of what factors they should review before possibly making a purchase.
- They likely ask critical questions which they expect detailed answers to.
- This customer likely makes one decision at a time during the purchasing process and wants to decide for themselves when to take the next step.

If the right hemisphere dominates:

- The customer is likely to make one or more spontaneous purchases if they feel the right emotions inside.
- They are more easily influenced by the seller or if they have someone with them in the store.
- The customer often looks at the seller's facial expressions to gain human contact and possibly affirmation that they are making the right choice.
- If the customer establishes an emotional connection with the product or service, they may be more inclined to make a purchase.
- More beautiful aesthetics and design may lead the customer to voluntarily want to buy a more expensive item than what you suggest.

You can always "turn the customer's dominant hemisphere" by creating an emotional reaction, which alters the customer's thoughts, thus creating a new unique feeling within them. This is because all customers are suggestible, as everyone makes decisions emotionally. (So use your superpowers wisely.)

What you can always influence are the chain reactions in the customer's brain through your emotional approach to customer interactions, which activates neurons in the customer's brain. Whatever you do or do not do, the customer is influenced by the external hospitality. If you are in a healthy culture and genuinely put yourself out in the customer meeting, the likelihood is extremely high (I would like to write 100%) that you and the atmosphere will emotionally impact the customer.

I see the "secret" to increased sales as: consciously, continuously, and focused effort to develop responses and strategies to the question:

"How can we increase the emotional value for our customers?" With the understanding of how incredibly different the two brain hemispheres "serve" and guide human beings, my recommendation is that you develop strategies in your work that address both hemispheres.

Your leadership is <u>the most decisive factor</u> in creating and maintaining a culture that generates and sustains loyal customers.

I conclude this chapter with some studies on the importance of good external leadership and what it creates:

2010 (The impact of service employees' positive mood and facial expression on customer satisfaction.) This study examined how employees' positive mood and facial expressions affect customers. The results showed that when staff expressed positive hospitality, customer satisfaction and the intention to return increased.

2007 (The role of customer gratitude in relationship marketing. European Journal of Marketing.) The study investigated how customer gratitude affects relationships with the company. The results revealed that the customer's experience of being treated with hospitality and gratitude led to increased loyalty and positive relationships.

2005 (Exploring the conditions under which gratitude leads to customer loyalty.) This examined how gratitude from customers affects their loyalty to the company. The results demonstrated that when customers felt they were treated with hospitality and gratitude, their loyalty and intention to return increased.

Reflection, Chapter 4

1. If you objectively, neutrally, fairly, and independently consider your team members' or customers' complete perspective and reflect on your external hospitality and how it is directly rooted in your culture and internal hospitality: What does your entity attract? What do they feel inside? What do they experience during a regular working day? Does it provide energy and engagement? Is it a pleasant and developing working environment? What kind of atmosphere does your customer enter and automatically receive? Is it well-being, laughter, joy, and good purchasing signals, or does the customer feel uncertain and critical? Do all your customers feel seen and acknowledged? Is the customer's feelings in focus? What do customers experience with you that creates their feelings? What do they take with them (because that feeling shapes your reputation)?

2. Reflect on how your time is allocated. What percentage of your time is dedicated to operational, strategic, and developmental leadership? If you have a role or position where your main focus is operational work, you can discuss opportunities for personal development in employee conversations with your manager and whether time can be reallocated to strategic and developmental leadership. If this is not possible, you can take personal responsibility for your own development by getting up twenty minutes earlier three days a week for 48 weeks a year to study strategic and developmental leadership. This equals six full working days of eight hours each per year, during which you invest in your own development, plus your new knowledge and insights will create more time in your operational leadership. *Thirty minutes a day equals nine full study days. What is your own development worth?*

CHAPTER 5

$$IH \dashrightarrow C \dashrightarrow EH : (E = potential^\wedge\infty) \dashrightarrow R = T$$

---

*Only when you are engaged do you leave a lasting impact
on people, results, and your legacy.*
Niclas Timmerby

We have arrived at the infinity of your potential.

We have reached the point in the formula where you can achieve the highest return. Here, you can sense how great your actual potential is.

You are fully aware of what creates the internal hospitality and how you, as a leader, bring out the best in it.

You are fully aware of the incredible power of your culture, the atmosphere you inhabit daily, "inhale," and are shaped by.

You are fully aware of how you can support, protect, and nurture the external hospitality both in the short and long term to maintain a healthy, safe, positive, and developing culture where people thrive, and loyal team members and loyal customers flourish.

You are now given this part of the formula: : (E = potential$^\infty$)

As you see on the previous page, this part is an extension of the external hospitality, which is a collective and always dynamic result of culture and internal hospitality.

All parts of the entire formula fluctuate continuously. The outcome after this part = "$\dashrightarrow$ R = L," is a result of the earlier components. *This means that you, as a leader, can always influence the outcome of the formula.*

First, you have a colon ":".
A colon in this context indicates that something is "weighted towards" or "influenced by" another factor and/or that the variable is dependent on or related to the other factor. The second factor in this context is that

everything that precedes leads to the current outcome of the external hospitality.

When I add the entire part of the formula: : **(E = potential^∞)**, the meaning is as follows:
- What is within the parentheses is weighted against the external hospitality.
- The potential of the letter E = raised to infinity.

The letter "E" in the formula stands for engagement.
The factor that brings team members, the entity, and results closer to the potential is the amount of engagement that is created, exists, and thrives within the entity.

A company cannot buy loyal customers. Loyal customers must be earned through genuine care. The same holds true for your entity. You can hire very capable team members, but that says absolutely nothing about whether they will be loyal to you or want to stay. *Loyal team members must be earned through genuine care.*

You have received many tools in the book for both short and long-term efforts that show you genuinely care about them, their well-being, and their development. This is genuine care.
You have a good view of humanity, which is genuine care. You put yourself out there as a leader, which is genuine care. Providing feedback and tailored coaching because you care about them is genuinely caring. Focusing on them, ensuring they feel seen and acknowledged, praising their contributions and who they are as individuals is genuine care. Listening to them and making them feel that they are your focus (e.g., by turning off your phone) is genuine care.

When they feel that you genuinely protect, nurture, and support a healthy and thriving culture, that they see you actively contributing to a pleasant working environment and an atmosphere that is enjoyable and pleasant to be in is truly genuine care.

If you reflect on the tools you have received, you will notice that none actually costs more than time. What you genuinely give of yourself will come back to you *(what you sow, you can reap).*

When you continuously and genuinely care about your entity's well-being and development, your team members perceive this as you showing _engagement_ towards them -> which creates _engagement_ and loyalty within them -> which fosters _engagement_ in the atmosphere that other colleagues and customers inhabit.

I wrote in the chapter's quote: *"Only when you are engaged do you leave a lasting impression on people, results, and your legacy."*

Why is it that you remember certain people who have impacted your life? Perhaps a teacher in school, maybe a boss from long ago, perhaps a partner, perhaps a relative, or maybe a colleague? Some people exhibit more engagement than others, which is perfectly normal since all people are different.

You likely have several memories of people who have impacted you deeply _negatively_ in your personal and professional life. They were deeply engaged in their cause and belief. (When you think of these individuals, you probably adopt negative body language, perhaps you feel down because negative hormones are released in your body, affecting you and those closest to you?)

You surely have several memories of people who have <u>positively</u> impacted and shaped you in your personal and professional life. They were also deeply engaged in their cause and belief. (When you think of these individuals, you probably smile, feel joy, experience a pleasant sensation in your stomach, and have positive body language because positive hormones are released in your body, influencing you and those around you?)

The common factor is the level of engagement they had in their cause and belief. *Genuine engagement is very powerful and has a significant impact on people. cultures, and results.*

<u>The more genuine engagement you can create within your entity, the more the atmosphere will be influenced by this x-factor.</u> *Numerous studies within psychology highlight the fact that when a person experiences feelings of engagement, there is a direct correlation to good relationships and positive results.*

The insight that leaders possess cannot be underestimated regarding the mental and emotional processes that influence a team member's participation and willingness to invest themselves in a particular activity, task, in people (such as customers), or in their entity.

When a person feels engaged in any of the above, they are motivated, focused, and willing to participate in achieving the entity's goals and the organization's vision.

The key to revealing parts of the entire entity's potential is the level of engagement. It is <u>the collective engagement</u> of team members that breaks barriers and achieves sales targets.

Hormones also play a significant role here.

When people in an entity share feelings of engagement and are involved in an activity, the following hormones are released:

- *Dopamine*, which gives team members feelings of *joy, pride, motivation, satisfaction, and belonging*.
- *Oxytocin*, which strengthens social bonds and creates feelings of *trust, connection, and affection* towards the entity.
- *Serotonin*, which is released when people feel included and recognized in an entity, leading to feelings of *well-being*.
- *Adrenaline*, in moderate doses, is released when people are engaged in a group and are collectively confronted with a common challenge or opportunity. This creates increased *focus and energy*.

There are also several studies that have examined the link between engagement and results within entities:

2010, Bakker and Leiter: "Engagement was positively correlated with job performance, customer satisfaction, and decreased employee turnover."

2012, Towers Watson: "Engaged employees were more productive, received higher positive feedback from customers, remained longer in the organization, and were less likely to seek other jobs."

2002, Harter, Schmidt, and Hayes: A meta-analysis showed that "Engagement was positively correlated with performance, customer feedback, profitability, and employee turnover."

2016, Gallup: "Engaged employees had 41% lower absenteeism and 17% higher productivity compared to disengaged employees."

2010, Rich, Lepine, and Crawford: "Engagement was linked to increased creativity and innovation in the workplace."

2015, Albrecht, Bakker, Gruman, and Macey: "Engagement was positively correlated with job satisfaction and well-being at work."

2006, Hakanen, Bakker, and Schaufeli: "Engagement was negatively correlated with burnout and stress, indicating that engaged employees had lower levels of these negative work-related conditions."

2006, Meyer, Becker, and Van Dick: "Engagement was positively correlated with organizational citizenship, meaning that engaged employees are more likely to contribute to the organization's success and prosperity."

Studies and research reports based on rigorous methods and analyses are important for making well-informed decisions based on facts and science.

However, it is essential to understand that the atmosphere cannot be "covered up" over time. The engagement that flourishes (in whatever form) directly affects the culture.

"The true atmosphere of a workplace cannot be concealed or beautified, as it is reflected in the organization's culture."
- Niclas Timmerby

Gallup conducted a study focusing on the 75th percentile of engagement:

The top 25 percent in the study, which measured the highest engagement, showed the following differences compared to others: 65 percent lower employee turnover, 37 percent less absenteeism, 21 percent higher productivity, and 22 percent higher profitability.

An uplifting engagement can be:

- *That team members feel inspired by you as a leader, motivated by goals, and enthusiastic about their tasks, roles, and responsibilities.*
- *That they have clear goals and expectations.*
- *Situational leadership.*
- *Feedback and coaching to challenge and develop them.*
- *That they experience intrinsic motivation; that is:*
  - *A sense that they have sufficient competence, making them self-sufficient.*
  - *A feeling of not being micromanaged, allowing them to grow and take initiative.*
  - *A sense of belonging, making them feel secure.*
  - *The experience of receiving personal responsibility, creating a sense of participation and belonging.*

A disheartening engagement can be:

- *That team members do not feel challenged enough, leading to a sense that they can take on more responsibility and contribute more to the entity, organization, and workplace than they are given the opportunity to, and that they could develop their skills if challenged.*
- *That they feel a lack of intrinsic motivation due to:*
  - *Insufficiently clear goals: When the perception is that the goals are not achievable, clear, concrete, measurable, applicable, developmental, and meaningful.*
  - *A lack of freedom under responsibility with the authority to influence and make decisions.*
  - *A lack of feedback in the form of affirmation, recognition, and challenging coaching necessary to reach personal and collective goals.*

- *That the perception is that the organization has a vision, you as a leader have a mission, and the entity has a set of values, yet this is not reflected in the daily work or atmosphere.*

As a leader, you can clearly see the signs of discouraging engagement:
- *Signs of low engagement when you delegate tasks.*
- *Signs of frustration and irritation.*
- *Signs of a lack of motivation and enthusiasm.*
- *Signs of a negative attitude.*
- *Signs of a tendency to seek faults instead of recognizing what is good.*
- *Signs of low energy, fatigue, and laziness.*
- *Signs that joy has less space in daily life.*
- *Signs that personal rules and routines are being created.*
- *Signs that productivity, efficiency, and quality are declining.*
- *Signs that team members willingly contribute less when you ask for help (indicating active passivity).*
- *Signs of reduced creativity when you ask for suggestions to solve daily problems and challenges.*
- *Signs of diminished interest in goals and outcomes.*
- *Signs of increased absenteeism and sick leave.*
- *Signs of tension and conflict within your entity.*

You see it directly.

At this moment, you can envision those who spread uplifting engagement within your entity and the atmosphere that influences the culture. These team members do this because they experience feelings of engagement.

And you see it directly.

You can visualize who in your entity spreads discouraging engagement within your entity and the atmosphere that impacts the culture. These team members do this because they do not experience sufficient feelings of engagement.

One of your most important tasks as a leader.

You understand the positive synergistic effects that a healthy culture creates. One of your most important tasks is to observe the type of engagement that influences the culture. Then comes the most important part: you need to dare to **act**. No impactful change can occur without active intervention, and all forms of change involve some form of development.

"Right focus, wrong focus, or poor focus is never a coincidence; it is a choice."
- Niclas Timmerby

When you use your entity's accepted tools, you can act in a natural and genuine manner.

You can praise and acknowledge, and you can adjust and correct.

You understand the significance of the right form of engagement. What you want from your conversations with your team members is to:

- Make visible, focus on, and acknowledge a truth that benefits the team member, the entity, the culture, and the organization.

- Or to make visible, focus on, and make the team member aware that there is another type of truth that could better serve their development and career, the entity, the culture, and the organization.

You have the tools.

As you know, all of this is influenceable. You can affect and create more feelings of uplifting engagement, and you can manage and influence feelings of discouraging engagement.

Three factors for understanding and influencing engagement that need to be in your awareness every day.

- *The iceberg.*
    - *All of us humans have a "why" that affects us. Even robots, computers, and all types of mobile devices have a "why" (their coding). Genuinely wanting to "see and understand" the iceberg in front of you highlights humility and understanding of people's differences, that everyone's individual coding/conditioning creates behaviours and attitudes.*

- *The four levels of feedback for all generations and cultures.*
    - *Your concrete tool for helping people develop and grow through small and large adjustments and corrections in daily life.*

- *Tailored coaching.*
    - *Your concrete tool for structured coaching conversations with A, B, C: asking questions and challenging. What is beneath the surface, what is the person's "why".*

Prioritise feedback and coaching to nurture and shape your entity's engagement, the potential for your entity's well-being, what your culture sends out, and the results you create together.

Two additional motivational factors that create uplifting engagement: Empathic leadership and participation.

These two factors have an equally strong connection as water and land. What empathic leadership does is influence the atmosphere on a human level. The effects of emotionally impacting people cannot be underestimated as it directly and immediately affects the form of engagement and the amount of engagement that spreads in the atmosphere.

1. Empathic leadership = You genuinely want to find out "why."

This form of leadership is about being curious, being aware of, and considering the team member's feelings, needs, and perspectives.

The more you know about a person, the more they dare to tell you (the iceberg), the more you will learn about the person and their feelings, needs, values, and perspectives.

2. You create a positive spiral of participation.

With small changes, you can create a positive spiral of improvements in many areas within the entity that also affects the entire organisation.

You create an accumulated effect in the form of feelings of participation that create engagement and intrinsic motivation that positively influence the atmosphere.

It is important that you have perseverance since it can take time before you see visible results in numbers; consider that you are reshaping the culture, which does not happen overnight. The reward, however, is more loyal team members and loyal customers who thrive in the atmosphere.

By continuously demonstrating genuine empathy and authentic engagement in the culture, you create a safe, human, inviting, and motivating atmosphere where it feels natural for team members to contribute the same factors: empathy and engagement. This is fantastic because <u>this is where the accumulated effect arises</u>.

When they themselves experience empathy and participation, it causes them to spread feelings of this around to everyone they meet. And then they create atmospheres around them of safety and humanity in their other entities. When they are secure and dare to be human/themselves, they permeate their other cultures, which creates further empathy, participation, inclusion, and motivation. Their self-concept, how they see themselves, also changes in a way that benefits them.

Courage.

To genuinely practice empathic leadership largely involves courage, that you create trust with trust.

Compare when you read a company's vision; does the vision express itself in the culture? Are there conditions on a human level to contribute to the vision, or are the vision just fine words?

Do you dare to take up the baton as a leader and show the way to empathy? Your entity will follow you, which benefits everyone.

Everyone is different, so some will take longer, and even if it does not show at all on people, the power of the culture will definitely create feelings inside. Over time, you will see positive effects on performance and results.

That you have the courage to shape the culture with empathic leadership also helps a lot in your feedback and coaching conversations.

If empathy and feelings of participation already thrive in the culture, it is more natural for team members to receive feedback and open up in coaching conversations when you as a leader pose challenging questions.

How do team members experience engagement created by empathy and participation from their perspective? Here are some examples:

- *I feel free to express my opinions and ideas without fear of being judged or ignored.*
- *I feel that my manager listens to my views and takes them seriously when making decisions.*
- *I have the opportunity to participate in decision-making and projects, which gives me a sense that my contribution is valuable.*
- *I am proud to be part of the entity and feel engaged in contributing to its success.*
- *I receive the gift of feedback that acknowledges my achievements and who I am and simultaneously motivates me to continue developing in my role.*
- *I am encouraged to take my own initiatives and to dare to fail; I feel a mandate built on trust.*
- *Collaboration, open communication, and having fun are part of our culture, which makes me feel involved and part of something larger.*
- *I feel seen and valued as an individual and as an important part of the entity.*

- *I am given opportunities for training to help me grow and become better in my role.*
- *I receive the gift of coaching to support my personal and professional development, which helps me identify my strengths and areas for improvement and gives me tools and resources to grow and reach my full potential.*
- *I feel involved in my own development and career, and I receive support and guidance.*
- *I feel safe sharing my thoughts and ideas without being judged or dismissed.*
- *I appreciate that the work environment is inclusive and respectful, where everyone feels welcome and accepted.*
- *My surroundings show empathy and understanding for my needs and challenges, which creates a sense of trust and safety.*
- *I have a positive and inspiring work environment that makes me feel motivated and enthusiastic to contribute.*
- *I feel personally included and involved in the organisation's various goals and vision, which gives me a sense of ownership, responsibility, participation, and engagement.*
- *I feel like a valuable individual, and that my thoughts and ideas are taken seriously and considered.*
- *I thrive in the atmosphere.*

You have in the book received concrete tools to include empathic leadership in your leadership. If you feel that this form of leadership feels foreign and that it would seem strange or false to "change style," here are some tips:

- Start with small, small steps.
- Draw support from the vision, your mission, and core values.
- Be honest; say that you have come to certain insights.
- Use the value-driven tools and workshops at staff meetings to practically demonstrate that you want to take the entity on a journey in a new direction.
- Consider what you can improve to be more present and attentive. Listening more actively to opinions, ideas, and concerns. With genuine interest and engagement, you shape the atmosphere so that the entity feels seen and heard.
- Create new forums for participation. For example, tell them that *"For the coming year, we will have a standing item on the agenda at staff meetings where we will brainstorm and discuss how we can create more participation. There are no bad ideas, and I will take everything to heart. I ask you to actively participate and contribute ideas and your perspectives."* This creates space in decision-making and problem-solving, fostering feelings of participation and engagement. *(Document what you come up with so you can follow up.)*
- Further develop your way of giving feedback and coaching in everyday situations by creating opportunities to give feedback and coaching. Support and encourage taking own initiatives and making decisions. Then provide feedback and coach on what you have encouraged through feedback at levels 1 and 3, as well as small challenges within coaching. This fosters a culture of participation and accountability.
- Reflect on what you can do in your communication style to create an even more pleasant atmosphere where team members feel included, significant, and valuable. This shows that you actively stand up for equality and against all discrimination and bullying. You shape a culture that contains respect and openness.

- Ask what your team members _want_ (you remember the word from coaching). By showing that you care about them as individuals and in their professional roles, you create many positive hormones in the atmosphere and team members experience feelings of participation and engagement.
- Show courage when negative cultural carriers with attitudes and behaviour suggest that _"it was better before"_ and purposely drag the train (the culture) backwards. Initiate encouraging conversations. If this does not help, provide developmental feedback at level 2; if that does not help, dare to give developmental feedback at level 4.

Everyone wants to feel the sensation of participation.
All the tools you have received in the book provide concrete opportunities to create a sense of participation or reinforce the feeling of participation among your team members, which is reflected in the culture.

You have likely experienced the feeling many times in your professional career when you are invited to have an impact. When a manager first asked you: _"Can you contribute your opinions or experiences?"_ How significant did that feel inside? I remember it almost as if I could feel all those wonderful hormones bubbling inside.

That you, as a leader, are almost "looking" for opportunities for your entity to contribute is purely positive. It causes you to reflect more, creating development and participation for you as well. And there is more. When you ask questions and create space around this, it energises your team members and makes them feel engaged because they have opportunities to influence the daily work.

Also, use concrete goal images; getting team members to feel involved through personal and shared goals or personal responsibility quickly creates motivation to want to contribute more. At staff meetings, take the opportunity to highlight common routines and checklists and ask your entity to contribute: *"Could you please suggest strategies and solutions to make the daily work and routines better?"*

By bringing out facts and then allowing your entity to brainstorm responses, maximum participation is created immediately.

How can they impact the atmosphere?
Ask them.

How can they impact the results?
Ask them.

How can they impact the daily work?
Ask them.

Additional bonus.
With your consistent, strategic, and genuine work to create participation through empathy, you also have greater opportunities to change habits in your workplace.

   When new daily routines become a routine, they have transformed into a habit. *This is significant because* <u>**habits are stronger than any external motivation**</u>. *When you combine your efforts to create intrinsic motivation with participation, you achieve a double effect on the engagement level.*

The gain for you.

And what about you, who, with genuine empathic leadership and all the other tools, helps the culture to thrive, allows everyone to grow and feel that they are developing, feeling significant, seen and heard, highly valued, and well?

The great gain for you is that you come closer to your own values, to what truly represents you. That in the near future, you can change your self-concept, your identity, and the image you have of yourself.

Many people play roles in their leadership to fit in and to be adequate, and when a person does this for a long time in their private or professional life, it will lead to unhappiness, because they cannot be themselves.

> *"An organisation changes in symbiosis*
> *with the pace at which leadership changes."*
> *- Niclas Timmerby*

To get the most out of the principles I describe in the book is not possible unless you do it with genuine engagement.

Self-awareness is the tool that everyone has within them that most concretely drives their own development. It is what makes a person stop a bad habit or start a good one.

Dare to show *vulnerability*; show that it is allowed to fail because that is when people and organisations learn and develop. Dare to lead your entity selflessly based on your values, considering your entity's values and letting your moral principles guide your choices and decisions.

Published studies have examined the relationship between:

(1) Participation and engagement.

(2) Empathic leadership and engagement.

(1) *A study in <u>the Journal of Applied Psychology</u> showed that "The higher the degree of participation an employee had in decision-making and tasks, the higher their engagement at work." A study in <u>the Journal of Occupational and Organizational Psychology</u> showed that "Employees who felt more involved and engaged in tasks and decisions were more engaged in their work and less likely to change jobs." A study published in <u>the Journal of Business and Psychology</u> found that "Participation and engagement were positively correlated, and that participation had a direct impact on employees' engagement."*

(2) *Dutton and Heaphy, 2003. The researchers found that "Leaders who demonstrated empathy and care for their employees had employees who felt more involved and engaged in their work." 2008, Eisenbeiss, Knippenberg, and Boerner. The study showed that "Empathic leadership had a positive effect on employees' perceived participation. Employees who experienced their leaders as empathetic felt more involved and engaged in their tasks." 2013, Grant. The study showed that "Empathic leaders who allowed and encouraged employees to express their opinions and voices contributed to increased engagement and performance."*

> *"A leader who is secure in their values allows their personality to shine, regardless of the situation, has the courage to stand up for people, and transforms cultures when everyone else says it is impossible."*
> *- Niclas Timmerby*

Reflection, Chapter 5

1. How do you, as a leader, daily influence the culture through your engagement? It spreads further in the atmosphere, so in what form do you demonstrate engagement and how do you spread it?

2. Reflect on how you can actively influence the entity's engagement through feedback and coaching?

3. Prepare for the next situation or event where you see or feel that a team member actively influences engagement positively or negatively. How can you plan your level of appreciative or developmental feedback at that moment? How can you already prepare what questions to ask when you coach in order to challenge the behaviour/attitude to learn more about the team member's "iceberg"?

4. Reflect on the gift and privilege of being a leader. For example, when you have worked with a team member for a period and see the person grow, develop and flourish before your eyes. How were you in those moments? What did you give of yourself to help the team member grow? Were you genuine? What tools did you use? Do you show appreciation for what you have done to yourself?

5. Do you have the courage to shape the culture with empathic leadership and invite participation? For people to reach a new state or a goal, change is required. Do you have the courage to challenge? No impactful change can occur without active action; all forms of change imply some form of development. You, as a leader, need to invite or take the first step.

CHAPTER 6

$$IH \dashrightarrow C \dashrightarrow EH : (E = potential^{\wedge\infty}) \dashrightarrow R = P$$

You don't need to explain what you have done.
Your reputation is doing that for you right now..
Niclas Timmerby

You don't need to speak when everyone already knows.
You need to act.
The significance of my quote on the previous page is that there is no need for a true leader to tell anything at all to their surroundings. What we spread as leaders does not need to be articulated in words, written on paper, or posted online.

Those who have been close to the leader know. They know what the leader stands for and defends. They know whether the leader talks, reacts, or acts. They observe how the leader treats those around them. They understand exactly what signals the leader emits in terms of hormones and neurotransmitters. They know if the leader has integrity, holds a positive view of humanity, is genuine, and communicates with those it concerns.

The leader expands perspectives.
Every person has *a subjective perspective*. Each individual has a completely unique perception and interpretation of their life (both personal and professional), their surroundings, the world, and even the universe.

This subjective perspective is based on a person's own values, emotions, background, and experiences. The subjective perspective influences interpretations and reactions to events and situations that arise in the individual's environment.

Every interpretation or reaction rooted in the subjective perspective significantly affects people's behaviours, attitudes, choices, and decisions. *One example is the individual's interpretation or reaction to stressful situations; while a person with negative past experiences may react more negatively to a stressful situation in the future, another person who has had positive experiences in a similar situation may respond differently. Another example is decision-making; a person with high self-esteem can make decisions that are more independent and less influenced by others' opinions, whereas a person with low self-esteem is more dependent on others' opinions and more affected by what others think.*

Thoughts turn into feelings, which create a reaction.
As a leader, it is crucial to understand that since all people have completely different feelings, values, experiences, and backgrounds, their subjective perspectives vary greatly. This can sometimes make it difficult to achieve a common understanding or agreement on certain issues. This manifests in tensions, irritations, and conflicts within the entity.

Here are some examples of what you as a leader may encounter and need to manage, along with the important "why":

When team members have different subjective perspectives, misunderstandings and misinterpretations can arise in communication. This can lead to frustration, irritation, and conflict when team members interpret and react to information and messages in different ways.

Since subjective perspectives are partially shaped by values, conflicts can arise regarding decision-making, resource allocation, and working methods.

During change initiatives, people may express resistance in various ways. It is the subjective perspective that causes this "rebellion." The subjective perspective does not understand the "why," which may relate to purpose or implementation. If you, as a leader, cannot help the team member understand the "why," it can result in long-term resistance to several details in the change process.

Sometimes you may not see, hear, or understand what causes the tensions you experience and feel from a team member.

In such situations, it is particularly important for you to have the courage to express what you feel in a conversation and to ask "why." One reason I have encountered in conversations as a consultant in various entities is that a team member feels their perspective is not taken seriously, that they feel they have been "run over," or that someone has "elbowed" their way forward while they have been humble and perhaps waited for their chance, but they do not say anything unless you ask "why."

If you understand the "why," you can manage the situation and develop your team members from the current state. If you do not understand the "why," the situation can quickly escalate into open conflict between team members. *Please feel free to revisit pages 158-162 and consider the subjective perspective that creates the reaction ladder when you provide feedback, and how it can be affected depending on whether the person you are giving feedback to reflects or ruminates.*

A fundamental insight for leaders (and human beings) is that all tensions and conflicts are inherently rooted in one or more individuals' subjective perspectives. If you understand the subjective perspective ("why"), you then understand the reasons behind it, and you comprehend the individual's perspective. From there, you can engage in a conversation with a shared perspective, and the intensity of the tension or conflict will diminish.

What can you do to prevent tensions and conflicts?
You have been given the broad strokes and the finer details. Most importantly, regardless of the brushes you have at your disposal and

where they came from, it is you who truly paints based on your own values and moral principles. If you do this, people will listen to you and want to follow you because they feel you are authentic and genuine, and that what you "teach" comes from within _you_.

How is the reputation of good leaders spread?

Through what they do, achieve, and accomplish. _With results-oriented leadership that influences the atmosphere and hospitality but does not challenge people's potential._

How is the reputation of true leaders spread?

Through how they genuinely care about and want to see others grow, seek to understand their "why," touch, motivate, inspire, and passionately lead and develop people into secure individuals who take responsibility for themselves, their time, their tasks, their colleagues, and the entity's goals and ambitions. _With values-driven leadership that impacts the atmosphere and hospitality while challenging people's potential._

Reflect on your (perfectly natural) subjective perspective.

How does it affect your team members and your entity? What daily situations do you face where your subjective perspective is challenged - and how do you react/listen? How do your perceptions and reactions affect the atmosphere and the entire entity, and how does your subjective perspective ultimately influence the culture and your shared results?

You are well aware that you can _consciously_ choose what types of hormones and neurotransmitters you emit to your surroundings, thereby affecting the culture. You also _unconsciously_ send signals to those around you. _Reflect on how you influence the culture._

Here are examples in daily life when your subjective perspective "infects" your entity and its culture:

If you are feeling good, are positive, enthusiastic, and engaged, it is likely that you unconsciously "infect" _your emotional tone and energy_ to your environment. Conversely, if you are not feeling well, are negative, in a bad mood, irritated, stressed, or downcast, you "infect" your surroundings with these signals.

If you unconsciously act and make decisions aligned with your moral principles, values, and a high ethical standard, you "infect" your culture with **integrity and responsibility**. On the other hand, if you unconsciously lack the moral principles you claim are important to you, and if you fail to act ethically and go against your values, the culture is "infected" with **feelings of undermined trust and morality**.

Unconsciously, you emit numerous non-verbal signals in the form of communication every day, such as body language, tone of voice, and facial expressions. If it comes naturally to you to communicate with openness, honesty, and empathy, your atmosphere will be "infected" with **trust and openness**. If it does not come naturally to you, or if you are unavailable, indifferent, or vague, the atmosphere will be "infected" with **a communication style that can create confusion, ambiguity, inquiries, and misunderstandings**.

When you unconsciously make well-founded and fair decisions, considering various perspectives and needs, your team members are "infected" with feelings of **fairness and trust**. However, if you prioritise your own interests over the entity or its vision, or make very quick decisions viewed as arbitrary without involving others, **feelings of distrust and frustration** may spread among team members.

If you allow your subjective perspective to influence your assessments of team members' performance, it will affect your way of giving feedback and coaching. If you have a genuinely **positive view of** *humanity, believe in your team members, and display a positive attitude when giving feedback and coaching,* you will "infect" the person in front of you who wants to develop with **motivation and trust**. This likely leads to them wanting to perform at their best and grow. Conversely, **if you send signals that make the individual in front of you feel judged or negative**, or if you enter conversations with preconceived notions, it will likely create feelings of **injustice and demotivation**.

Your subjective perspective can influence conflict management. **If you are attentive and objective when conflicts arise**, your team members will be "infected" with the **desire to resolve conflicts in a fair and constructive manner**. If it is perceived that you **take sides early on or avoid addressing conflicts** effectively, feelings may likely spread that could lead to the **escalation of conflicts and soon create a negative, demoralising work environment**.

If, as a result of your subjective perspective, you encourage and support various viewpoints, ideas, and angles, you "infect" the environment with **feelings that stimulate creativity and innovation**. However, if your perspective is interpreted as a narrow view of what is right or wrong, or if you interrupt and restrict discussions, it is likely to **stifle creativity and the courage to take initiatives. This can also affect the sense of responsibility within the entity**.

When you are engaged in your team members' progress, provide them with appreciative and developmental feedback, and give them opportunities to grow, you "infect" your entity with **motivation and engagement, contributing to them achieving goals and growing in their roles**. Conversely, if it appears that you, as a leader, favour certain team members or show that you have biases or judge people, or speak ill of others behind their backs, **feelings of unfairness and demotivation are likely to spread throughout the entity, negatively impacting their wellbeing, trust, passion, engagement, and performance**.

Your subjective perspective "infects" the culture every second, which affects the work environment and wellbeing. If you genuinely promote respect, openness, trust, cooperation, participation, and care for each team member, you "infect" them with the willingness to contribute to a positive and healthy work environment where everyone feels safe and valued. Conversely, if you display dominance, lack of fairness, are perceived as confrontational or have a negative attitude, it will likely create an adverse work environment with frightened team members, negatively impacting the culture.

The Psychological Concept.

The concept of subjective perspective is a central idea in psychology. Wilhelm Wundt (1832-1920), considered one of the founders of modern psychology, emphasised the significance of individuals' subjective experiences and introspection as a method for understanding psychological phenomena.

Later, psychologists such as Sigmund Freud (1856-1939) **"It's like having the water bottle but not the water."**
- Eva Timmerby, on subjective perspective.

highlighted the importance of the unconscious and how it can affect our subjective perspective and behaviour, while Carl Rogers (1902-1987) contributed to the understanding of subjective perspective. Rogers focused on individuals' self-perception and emphasised the importance of understanding and accepting each person's unique perspective.

Today, the concept is relevant in sociology and philosophy, as well as in areas such as **cognitive psychology** *to study how thoughts, perceptions, and interpretations of the world shape people's cognition and mental* *representations, how this affects perception, memory, reasoning, and decision-making.*

*In **social psychology**, the term is used to investigate how people perceive and interpret social situations and interactions individually, and how perceptions and experiences can influence how we understand and react to social events.*

*In **pedagogy and education**, the concept is used to understand how students perceive and interpret their learning environment and teaching. Considering individual differences, experiences, and perspectives is crucial for creating a meaningful and effective learning environment.*

*In **psychotherapy**, the concept is used to understand and explore individuals' unique experiences and interpretations of their own reality.*

*Within **organisational psychology**, the concept examines how individuals perceive and interpret their workplace, job tasks, and work relationships. It focuses on how individual perceptions and experiences affect work performance, motivation, engagement, and wellbeing.*

When you receive a questionnaire or form at your workplace, it is grounded in organisational psychology, as management wants to become aware of what employees subjectively believe and think on important issues to identify problem areas and develop strategies for change and development.

*Those who first used the term organisational psychology include the psychologist and author Edgar Schein, who is also known for his work on **organisational culture**; he is currently an emeritus professor at the Massachusetts Institute of Technology (MIT) and still contributes to research and development in the field. The other was Chris Argyris*

(1923-2013), whose contributions live on through his theories and ideas about organisational learning and change, which are still applied in organisational development and leadership today. Argyris argued that organisations often become stuck in old behaviour patterns and that it is crucial to identify and break these patterns to create change. (You may recognise this in my discussion of line organisations and flat organisations in section C: Control Systems, or passion and will.)

Are you consciously working to open up the culture?
Tensions, disagreements, irritation, and conflicts arise when one subjective perspective does not align with other team members' subjective perspectives.

The path to creating an objective perspective in a team member goes through your leadership and the culture you contribute to.

For your own reflection:

- Do you make your team members feel seen and heard?
- Do you encourage them to challenge old truths/paradigms, their own thought patterns and perspectives in your coaching conversations?
- Does the culture promote trust and respect for differences?
- Is there space in the atmosphere to "question" established truths in daily work and objectives?
- How good are you as a leader at listening without interrupting?
- Do you encourage open dialogue in meetings and conversations to incorporate multiple perspectives? Or is there no space to openly discuss/improve your proposals and decisions?

Your Traffic Light.

Imagine you have a traffic light accompanying you through life, both privately and in your professional life. Only you can see the traffic light.

This traffic light reflects <u>your perspective</u>, and every time you face a situation where your subjective perspective is challenged (which happens countless times every day), a colour clearly appears, so strong that you almost have to squint your eyes.

<u>Red</u> color is when you directly oppose the other person's perspective, and the person sees it in your communication and feels it in what you emit.

<u>Yellow</u> color is when you directly oppose the other person's perspective, but you say nothing and keep it inside (and perhaps tell others about it).

<u>Green</u> color is when you listen attentively without looking for faults, assuming, or interrupting. You give acceptance to the other person's perspective by showing genuine interest and demonstrating through your focus, eye contact, and body language that you are truly present. You ask follow-up questions, show that you want to understand, and exhibit empathy by putting yourself in the other person's perspective.

The symbolism of the "traffic light" came to me during a feedback conversation with an employee that caused tensions within the entity. When I asked the person to describe their traffic light at home and in the workplace, we became closer than ever before. If you wish, use "Niclas's traffic light" as a tool when giving feedback, coaching, or in a one-on-one conversation. Or why not for your own development and to strengthen your self-leadership?

What colours emerge in your private life? And in your professional life? In what situations? Are certain colours more frequent with certain people, and why is that? Do you promote an objective perspective at home and in the workplace? Do you have a good view of humanity? Are you genuine?

The Paradox of the Binoculars.
Looking through binoculars provides a perspective that is very clear and distinct, significantly better than with the naked eye. But have you considered that what is really being demonstrated when a person looks through binoculars is *an extremely subjective perspective*?

The paradox I see with this is that the person looking into the binoculars sees precisely what they are focused on with good clarity, but they can easily miss everything around what they see through the binocular lenses. I want to illustrate this with the image here to the right.

A paradox is something very useful because it challenges our logical thinking and opens us up to new perspectives, insights, and reflections. Thus, with this image, I want to remind you of the paradox of binoculars so that in your leadership role, you carry with you the insight and importance of an objective perspective to promote culture, the entity, and outcomes. Also, use "the paradox of binoculars" as a concrete tool in your daily life, do you understand everyone's perspective?

A person's normal total field of vision is about 180 degrees horizontally and 135 degrees vertically. A standard-format binocular has about seven degrees of total field of view. The area that the user cannot clearly see through the binoculars is called "binocular parallax."

If I were to take this to its extreme and create a fictional example by comparing what a person "misses" with a subjective perspective and call it "the subjective horizontal parallax," it means that a person sees seven degrees of the objective perspective, which leaves 173 degrees that the person does not see objectively.

(If a plane were to fly as the crow flies from southern Sweden in Kristianstad, where I am, to Stockholm, the distance is about 40 miles.

If the plane were to fly 173 degrees off course over this short distance, it would miss Stockholm by around 80 miles. So it is good that pilots do not make final important decisions based on emotions and their subjective perspective in choosing, for example, a direction or runway.)

When you broaden perspectives, you create <u>real</u> change.
Expanding a team member's perspective is how you can concretely influence their view of their subjective reality. When this happens, you have come a long way in your leadership work, as this creates profound, lasting development within the individual.

You help by challenging the individual to better understand themselves when they reflect on unconscious thought patterns.

With the line and arrow at either end on the previous page, I want to illustrate what you see subjectively and what everyone in your surroundings sees subjectively. Consider the challenging and developing idea that you can slightly broaden your subjective perspective. Do you listen better to people then? Do you challenge your own paradigms more often? Do you become more insightful and open to differences?

Now think of the idea that it can be your task as a leader, in conversations with your team members and through your genuine leadership, to broaden the entire entity's perspective. What positive effects could that create in the work environment, acceptance of differences, responsiveness, community, trust, culture, external hospitality, and reputation?

By broadening your entity's perspective, you directly impact the possibilities for internal hospitality and profound development. The significance of profound development for leaders and employees and its effects in terms of personal and professional growth is well documented in many studies. The conditions are there: if leaders consciously develop their entity in depth, it can create a more engaged, competent, and productive workforce that achieves professional goals. *As you can infer, coaching, feedback, and clear personal goals combined with the leader having resources in terms of time for conversations are prerequisites for significant growth.*

*In 2021, "The Effectiveness of Deep-Level Developmental Feedback on Employee Performance and Motivation" (Wang, Liao) found that "deep developmental feedback can improve **employee performance and motivation**."*

In 2018, "The Role of Deep Developmental Coaching in Enhancing Leadership Effectiveness" (Grant, Curtayne, Burton) found that "deep developmental coaching can enhance **leadership effectiveness and personal growth in managers.**"

In 2021, "The Role of Deep-Level Developmental Goals in Enhancing Work Engagement and Well-being" (Xanthopoulou, Bakker) showed that "deep developmental goals can increase **employee work engagement and well-being.**"

In 2021, "The Role of Deep-Level Developmental Job Resources in Enhancing Employee Resilience and Well-being" (Bakker, Demerouti) demonstrated that "deep developmental resources in the workplace can increase **employee resilience and well-being.**"

Research exists on the connection between **profound development from an objective perspective**. Here too, the importance of allocating time for conversations, coaching, and feedback is significant.

In 2015, "The Impact of Leader Empowering Behaviors on Employee Development and Performance" examined how leader empowering behaviors affect employee development and performance. **"Leaders who delegate responsibility, empower, and support employee independence promote their profound development and performance."**

In 2014, "The Role of Leader Feedback in Deep-Level Employee Development" explored how feedback from leaders affects employee development. **"Leaders who provide constructive and specific feedback promote employees' capacity for profound development by identifying areas for improvement and offering support and guidance."**

In 2019, "The Role of Leader-Member Exchange in Deep-Level Employee Development" examined how the relationship between leaders and employees affects profound development. *"A high-quality relationship, known as leader-member exchange (LMX), promotes employees' capacity for profound development by providing support, feedback, and challenges from the leader."*

In 2012, "The Impact of Leader Trustworthiness on Employee Development and Performance" investigated how leader trustworthiness affects employee development and performance. *"Leaders who are credible, honest, and fair promote employees' capacity for profound development by fostering trust and a positive work environment."*

In 2018, "The Effects of Leader Humility on Employee Development and Performance" examined how leader humility affects employee development and performance. *"Leaders who demonstrate humility and openness foster employees' profound development by creating a culture of learning and growth."*

In 2017, "The Role of Leader Authenticity in Deep-Level Employee Development" explored how authentic leadership affects employee development. *"Authentic leaders, who are genuine and transparent in their communication and actions, promote employees' ability to develop profoundly by building trust and openness in the work environment."*

In 2011, "The Role of Leader Supportive Communication in Deep-Level Employee Development" examined how leader supportive communication affects employee development. *"Leaders who communicate clearly, listen actively, and provide support and encouragement promote employees' profound development by creating an open and supportive communication culture."*

*In 2016, "The Impact of Leader Emotional Intelligence on Employee Development and Well-being" investigated how leader emotional intelligence affects employee development and well-being. "**Leaders with high emotional intelligence (who can understand and manage their own and others' emotions) promote employees' profound development by creating a positive and supportive work environment**."*

"Ultimately, there is one decisive factor that remains.

A decisive factor that your employees will remember for the rest of their lives, that they carry with them and share with others.

It is your leadership."

- Niclas Timmerby

It is fundamentally important that you, as a leader, have conscious strategies to ensure that your team members always have a crystal-clear map of where you are going and a clear direction on how to get there.

You, as a leader, need to be prepared to act rather than react when events or situations arise that become obstacles on your way towards the vision.

You have been provided with the tools in the book. Whenever you perceive that you are off course from the vision, mission, or values, or as soon as you sense that tensions arise and the atmosphere is uncomfortable, you know what the cause is. Something has occurred in the internal hospitality that creates imbalance, and it is highly likely that not everyone is adhering to your shared foundation of values.

You need to clearly repeat the long-term tools and expectations you have for everyone in your entity during meetings. You need to prioritise one-on-one conversations, coaching, and feedback as daily tools to guide your team members in steering the culture in the required direction. You should also have discussions with everyone in your entity to identify feelings and causes.

What are the underlying reasons? Ask them:

- *Lack of cooperation / Lack of trust.*
- *Communication problems.*
- *Feelings of unfair work distribution.*
- *Unclear expectations / Unclear goals.*
- *Stress / High workload.*
- *Harassment, bullying, discrimination.*
- *Competition within the entity.*
- *Lack of resources to achieve goals.*
- *Uncertainty / Insecurity about the future.*
- *Negative cultural carriers affecting "the Gold."*
- *Poor leadership (lack of conflict management, insufficient coaching, feedback, one-on-one conversations, developmental discussions, lack of respect for work/life balance, clarity, unfavourable work environment, signals sent to the entity).*

Stabilise the internal hospitality - staff meeting (2-3 hours).
Regardless of the reasons that emerge in your conversations, you as a leader need to act promptly to stabilise the internal hospitality that affects the team members and the entire formula.

1. After having your conversations and gaining an understanding of the reasons causing tensions within the entity, it is time to gather your team

members for a mandatory staff meeting. *(It is relatively common for those you want to attend to find reasons not to show up. Find ways to start with when they can attend before you schedule the formal meeting. If some still do not attend the meeting, make detailed meeting notes and invite those who did not attend to a separate meeting as soon as possible. Find constructive ways to resolve this expeditiously so that everyone receives the same information ideally within a week.)*

2. Start the meeting by mentioning that you have now spoken with everyone because you have sensed clear tensions within the entity that you consider to be a significant risk to wellbeing, the work environment, cooperation, communication, efficiency, productivity, and the risk of not achieving your entity's and the entire organisation's goals.

3. Express that your intention for the meeting is to openly raise this for discussion where everyone can voice their opinions and what they perceive as obstacles, problems, or concerns. Clarify that the room is a safe and respectful environment where everyone should feel comfortable sharing their views.

> *"If you want to make everyone happy, don't be a leader.*
>
> *Sell ice cream."*
> *- Steve Jobs*

4. Begin by presenting your vision and your mission (why you all go to work and what you strive to achieve together). Start an open discussion in the room. (1) What risks are currently present that might prevent us from achieving our vision and mission? (2) What are the solutions? (3) How do we implement the solutions? (4) What must everyone commit to here and now?

5. Continue with the shared foundation of values, going through it step by step and repeating the four questions from point 4 on the previous page.

6. Conclude with the expectations you have communicated in your emotional information regarding all team members, as well as the expectations you have conveyed that they can have of you as a leader. Repeat the four questions.

7. Thank everyone for their valuable input and feedback.

8. Clearly communicate that everyone has a significant individual responsibility in solving problems and potential conflicts. Tensions affect the entire entity and how people feel before you, as a leader, may become aware and can act - which you will do. *As a leader, you will always protect the entity, uphold the culture, stand up for injustices, strive toward the vision, and uphold the shared foundation of values.*
    This clarifies responsibilities and ensures that everyone fully understands what it means to be part of the entity and what you expect of all.

9. Be clear that you are a reference point if any of them do not dare to raise the tension or conflict with the person involved. In that case, you will call for a conversation where you act as a neutral mediator, solely with the organisation's vision as your goal in the discussion. *(The vision is your strongest concrete tool for building teams, achieving goals, and overcoming conflicts. The vision is your guiding star in daily work when making choices and difficult decisions)*

10. Emphasise the importance of mutual respect and listening to each other's opinions and viewpoints. It is crucial to create an environment where everyone feels seen and heard.

11. Stress that cooperation is fundamentally important to your culture because it allows everyone to benefit from each team member's individual strengths and competencies. That you are strong together. *Make the connection to your common goals and how these goals can only be achieved by working together.* It is essential that everyone understands that their individual successes are directly linked to the entity's and organisation's success.

12. *Conclude, if you feel comfortable doing so, by discussing research related to subjective and objective perspectives.*

Emphasise that in a conflict, it is not the person who is "at fault," but rather the communication.

When we do not understand each other or disagree, we simply see the "issue" from two different subjective perspectives, and our task in an entity is to create a shared viewpoint, a common objective perspective to move forward, or alternatively to acknowledge that we see the "issue" differently, which is perfectly okay as long as our individual and collective goals are not compromised.

Self-reflection.

You also need to reflect on yourself. Have you been unclear? Have you lost your engagement? Do you feel stressed/pressured that your entity is not meeting goals? What is your traffic light saying? Are you attentive? Do you have the courage to give feedback? Do you coach your team members? Do you create participation? Do you make your entity feel significant, seen, and respected? Are the goals applicable?

Do you have a good view of humanity? Are you following the vision, your own mission, the shared foundation of values, and the expectations you emotionally communicated that they can have of you as a leader?

In crises and times of uncertainty, your reputation as a leader is determined.
Everyone goes through both minor and major crises, and this includes all entities.

Daily, you, as a leader, put out small fires and build long-term strategic firebreaks to facilitate daily work and counteract obstacles and tensions. Sometimes you need to bravely give clear feedback at level 4; at other times, coaching conversations become very emotional, which naturally affects you as a person.

You may come into conflict with a team member; do you have a clear strategy for that? You may need to mediate between two team members who have a conflict; do you have a clear strategy for that?

"Regardless of what happens in the world and what the people around you think, feel, do, or say, you always have a choice.

What do you do?
What do you emit?
What legacy do you leave behind?

That becomes your reputation."
- Niclas Timmerby

You always have a concrete tool right in front of you: Your vision.
All communication in your entity should lead to your vision. What really moves a team member, two team members, or the entire entity forward? *That is the goal of communication.* The goal of communication in all entities should be, in every situation: *the best possible common solution to achieve the vision.*

To achieve the vision, it is not important what one team member says, what another team member thinks (with their subjective perspective), or what you as a leader say, think, or write from your subjective perspective.

All communication, whether spoken or written, everything that is discussed and ventilated, must have a (1) clear goal: *How can we together achieve our vision?* This is crucial because all communication plays a decisive role in achieving essential tasks, strategies, goals, and ambitions in the pursuit of the vision.

Small and large things happen every day that build your reputation as a leader. How do you act in stressed and pressured situations?

It is very easy to lead in good times; *it is during turbulent times that leadership is most important.* You may have consciously and unconsciously built your good reputation as a leader for many years, but then you lose your patience for a second when you are provoked, when goals are not met, or when you do not uncover a team member's "why" and instead impose stricter demands with the same conditions.

It is in these situations that your reputation can change in an instant.

So, my warm advice to counter potential tensions, protect the culture, and clarify/visualize everyone's direction and map is again to strategically and consciously use your vision and mission. The shared foundation of values work for you in the background as the entity's established ground rules.

If you find yourself in a situation where you feel you are about to lose control and potentially headed into an impending conflict, here is my best tip: *extinguish the negative energy by saying, "I want us to start over, now."*

If you are in a situation where you need to mediate and negative energy is flowing in the room, say: *"I want you to start over, now."* Then ask them: *"What do you need to sort out to move forward?"*

When you know the "why," you can concretely work your way forward in the conversation. Elevate the vision in the discussion: *"This is why we come to work, to strive toward the vision. You need to sort out your discrepancies because this does not bring you, me, or your team members closer to the vision."*

The vision cannot be questioned.

If a team member does not want to stand behind the entity's pursuit of the vision, you as a leader need to have separate conversations with the one who does not want to support the pursuit.

This continues until the team member fully understands and accepts that all operational and strategic work being carried out in the organization has a function: to promote and support the achievement of the vision.

This is because the organization exists to ensure that the pursuit and intention is to achieve the vision.

The vision is the guiding star.

The opposite of acting on impulse is the importance of reflection.
When you are provoked, challenged, or irritated is when you need to be a true leader and not act on impulse. The British preacher and author (he wrote over 140 books) Charles H. Spurgeon said in the 1800s: *"You get the reputation you deserve, and you deserve the reputation you get,"* and this is precisely how it is. All leaders are sometimes provoked and irritated. But that does not automatically mean we understand "why" the situation has arisen, or the leads that have led to the visible behavior or attitude you clearly feel, or that you see that goals are far from budget/being fulfilled.

Once, when I was called to my son's school and they told me that my son had thrown stones (very small ones) at students, it was the visible, obvious behavior that is absolutely not okay. Unfortunately, the school did not have the formula or structure that indicated an atmosphere that included bullying, and that other children, among other things, had tied my son up around the neck and were violent towards him (which my son disclosed five years later). When this happened, I trusted the school, whose only point on the agenda was that he had thrown stones (= the visible behavior). I strongly questioned my son's behavior at that time. I have apologised to my son, but this will be something I feel bad about for the rest of my life.

The only positive outcome of this in my life is that I do not act on impulse and truly do everything to understand the entire process/story/ perspectives underline before underline I act. underline I want the person in front of me to tell me "why." underline And that person will only do so if he or she feels underline trust in me as a person underline. Therefore, trust means so much to me in an entity. (You can read about the positive synergistic effects of a consciously trust-based leadership, combined with sections A-E, in section G.)

When I receive something that directly harms people or the culture, I act immediately by calling for a conversation or by visiting the team member to create a fact-based picture of what I have heard or seen.

When I receive things that are provocative, irritating, or similar, I turn off notifications on my phone and reflect.

When I reflect, I simultaneously take notes, and I want to offer that as a warm tip to you as a leader.

When we write down what we think, it becomes much clearer than when thoughts float away in our heads (you have about 35-48 conscious and unconscious thoughts per minute, which is incredibly hard to sort out well if you are irritated or provoked).

I have made a decision within myself that if I am in a meeting and I become provoked or irritated, and feel there is a risk that I might say something in the heat of the moment, I leave the meeting. This way, I can reflect and then return with a balanced response.

(As a consultant, I have sometimes had to act as a representative for employers in local and central negotiations with trade unions. In these negotiations, there is a wonderfully wise tool.

You can request to adjourn the negotiation virtually any time during the meeting to allow for a pause for reflection and consultation with your representatives.)

The formula is your concrete visible tool.
I clarify the formula again and want to emphasise that my view is that
the formula structurally creates the outcome of the reputation.

$$IH \dashrightarrow C \dashrightarrow EH : (E = potential^{\wedge\infty}) \dashrightarrow R = P$$

*It is <u>so easy</u> to see a behaviour, feel an attitude, or see a result that does
not meet the goal. And then immediately question, complain, or hold
meetings about what you see, hear, or experience.*

But have you then taken in the whole perspective?
- *Do you know "why"?*
- *Have you asked the team member how he or she is feeling?*

*If you have provided feedback and had coaching conversations, I can
guarantee that you could have caught early on what burdens and
therefore affects your team member's behaviour/attitude/result.*

*It is so important to capture feelings and well-being in conversations at
an early stage. Imagine if your team member had shared this with you
and could then release feelings naturally; you could have supported and
potentially helped through efforts from the organisation.*

*The paradox is that if you do not have trusting conversations, you later
see a behaviour/attitude/result that you do not understand, or in the
worst case, that the capable loyal team member leaves without stating a
reason.*

As a leader, you are continuously creating four reputations that together build the reputation of you as a leader:

1.Your reputation as a leader.
Are you someone whom people seek to work with?
You are more than a manager who directs employees.
You are a leader who has the reputation of being a person who develops people and organisations.
You may even have built a reputation as a mentor, developing existing leaders and creating new ones.

2. The reputation as an employer.
Culture spreads like the wind; what does the atmosphere you have contributed to building convey? Is it a culture in which people want to be a part of, be shaped by, and develop?
How people thrive, how they treat each other, how they feel, how they work together, whether there is a good atmosphere and community, and how you are in your leadership.
All of this creates the reputation of your organisation as an employer and of you as the leader of the work.
Your reputation creates loyal team members; are your good qualities as a person and your good leadership what your team members talk about when you're not present?

3. Your reputation is as a leader with loyal team members.
People outside your organisation know you and your leadership. They know that you have a self-sufficient, motivated entity that thrives. They know that you care for your team members, that you see each individual as a person, you know the names of their family members and maybe even their pets, you are aware of their personal challenges and

backgrounds, and you make everyone in the entity feel very significant.

You nurture the culture more than anyone else; you create safety, care, and joy around you.

You are well aware that younger generations almost demand engagement, that they experience commitment around them and from the leadership. (Brilliant Future demonstrated in a study that what creates engagement is that you, as a leader, strive for a balance in your leadership that allows your entity to feel evenly proportioned energy and perceived clarity); these two elements need to accompany you in your daily leadership to foster engagement.

You have the ability to start from everyone's needs and create a well-functioning whole that collaborates and pulls in the same direction, regardless of age, experience, and background.

4. Your reputation as a leader creates loyal customers.

You, as a leader, are the one who most influences the culture, which is why you also impact the external hospitality the most.

You use feedback and coaching as daily tools to shape the atmosphere in alignment with the vision and your mission.

Your team members trust that you are leading them in a clear direction.

Everything you do, for and with your entity, is noticeable to customers in the external hospitality as soon as they experience your culture.

If the atmosphere is pleasant, authentic, caring, trustworthy, and professional, mixed with genuine joy, and your team members dare to put themselves out there - you can almost see and feel in real-time that what you have built, nurtured, and stood up for reveals itself before your eyes. Be proud.

Studies that demonstrate that your reputation is crucial for attracting and retaining good team members, as well as attracting loyal customers:

In the study *"The Impact of Leader Reputation on Employee Trust and Engagement: A Multilevel Study"* by Dirks, K. T., and Ferrin, D. L., the researchers examined how a leader's reputation affects employee trust and engagement.

They found that *"a positive leader reputation was associated with higher levels of employee trust in the leader, which in turn led to increased employee engagement."*

The study emphasised the importance of leaders building and maintaining a positive reputation to foster trust and engagement among employees.

In the study *"The Impact of Leader Reputation on Attracting Job Applicants: A Field Experiment"* by Cable, D. M., and Turban, D. B., the researchers conducted a field experiment to investigate how a leader's reputation affects the ability to attract employees.

They found that *"a leader with a positive reputation was more successful in attracting qualified job applicants, and these applicants were more likely to seek employment with the organisation."*

The study showed that a leader's reputation played an important role in creating an attractive employer and attracting qualified talent.

"A fundamental prerequisite for motivating and developing people is that you, as a leader, know and respect everyone's "why."

If your team members do not have a higher VALUE than security/salary in their WHY, there is a significant risk that they will leave your entity as soon as they see a greater WHY that offers them a higher VALUE elsewhere."
- Niclas Timmerby

Reflection, Chapter 6

1. Reflect on everyday situations in your workplace where you can later broaden team members' subjective perspectives in coaching conversations. After addressing the factor individually or for your entire entity, you can also utilise feedback on all four levels. Using both of these tools in this context creates profound change and genuine development.

2. Reflect on how your subjective perspective influences your decision-making and your interactions with managers and your team members. Can you influence your thinking in different situations to create a higher objective perspective? Can you "adjourn" a conversation or meeting to avoid acting or responding on impulse? Reflect on how your insights can help you enhance your understanding of the people around you—their behaviour, attitude, actions, choices, and decisions. Are there any preconceived notions or biases you can become aware of that may hinder you in your leadership role, and that you can therefore work to overcome?

3. Reflect on how you can actively practice and develop a more objective perspective and become more aware of how your behaviour and attitude ultimately affect people and results. What strategies can you employ to become even more attentive, fair, and inclusive? Perhaps "Niclas' traffic light" or "the paradox of the binoculars"? What is it that you see clearly with your subjective perspective, and what is it that you miss?

4. Take a moment and let it sink in. How incredibly significant you are as a leader. What a privilege it is to lead others and to help them grow as individuals and in their professional roles.

CHAPTER 7

IH ⇢ C ⇢ EH : (E = pctential$^{\wedge\infty}$) ⇢ R = P

Profitability and growth are ultimately measured
by how many people you have developed.
Niclas Timmerby

P = Profitability.
We have now reached the final part of the formula, the letter P.

Profitability is an important tool that measures the economic health, return, and success of an entity. Profitability results from good outcomes, and good outcomes arise from the people in the team. The better you, as a leader, can develop your team members' competencies, knowledge, and skills through the tools you've gained from this book, the greater growth your entity has the potential to achieve. Because the more a team member grows, the more they can contribute to positive results.

Growth = profitability.
Satisfied customers create the conditions for a business to survive. *Loyal customers* create the conditions for profitability in the business. Creating growth within the people in your entity generates conditions for loyal employees and customers, which in turn creates conditions for profitability. Profitability creates good conditions for continuing to foster growth in people. Therefore, growth is inherently linked to profitability.

Growth can represent many different positive parameters for various types of entities: development of teams, people, and leaders; development of entire organizations; development of results in terms of profitability, liquidity, and solvency; cohesion, trust, confidence, collaboration, and joy - which contribute to workplace environment and climate; growth of new loyal customers and team members; opportunities for diversification of the business; engagement, efficiency, and productivity; results and increased profits (in sports); sustainable growth, digital growth, capacity growth, brand growth;

increased market shares, internationalisation, acquisitions/mergers, new partnerships/new collaborations, social responsibility; e-commerce growth; reputation as an employer and organization.

These parameters are inexorably created by the formula:

$$IH \dashrightarrow C \dashrightarrow EH : (E = potential^{\wedge\infty}) \dashrightarrow R = P$$

If your organization does not have the level of profitability or growth that management/shareholders expect, it is important to review every step in the formula and start from the beginning.

Does the internal ownership create conditions for a healthy and productive culture?

If so, it creates the conditions for customers to perceive positive and genuine external hospitality.

Is there engagement, the X-factor that creates the unique appeal, specific to each entity?

Engagement is the immeasurable potential that summarises the first four steps of the formula, which creates the reputation.

How does the organization want to be perceived?
And is this the same as how the organization is actually perceived by its employees, customers, suppliers, and other stakeholders?

This is an extremely relevant question that all organizations need to continuously ask themselves.

"Without good self-awareness, goals are merely dreams.

Only through action, self-reflection, and determination
do dreams become reality.
- Niclas Timmerby

Here are relevant questions that I believe should be continuously discussed, documented, and followed up in each department/team:

- Why should the customer choose to come to us?
- What differentiates us from our competitors, what is our competitive advantage?
- What do we want the customer to feel when they leave us, regardless of whether a transaction has taken place?
- What do our customers tell others after visiting us, regardless of whether a transaction has occurred?
- How do our suppliers and other stakeholders perceive us, and what do they say about us to others?
- Are we following our vision, mission, and shared foundation of values?
- How is our corporate culture reflected to the outside world?
- What events or incidents may have negatively impacted our reputation?
- Is our self-perception the same as how customers perceive us?
- What do our customers expect from us?

It is crucial in leadership to always see people before results.
Results do not come by themselves; it is always people who, in some active form, create the final outcome. It is very easy in a leadership position, when the results are not as expected, to look at what people are doing or not doing rather than analysing the underlying reasons for behaviours, attitudes, and results.

It is akin to taking a medication for a headache when we know that we have not consumed enough fluids on a hot day. We are treating the symptoms, the disruption in the body that has arisen because we have not addressed the obvious underlying cause.

As a leader, you see symptoms every day; the less you work on the underlying causes, the more symptoms you will have to address afterwards, and the more fires you will have to extinguish.

Maintain an unyielding mindset that observes the causes.
If you, as a leader, want your entity to perform at the highest level every day and in every situation, you need to act before symptoms that could damage your entity's reputation reveal themselves. You need to have the ability to sense how your entity is doing, and to do this, you need to know all your team members deeply.

Your entity is your greatest asset because the team allows you to reach goals faster than you could achieve alone. If you focus on your greatest asset, that asset will generate more and more benefits for you.

When you have developed an unyielding mindset that focuses on identifying and understanding the causes of symptoms; various situations, problems, performances, collaboration, results (both positive and negative factors) that arise, you can focus on development instead of extinguishing fires.

You have previously read about working with the "iceberg" to understand what causes behaviours, attitudes, and provides insights about people's differences. When you take the time to analyse, identify, and evaluate beyond merely treating symptoms, you can start to work proactively in your leadership, addressing the root causes, changing working methods, conversation forms, and strategies to create long-term and sustainable solutions. While products and services can create a good reputation, it is always people who are co-creators somewhere along the way.

So what can you do as a leader to get the most out of your team members to create an even better reputation than what you have already read in the book? You know that reputation largely depends on how your team members feel.

"A person is truly rich when they shift their focus from what they want to what they have."
- Niclas Timmerby

So, do you know how they feel?
- *Do you ask them if they are happy?*
- *Do you inquire about what is difficult in their lives?*
- *Do you ask what their drive and motivation are?*
- *Do you ask how they feel in their relationships?*
- *Do you ask about their personal goals and dreams?*
- *Do you ask what experiences in life have shaped them into the person they are today?*

"How your employees feel is how your customers will feel."
- Sybil F. Stershic

Often, as a leader, it is enough to listen, showing that the person in front of you is important and meaningful *to you*. Your team members can immediately sense whether you are genuinely interested in listening to them.

One of my warmest pieces of advice in leadership is to always see the person before seeing the employee. The more genuinely interested you are in and treat them as a human being, the more they will contribute as an employee and team member.

Maslow + Employee Conversations = "Why" = Profitability

In addition to coaching and feedback conversations, you have another concrete tool to enhance your relationships with your team members related to internal ownership: the employee conversation. It's a fantastic structured and recurring tool where you and your team member can prepare, speak openly, honestly, and forward-looking, while focusing on motivations, obstacles, needs, vision, and goals.

I have yet to find a conversation format that is more concrete, developmental, and that brings teams together in a common direction.

Unfortunately, employee conversations are a tool that is often not used systematically and sometimes viewed as unnecessary and time-consuming; this is something I have understood in my conversations with both managers and employees. I think it is a shame that this opportunity to get closer to one another, create better understanding, and clarify the direction forward is not seen as more valuable.

There are many positive synergies with a structured and well-prepared employee conversation where everyone develops: the team member, the leader, and the entity as a whole.

What I have discovered in my work to create loyal teams and in change processes is that it is particularly beneficial to study the American psychologist Abraham Maslow (1908–1970). Maslow was a leading figure in humanism, and his most famous legacy is the hierarchy of needs, which he developed to create an understanding of human motivation and behavior.

Humanistic psychology focuses on human potential, self-actualization, and personal growth. His theory posited that human actions are born out of motivation directed towards a goal that meets human needs. He emphasized the importance of understanding a person's intrinsic motivation and how their needs influence their behavior and goals.

He concluded that by identifying and fulfilling people's needs, you can foster their motivation to achieve goals and realize their full potential.

I have many favorite quotes from Maslow that are very insightful:

"We do what we are, and we are what we do. A musician must make music, an artist must paint, a poet must write, if they are to be fully at peace with themselves."

"If you plan to be anything less than you are capable of being, you will surely be unhappy for all your days."

"Be independent of other people's good intentions."

"We can orient ourselves towards defense, security, or fear. But on the opposite side lies the opportunity for growth. Choosing growth rather than fear twelve times a day means moving towards self-actualization twelve times."

"People are not bad; they are unhappy."

How does Maslow's hierarchy of needs relate to profitability?
What Maslow means is that everyone has choices to make every day. **"Either you will take steps forward towards growth, or you will take steps back towards safety."** This is a fantastic thought to carry with you into all conversations in your self-leadership and in all individual conversations with your entity.

Individual conversations with your team members are highly significant; the answers you receive in a coaching, feedback, or employee conversation provide insights into human needs and motivations, which gives you a deeper understanding of individual drivers.

Through your questions, you can promote each team member's self-awareness and growth.

As a leader, you can he p your team understand themselves better by encouraging them to identify their own needs and motivations.

This is among the most rewarding aspects of leadership - helping people grow and want to get more out of their lives.

The essence of Maslow's work is that all motivation is based on a need, and since every person is unique, everyone has different needs and, therefore, different motivational factors.

"Every time you expect or ask an employee to do "that little extra," you should ask yourself if you are doing "that little extra" as an employer."
- Hamid Eslami

The reason I mentioned the quotes is that they can be helpful during an employee conversation. The more you develop in your self-leadership, the more you can develop your team Take every opportunity for self-reflection and personal growth.

The answer to the question at the bottom of the previous page is that the hierarchy of needs is an excellent tool to unlock each team member's "why." When the person in front of you shares their "why," which they may not have disclosed to anyone else, you understand their driving forces, obstacles, motivational factors, and personal goals.

This provides you with a deep understanding of each individual's unique needs, giving you the opportunity to lead, motivate, and develop each unique team member successfully.

Maslow's hierarchy of needs is fundamentally about <u>needs</u>.
Throughout life, we humans find motivation in fulfilling our needs. When we feel satisfied with meeting the most basic human needs, we strive to achieve higher needs to reach our potential as individuals.

Here is a basic representation of Maslow's hierarchy of needs.

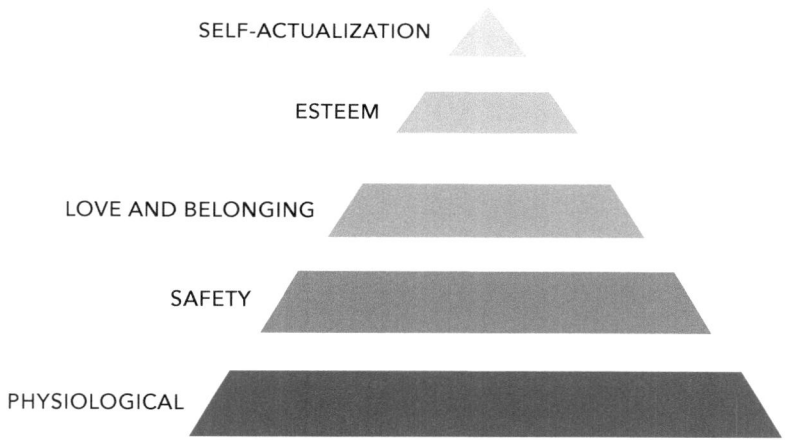

SELF-ACTUALIZATION

ESTEEM

LOVE AND BELONGING

SAFETY

PHYSIOLOGICAL

As a leader and fellow human being, *<u>you can never make another person want to climb the hierarchy if they do not wish to do so themselves</u>*. They will only ascend when they feel their needs are satisfied, and they can only feel their needs are met through intrinsic motivation - that is, by fulfilling their own needs. Unfortunately, a person can be pulled down the hierarchy by their own thoughts and/or the influence of others.

Therefore, your work with negative cultural carriers, which I have written extensively about in the book, is crucial. If you have a negative cultural carrier, there is an overwhelming likelihood that those who want to climb upward will feel significant obstacles to their own development and motivation.

Your understanding of the hierarchy and your willingness and ability to develop and motivate your team members are therefore fundamentally important in all change efforts. *You cannot change people, but you can inspire them to want to make a change within themselves.*

Your task as a leader during various conversations with each team member is to find out which needs are fulfilled and, through well-asked questions, challenge old truths. This way, you can create motivation and inspiration within people, enabling them to identify new needs they want to satisfy and autonomously want to climb higher. *This is true leadership.*

Your work as a leader to understand needs and create motivation fosters engagement, which is the immeasurable potential within your entity. How much engagement can you create as a leader?

On the next page, I have created an open table where you can fill in the positive and negative factors currently affecting your entity. Factors could include: time, people, resources, your leadership, as well as the organization's functionality, governance, meeting structure, and maturity. Consider the table as a risk matrix where you rate the factors by placing them as follows:

Low/short-term risk: *High sense of trust and motivation.*
High/long-term risk: *Low sense of trust and motivation.*

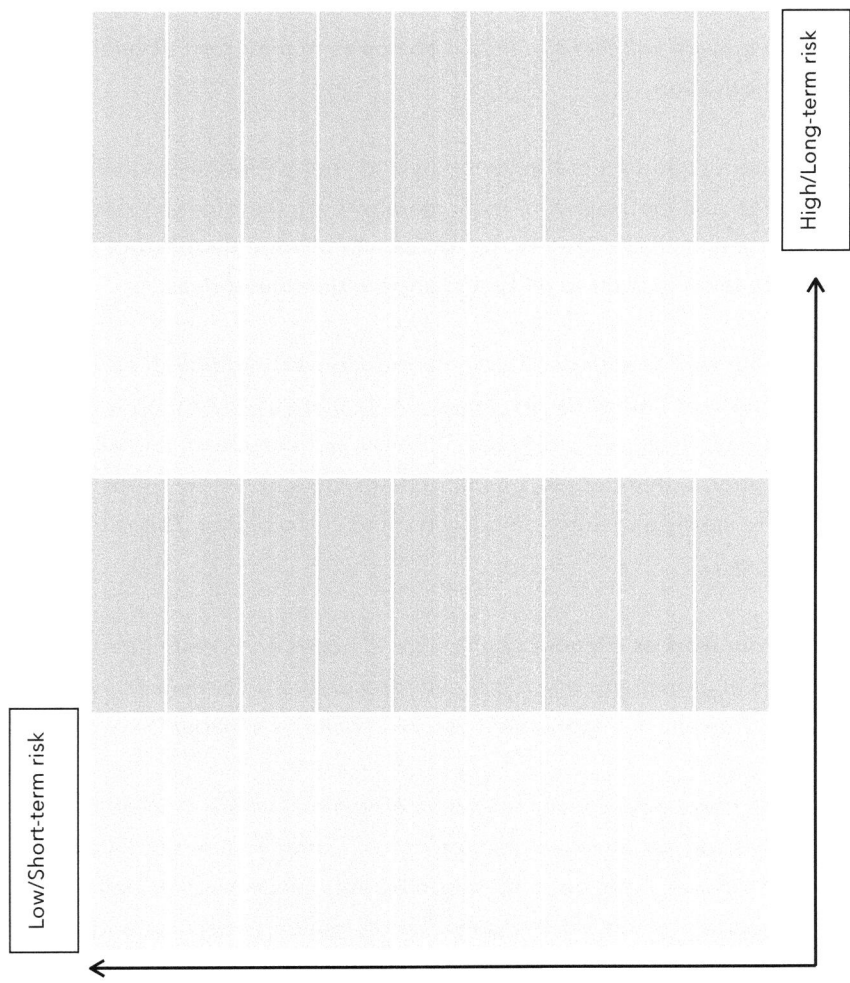

I have adapted Maslow's hierarchy of needs to reflect how a team member might experience their situation and feel in their workplace and team. At the top is Maslow's basic model, and below it is the perspective of a fictional team member.

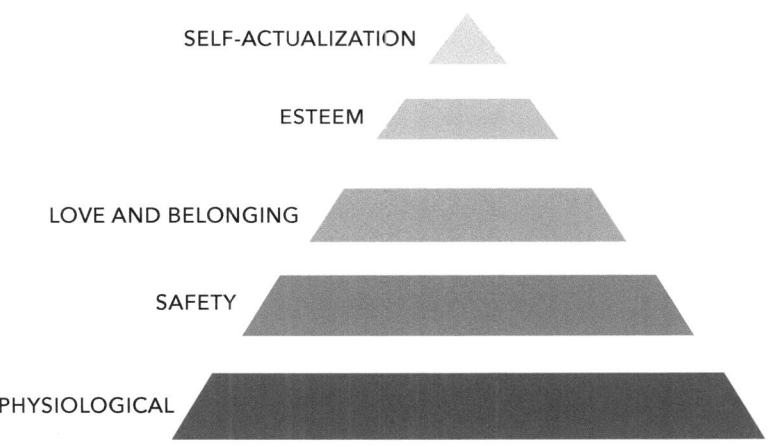

SELF-ACTUALIZATION

ESTEEM

LOVE AND BELONGING

SAFETY

PHYSIOLOGICAL

I have the opportunity to contribute, develop, and make a significant difference.

I feel appreciated at the workplace and am satisfied in my role.

I feel a sense of belonging because I am included in the team.

I feel secure because I receive a salary and am treated well.

I don't have to worry about losing my employment.

If you read through the lower hierarchy on the previous page and reflect on your entity, at what place in the hierarchy of needs do your team members find themselves?

And if you take a moment to consider yourself, where do you find yourself in the hierarchy? What is your current state? When you see your starting point in the hierarchy, write down what you would need in your professional role to climb to a higher place.

What you have just contemplated for yourself is important. This self-reflection creates insights and new motivation.

This is precisely what you need to do during and after your conversations with your team members: reflect on their perspectives.

- *What are their needs*
- *How do they feel?*
- *What do they want?*

What can you do as a leader to help them feel differently, see new needs and opportunities, develop stronger feelings of motivation, and begin to feel differently in their work roles?

Simply telling your team that you appreciate them creates a strong sense of security is the simplest and most obvious thing to fulfil their need for security, level two in the hierarchy of needs. These words can inspire them internally to climb to step three in the hierarchy of needs.

It is incredibly important as a leader to understand that if a team member is not satisfied with their needs at one level, they will not be satisfied with any of the higher levels. Therefore, as a leader, you need to confirm in your conversations that each respective need is fulfilled. Consider that the right salary and praise/appreciation (feedback at level

1) are sufficient to meet a team member's needs at level two, making them feel secure.

Level two is the critical turning point.
I see level two as the central level from a developmental and employer perspective. Level two is crucial for whether the team member is at the workplace solely for the sake of the salary. When a person's needs at level 1 and level 2 are met, the organisation, leadership, and team member are at a critical turning point.

If the leader has discovered the person's 'why' through conversation - their drives, obstacles, motivation, and needs - it may well be that the team member is at the workplace solely for the salary.

At that point, it is up to the organisation how many resources should be allocated. Is it functioning well for the person to come to the workplace for the salary alone, and are the tasks being performed as expected while the person operates satisfactorily with their team members? Or does it require more from the individual?

It is often at this turning point that I, as a consultant, have been asked for consultation for various reasons, such as: *The employee is not doing what they are supposed to do. The employee is not functioning in the group. The employee is spreading a bad atmosphere. The employee is late for work. The employee is rude to customers, etc.*

It is fundamentally important to understand that if a person finds themselves in situations like those examples above, they do not feel they are at levels 3, 4, or 5. Examples from the team member's perspective from page 335:

<u>Love and belonging.</u>
I do not feel included in the team; I do not experience feelings of belonging or participation. I do not feel genuine connection or community.

<u>Esteem.</u>
I do not feel appreciated as a person and am not fully satisfied with my role.

<u>Self-actualization.</u>
I do not feel that I have the opportunity to contribute, develop, and make a significant difference.

If a person does not experience satisfaction beyond level two and does not see within themselves the potential to reach level 3.

<u>How can employers believe that they can get the team member to:</u>
- Perform better?
- Be a source of joy at work?
- Arrive at the workplace on time?
- Function better in the group?
- Be nicer to customers?

*This is purely a matter of leadership. Understanding and insight into this reality distinguish great leaders from mediocre ones. **For how can we place demands on a person if we do not understand them, know what they need, and motivate them?***

You have previously read in the book about a person's self-concept, human identity, which is how they perceive themselves. The psychology underlying this is crucial to understand as a leader.

Can you, as a leader, motivate and inspire a person at level 2 to want to grow and develop by helping them envision their identity changing into something else, something they are not today?

If so, you have likely created the inner motivation required for the individual to feel new needs that they want to satisfy as a person and in their professional role, thereby striving to reach higher in the hierarchy of needs.

You need to constantly motivate and inspire.
I will reiterate the hierarchy of needs: what are your team members really saying to you in their everyday interactions? When they speak, and considering what you see and hear in their behaviour, attitude, and performance levels?

This _may_ encompass what they feel and want to convey to you.

Please help me reach my full potential.

Make me feel appreciated, valuable, and significant.
This boosts my confidence and enhances my self-esteem.

Make me feel accepted in the team so that I can be myself.

Make me feel secure.
When I feel that I can fail, I am more willing to take risks and can contribute more.

Treat me with respect.

The ability for you, in your leadership role, to help another person change their identity to someone they never thought they could become is incredible.

On page 336, I asked you to contemplate where you and your team members currently find yourselves in the hierarchy of needs. What are your respective starting points and current situations?

Your task is to ascertain your team members' current situation and strategically develop them into a new position where individuals grow as human beings and evolve to new levels in their professional roles. When you know each person's current situation, it's through your conversations that you motivate, inspire, and develop. Below, I break down Maslow's hierarchy of needs from a team member's perspective into the simplest descriptions from a "I" perspective: What is your and your team members' current situation? Ask in your individual conversations with your entity what they feel and then ask challenging follow-up questions until you know exactly where they are and what they want.

I develop others and our operations!

I am passionate!

I will lead us forward!

I want to, and I can!

I must!

As you can see, the will and knowledge are already present at level two. Your job as a leader is to create security and motivation so that your team members feel a strong need to climb higher. Your ambition is to create feelings of drive and determination.

What behaviours do you want in the workplace, what attitude do you want? Exhibit what you desire every day, and it will follow you if you listen to them, understand their "why," build trust, challenge them, and develop them. They want to follow a role model and an example. Be the one who points out the direction and shows them the way.

Curiosity: Abraham Maslow first described his model and theory in 1943 in an article titled "A Theory of Human Motivation" and expanded it in his book "Motivation and Personality" in 1954. Since 1970, there has been a debate about whether the theory should be expanded to eight levels. The additional three levels described are:

- *Cognitive needs*: A hunger for knowledge and an understanding of the world and our place in it. A strong inner drive and curiosity to learn, develop intellectually, and a strong desire to explore new ideas and concepts to create a higher sense of meaning and predictability in life.
- *Aesthetic needs*: Beauty, form, creativity, and artistic expression. Humans fulfil this need through the creation of art, music, literature, theatre, and other forms of aesthetic creation to evoke feelings of harmony and visual pleasure.
- *Transcendent needs*: Humans feel the need to understand and discover things beyond the mundane and material, as well as a strong drive to find meaning and purpose in life through deeper connections to spirituality, spiritual development, and the transcendental. Here, there are questions about existence, consciousness, and a cosmic order/spiritual dimension.

(Maslow + Employee Conversations = "Why" = Profitability)

Allow me to return to the title before the section on Abraham Maslow. I wanted to share my thoughts on the hierarchy of needs before discussing my methodology regarding employee conversations. *This is because the better you understand your team members' needs, the better, more concrete, and individually tailored employee conversations you can hold.* When you have well-prepared employee conversations, you consciously tie together feedback, coaching, and delegation into a cohesive whole that you systematically drive forward.

The employee conversation is the perfect opportunity for you as a leader to make your team members feel extra important, seen, and significant.

You take the time for them, you listen to them, they get to be in the spotlight, and they can give you feedback.

You have the opportunity to shape, fine-tune, and align your entity so that everyone together creates a whole.

- They get time to prepare and express how they feel as individuals and as a team, how they experience their working situation, their tasks, and their goal images.

- You can invest time in private conversations that are individually tailored so that everyone in your entity understands more about the bigger picture, sees the broader perspective, and thereby grasps the importance of all team members and all tasks being significant.

- You will have the opportunity to create an open discussion forum around the vision, mission, values, and your soft values.

- You will have the opportunity to express how you believe they contribute to the team and results, as well as how they have performed individually and functioned within the team since your last employee conversation.

- Together you get time to set individual goals and sub-goals for the next conversation, as well as to determine how often, when, and in what form you will follow up.

- You can talk about how the team member experiences it when you coach and provide feedback.

- You have an excellent opportunity to motivate and challenge.

Maintain the mindset that all your team members are puzzle pieces. Not everyone can excel at everything, so all puzzle pieces will look different. It can and needs to take time to fit all the puzzle pieces together. *What you know before the employee conversation are the insights you've gained in your previous conversations with each team member. You certainly know more about the "iceberg" and their needs in certain cases than in others. This is an ongoing process; people change, icebergs change. Emotions, goal images, motivations, and the obstacles people perceive to reach their goals change.*

What you need to have clarified before you schedule employee conversations is exactly what you rely on your entity to deliver together. You need to paint a picture of your completed puzzle in front of you and how you will contribute.

What is required for the expectations from your organisation of you in your role to be fulfilled, and what is needed for the puzzle to be complete? What must be done daily for the puzzle to be completed, and what is not being done? What kind of culture do you want to contribute to every day?

You know that it is likely that some in your entity today go to work for the salary and do not feel the need to contribute more or climb higher. You also know that it is likely that some in your entity want to contribute more and aim higher than you are aware of. The employee conversation gives you the opportunity to dig deeper and become more aware. The more aware you are, the better you will fit the puzzle pieces together.

Everyone wants to experience energy and feel secure; *everyone* wants a clear direction. This is something you can ensure in your employee conversations. Take the time to discuss the vision, your mission, the feedback culture, ambitions, and goal images.

Also, refer back to your notes from coaching conversations to reinforce that you remember what has been important to each team member in terms of personal motivation, goals, and obstacles. This creates energy, provides security, gives everyone a common, clear direction, and this wholeness fosters motivation and engagement.

Regardless of where your team members are in the hierarchy of needs at their current state, you can create motivation and engagement with the right goals and sub-goals.

There is much talk about goals; my opinion is that the most important factors in achieving goals is that they are individually tailored and applicable, and that results are followed up.

Example for a team member at level 2:
This team member should receive clear, achievable goals as well as a challenging goal.
- *Make common team goals and ambitions visible, and from this, develop one or more individual goals.*
- *Follow up on checklists, discuss execution and quality.*
- *Talk about general tasks and what is required for them to be considered completed.*
- *Hold the team member accountable for an achievable goal.*
- *Set dates for all follow-ups.*

This team member needs praise, guidance, and clarity. Tell them: "I know what you are good at, it is 'this', 'this', and 'this'. What I require from you every day is exactly that: to be on time, to be nice to your colleagues, and to share our vision. I require that of you every day. I believe in you and that you can develop significantly. I am here for you."

Example for a team member at level 3 or higher:
This team member should receive individual, very challenging goals.
- *Ask them: "What do you want to learn?"*
- *Suggest tasks you are doing today that you can delegate to the team member.*
- *Give the team member time to develop alternative goal images that you can discuss together. Which can be implemented in the operations? You challenge the goal images.*
- *The team member sets timelines, and you challenge the timelines.*

- *Set dates for all follow-ups.*

This team member needs praise and follow-ups. Tell them: "I appreciate what you do for me and the organisation; you are significant. I see that you have great potential, and I will challenge you because I want to see you grow."

Recommendations for an employee conversation:
- Allocate sufficient time and have a little buffer.
- Hold the conversation in a place where you will not be interrupted or stressed.
- Listen much, much more than you speak during the conversation.
- Take handwritten notes during the conversation to keep it at a human level; this opens up for deeper discussions.
- And of course, do not have your mobile phone in the same room. Otherwise, the mobile phone is more important than the person in front of you. As a leader, you develop people, not mobile phones.

After an employee conversation:
Once new goal images are set, inform them that you will follow up and use feedback and coaching as you want to see the team member exceed the goals.

As a leader, you want to energise your team members.
A person can be motivated or demotivated solely through words. Words that show the individual that you believe in their skills, see their potential, and have high expectations that you know they can fulfil.

This is referred to in psychology as the Rosenthal effect (also known as the Pygmalion effect). This demonstrates that expectations (both others' and one's own) influence a person's performance. Robert Rosenthal said, *"If I change my thoughts about a person, I can influence and change that person's outcomes, both positively and negatively."* He also stated, *"My belief or thought about a certain individual affects that person's behaviour. Thus, my thoughts and attitudes are not solely my own; they influence others."*

If you articulate clear expectations and provide your team member with support, encouragement, and resources, it can lead to them performing in the expected manner.

Do not be afraid to think more of your team members than they do of themselves.

Challenge their identity as much and as often as you can to help them grow and develop.

Michelangelo Buonarroti (1475-1564) has expressed many wise, thought-provoking, and inspiring quotes about potential.

> *"The greater danger for most of us is not that our aim is too high and we miss it, but that it is too low and we achieve it."*
> *- Michelangelo di Lodovico Buonarroti Simoni*

"I just sculpt away the excess material to reveal the sculpture that is already there."-
Michelangelo di Lodovico Buonarroti Simoni

Reflection, Chapter 7

1. Reflect on how you have fostered growth and developed individuals, how you are currently working strategically, and what you can further develop.

2. Reflect on how often and in what form you create documented forums for discussion linked to profitability that are followed up. What can you improve?

3. What mindset do you have, and how do you work strategically? Do you spend most of your time, energy, and resources on symptoms that arise (fires you need to put out), or do you analyse and address the underlying causes of the fires?

4. Are you working to map your organisation by creating a risk matrix, as shown on page 334, where you assess the factors in your organisation that create "*Low/short-term risk: High sense of trust and motivation*," and "*High/long-term risk: Low sense of trust and motivation*"? This is a tool for you to work strategically on the underlying causes, i.e., "High/long-term risk," the factors that may not affect your entity and operations the most today but could create significant long-lasting costly issues in the future.

5. Reflect on the importance of you as a leader fully understanding your team members' "why" and its connection to the human and professional hierarchy of needs = How can you individually motivate them towards development? Additionally, reflect on your own "why" and how it connects to your human and professional needs = What motivates you to develop, and what is your next step?

6. Reflect on and analyse the employee conversations you have conducted. Are they structured? What can you develop, and can you challenge more?

F

Can you see the stones?

It is in the moments you challenge yourself
that you can achieve more than you believe.
Niclas Timmerby

If I may return to my quote at the beginning of the previous chapter: *Profitability and growth are ultimately measured by how many people you have developed."* What I mean by this quote is that profitability and growth can only occur when the leader challenges and develops themselves and their team members. There is no other way.

Can you see the stones, how everything is interconnected?
To develop in your leadership, you need to do things you are not doing today; you need to listen in a way you are not doing today; you need to speak in a way you are not doing today. You need to do many things you are not doing today. Development requires courage.

I often explain this by painting a scenario. It is foggy outside and you are safely standing on a very stable stone. The stones closest to you are visible and clear, so if you were to take a step towards any of them, there would be no risk for you. But the further away you look from where you stand, the harder it is to see the stones in the fog, and a bit further from where you stand, you cannot see the stones at all. So for every step you take, you need more courage. ***This, is your leadership.***

The stone you stand on and those you can see clearly are the things you have fully mastered, that you are not worried about, and that everyone in your entity knows you do well. *This is not where you develop.*

The stones that are a bit further away are ones you can easily jump to, but you do not see them clearly, and there is a risk that you might miss. *This is where you develop, when you expose yourself to situations and tasks that you do not feel comfortable with. This is where you build your confidence and self-esteem.*

Then there are stones that you can only glimpse and those you cannot see at all. *This is where you develop the most. This is where you create a new image of yourself, a new identity, a new self-image; parts of your self-concept. Leadership is the courage to become something you are not today. Be grateful and curious when situations arise that you are not used to handling. Think: Now I have the chance to develop.*

You remember the section about your comfort zone on page 106?
In all the situations where you dare to challenge yourself, your (and others') old truths, your routines, and the habits you are comfortable with - this is where you develop. It is there you take steps towards a new identity; it is there you take steps up Maslow's hierarchy of needs; it is right there that you change your self-concept. How you see yourself today is not how you necessarily need to see yourself tomorrow. The choice is yours.

G - I - F - T
The leader is the one everyone sees as the person who should show the way forward. It is a vulnerable position. Many look at the leader with

scrutinising and critical eyes. Are you a role model? Are you a good person? Do you motivate and inspire? Do you follow the vision and act in accordance with the values?

Be kind to yourself, be proud of every step you take on your journey of self-leadership and leadership, and be consistent in creating space for self-reflection, even if only for a few minutes. Here, I share the full theory I have worked on for over fifteen years: "G-I-F-T." This comes after I have reflected on what I need to do as a person to feel a sense of peace within and how I need to think and act in daily situations. This is a form of personal development in everyday life, where I get a good image of myself and only measure myself against myself. G-I-F-T creates self-awareness and good habits.

The letters stand for Generosity, humillty, thankFulness and responsibiliTy,

"It takes 20 years to build a reputation and five minutes to destroy it. If you think about it, you will do things differently.
- Warren Buffet

These qualities are like your character traits that reflect your moral compass in front of others who observe your behaviour and sense your attitude. To develop, nurture, challenge, feel, and balance these qualities helps you in your self-leadership, creates security and inner peace, builds your reputation, and fosters long-term positive relationships with others.

I have written brief sections about each quality to provoke thoughts and create self-reflection within you. How can you more consciously use and develop these four qualities? See this theory as an accessible methodology and a tool in everyday life both personally and professionally. There will come times and situations when you feel you are drifting away from the person and leader you want to be; then G-I-F-T is a simple and effective way to find your way back to the direction you want to maintain.

G - I - F - T - Generosity

The word "generosity" comes from the Latin word "generōsus," which can be translated as "of noble birth." I believe the fundamental meaning fits perfectly into our society, for what could be nobler than being generous? The Danish-French artist Jacob Abraham Camille Pissaro (1830-1903) wisely said: *"Blessed are those who see beautiful things in simple things where others see nothing."*

If you want to feel good inside, the choice to be generous must be one of the most enjoyable. Few things make us feel as good as when we, through words and actions, give of ourselves to other people.

Giving to a fellow human brings you happiness, self-esteem, energy, positivity, and well-being. Generosity comes in two steps:

1. You receive when you give in words and actions. *We can donate money to charity events on television and similar causes, which is great, but giving of yourself through words and actions is something entirely different. When you give of yourself as a person, rather than in the form of material things, you receive a genuine sense of happiness and pride in return.*

2. You receive the most when you do not demand or expect anything back. *Everyone feels good receiving appreciation and recognition, but as psychologist Wayne Walter Dyer said, "If you need approval, you are on dangerous ground."*

If you are generous and become angry, sad, frustrated, or upset when you do not receive anything in return, there is a risk that you will suffer from your action instead of it benefiting you. The interesting thing is that the person who does not thank you for your generous act has no idea of the reactions it causes. So, be generous in words and actions without expecting people to thank you. Be proud of your actions and take the opportunity to praise yourself. When people see and appreciate your generosity, just enjoy it.

Telling people what they can become and what they can achieve is among the finest and most generous things we can do for another person. Unfortunately, people's own negative thoughts often set barriers and limitations in life. This is where you, as a leader, can create wonders. When you show that you believe they can reach further and higher, you provide the positive effect that can make the difference for that person to find the path to a new identity.

G - I - F - T - Humility

The very word comes from the Latin word "humilitas," which derives from the word "humus," meaning the earth. Humility is a significant and important trait. Common synonyms for being humble include being unpretentious and respectful. People perceive humble individuals as extraordinarily kind and sympathetic. They are easy to like because they do not trample on others and do not speak ill of others. What characterizes people with humility is that they are free of pretensions; they have no need to assert themselves before others.

When I coach in the sports world, I often say that the first rule is to always display "humble authority"; to always present the player/person you want to be. You should never deviate from the image of what you want to be and never lower the minimum standard you want to maintain. When you act with humble authority in every training/session, you will ultimately come to truly believe that you can become exactly the player/person you aspire to be. The player will want to train like the player they want to be, and they will adopt the same posture and body language as the player they wish to emulate. What kind of leader do you want to be? Enter every situation with humility, and you will automatically gain self-awareness.

Mohandas Karamchand Gandhi believed that it is impossible to be true without humility. (He received the title "Mahatma" as an honorific after his significant work for India's independence movement and his commitment to non-violence and peace. "Mahatma" comes from Sanskrit and means "great soul" or "great spirit.")

Taoism describes a wise person as someone who has achieved "Tao"; "To achieve harmony and balance with the universe. A wise person acts without claiming the results; they achieve their worth and display no arrogance – they do not wish to show their superiority." I translate this to mean that a humble person is secure within themselves and therefore has no need to boast or insist on being right, which benefits them in all social contexts in life.

A study in the Harvard Business Review by Jim Collins and his colleagues demonstrates that humility is a multidimensional leadership trait, which includes self-awareness, self-insight, openness, and the ability to have perspective.

*The Spanish priest Josemaría Escrivá de Balaguer y Albas (1902-1975)
identified signs of a lack of humility. Here are fifteen of them:*

1. Believing that what you say or do is better than what others say or do.

2. Always wanting to go your own way.

*3. Arguing with stubbornness or audacity, whether you are right or
wrong.*

*4. Giving your opinion when others have not asked for it, or when love
does not require it.*

5. Looking down on someone else's viewpoint.

6. Not viewing your gifts and opportunities as a loan.

7. Using yourself as an example in conversations.

*8. Speaking ill of yourself so that others will think well of you or
contradict you.*

9. Excusing yourself when you are corrected.

10. Taking pleasure in praise and compliments.

11. Becoming upset when others receive more recognition.

12. Refusing to perform lesser tasks.

13. Seeking to stand out.

*14. Referring to your honesty, genius, skill, or professional competence
in conversation.*

15. Being ashamed of lacking certain possessions.

G - I - F - T - Thankfulness

> *""He who is not satisfied with what he has
> will never be satisfied with what he gets."*
>
> *- Socrates (c. 469-399 BC)*

When genuine thankfulness exists within us, we feel good inside.
Socrates' quote illustrates that the same concerns existed before our
calendar era, albeit in different forms. People walk around complaining
instead of being deeply thankful for what they have, which is tragic. In
our society, it is very easy to always chase something, to always want
something better, newer, or finer. It's easy to see that this "chasing" is
not beneficial for us as humans.

Ask yourself whether you are satisfied with what you have, that you do
not urgently need anything more. If your answer is yes, right now you
have a feeling of thankfulness within you. In this moment, you are
experiencing an increased production and release of the following
wonderful hormones and chemicals: dopamine, serotonin, endorphins,
and oxytocin. Be genuinely thankful often; it benefits you by improving
your mood, reducing your stress, and creating a sense of well-being
within you.

*"Do not spoil what you have by desiring what you do not have; remember that
what you now have was once among the things you only hoped to attain."*
- Unknown."

You determine what happiness is.
There is so much external influence in our lives, so many people who
want to affect us, telling us what we should feel and think. A sense of
thankfulness here can be that you actually determine this for yourself.
Why should anyone else influence you and dictate what makes you
happy? No one but you knows what happiness means for you.
Happiness can be many different things—such as the ability to breathe,
walk, see, hear, having a job, and so on. You decide when to turn off the
TV commercials, when to stop scrolling, and when to minimize the

impact of social media on you. It is often said that money cannot buy happiness. I believe this to be true. Money can never create genuine, long-lasting happiness. Money can certainly provide material happiness but never spiritual happiness.

G - I - F - T - Responsibility

If we do not take the responsibility we feel we should in our personal and professional lives, we do not feel good; it is about our character. It is what we want to stand up for, an inner human drive and pride combined with the desire not to disappoint others.

"Only when we fully take personal responsibility for our attitude and behavior do we change our lives in the direction we want."
- Niclas Timmerby

You can only take full responsibility when you understand.
In your role as a leader, it is essential to have full awareness of goals and ambitions. It is your task to continuously ask your immediate supervisor: *"Is there anything that has changed regarding our entity's goals and ambitions?"* This ensures that you can work proactively and with good foresight for your team members.

If you do not fully understand a goal, take responsibility.
Ask follow-up questions until you are fully aware of exactly what is required in terms of time, quality, and specified criteria for the goal to be considered met in terms of results or outcomes.

If you are uncertain about your mandate, ask questions. If you are unsure about when follow-ups should occur and in what form, ask questions. If you are uncertain about which non-economic (personnel, equipment, materials) and economic resources (specific budget, financing) have been allocated to achieve the goal, ask questions.

*Request to be involved when the allocation of resources is set up, ask to be part of the planning process and risk assessments. **This is taking responsibility for goals.***

Then, as a leader, it is your task to establish strategies, plan the daily work, and allocate tasks within your entity effectively so that the goal is met.

My friend Tina Thörner wrote in one of my earlier books that when she decided to become one of the best in the world in co-driving in rallying, a mental trainer told her that there is a formula that would help her on her journey. The formula was: "**Take 100% RESPONSIBILITY—for everything you say, do, act, and react while eliminating excuses and justifications.**"

I consider this to be a magical formula for *those who are the best at talking us out of situations and opportunities* - it is <u>always</u> ourselves.

"Whatever you hear or see is not true until you tell it to yourself.

How often you then repeat it to yourself determines how much impact it will have on your life."
- Niclas Timmerby

Taking responsibility as a leader requires every day one or more of the following factors: courage, integrity, and the ability to stand by your actions. The more you work on your self-leadership, the better you can handle responsibility in these situations. Good self-leadership gives you a greater ability to manage and regulate your emotions. The better your ability, the better you can handle stress, pressure, difficult decisions, and daily challenges in a balanced and constructive manner. This ability is referred to in psychology as having good emotional regulation.

Your interpersonal skills.

Do you have the ability to listen actively and adapt your behavior and communication style to different situations and people? Do you communicate clearly, handle conflicts well, and build positive relationships with others? If so, you possess strong interpersonal skills and have excellent conditions for creating a positive work environment and developing people.

Interpersonal skills refer to the ability to interact and communicate effectively with others.

We all have different circumstances; we all carry different types of emotional baggage in life in the form of memories or experiences from our childhood and youth.

Some things we do not forget, and these shape how we consciously and unconsciously take responsibility and how we handle what we go through in life.
Sometimes we are aware of this, and sometimes we are not.

These memories and experiences influence our interpersonal skills, or as it can also be expressed: social competence.

"Do not complain about your circumstances when there are others who have none."
- Niclas Timmerby

Your interpersonal skills can be developed:

- Practice active listening and ask follow-up questions.
- Develop your empathetic ability by practicing humility.
- Continuously seek honest feedback at levels 2 and 4.
- Develop your self-awareness in interpersonal situations.
- Conflicts are training opportunities.
    - *Do you show respect?*
    - *Are you open to dialogue?*
    - *Are you attuned to what the person is feeling?*
- Practice how you communicate verbally and non-verbally. View yourself from an outside perspective:
    - *What body language do you have?*
    - *What tone of voice do you use?*
    - *Do you adapt your communication to the situation and the person/people involved?*
- If you want to understand other people's perspectives, behaviors, and attitudes, you really need to want to understand their needs and conditions.

Every time you consciously prioritize other people's needs and interests over your own, you concretely practice your interpersonal skills.

Taking responsibility is an active, conscious, free, and voluntary choice that only benefits you. The same applies to humility, generosity, and thankfulness.

Deliberately and continuously develop these aspects within yourself and watch how you change, how your relationships change, how your professional life changes, and how you transform your future.

Reflection, Section F

1. Reflect on a typical working day and consider how often you challenge your thinking. When you challenge your thinking, you also simultaneously challenge your feelings of security. Use my tool if you wish: In every situation that arises, both personally and professionally, try to listen more than you usually do. I see this as the simplest path to development. *When I am in nature, I sometimes stand completely still and close my eyes; something truly magical reveals itself. The more I focus on just listening, the more I hear from my surroundings.* It is exactly the same in all situations in life. *"If you want to derive concrete and long-term value from a conversation, choose your words carefully or refrain from speaking."*

2. Reflect on the four qualities I describe: Generosity, humIlity, thankFulness and responsibiliTy. Reflect with great self-awareness on the situations in which you utilise these qualities, how you employ them, and how you can use this theory in your daily life as a tool in your leadership.

3. How often can you practice your interpersonal skills? The most critical factor for all forms of growth, profitability, and success in any type of entity in the world is as follows: ***How leadership creates a healthy culture, builds trust, and simultaneously challenges the people in the team to their own development.***

If an entity does not achieve the desired results, the solution lies in the factor I mentioned in italics above (3). This is my own experience after working as a leader, consultant, and leadership developer for over 20 years.

G

Trust-based leadership: you are building a house.

———————————————

A leader does not raise their voice; they raise the level.
Niclas Timmerby

In Chapter 1, I wrote that later in the book I would present the final decisive factor for **the Foundation**, and that last factor is trust-based leadership. First, allow me to summarise. <u>The Foundation</u> consists of the five sections in which you make your choices as a leader. It is crucial for you in your leadership to be aware of what your choices are likely to lead to; this is what I have described in sections A-E, which aim to create awareness and active choices.

<u>Your conscious active choices build the Foundation,</u>
<u>which is the culture.</u>

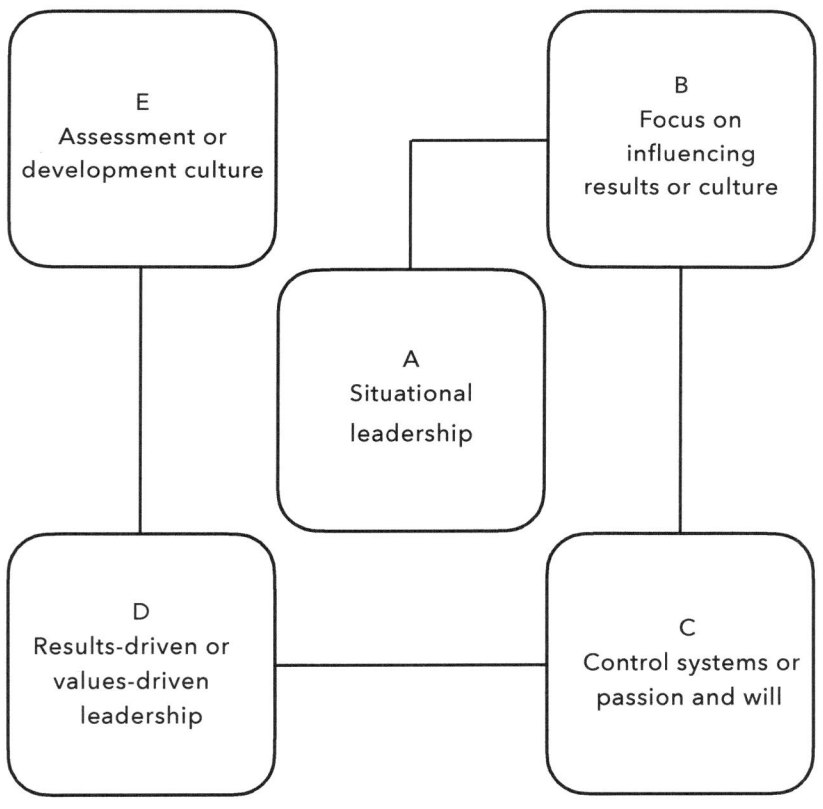

Once **the Foundation** is established, the next part of the book will address **the Process**, which creates *the Formula for profitability, growth and development.*

$$IH \dashrightarrow C \dashrightarrow EH : (E = potential^\infty) \dashrightarrow R = P$$

Trust vs. Confidence.

There are numerous articles and research studies that explore the differences and similarities between trust and confidence. A Google search on the difference in English yields over 250 million results. The difference can be summarised as follows:

<u>*Trust* is based on emotions; it is an emotional phenomenon.</u>

<u>*Confidence* is based on actions and performance.</u>

I want to clarify that my thoughts on the importance of trust are my own theory, grounded in my work as a consultant and leader, as well as the results I have achieved with various entities and individuals.

Confidence is good, but trust is on a completely different level.
Confidence is very beneficial; we can have confidence in someone's experiences, knowledge, reliability, integrity, title, behaviour, and various abilities that generate good results. Confidence is built through what has been experienced and/or observed.

This is certainly good, but it is <u>not</u> confidence that drives team members to run through fire for one another. It is <u>not</u> confidence that leads soldiers to trust each other blindly and without hesitation in battle. *<u>It is trust. It is emotions.</u>*

That is why a title can never create trust; a title can only create confidence. A person with a title can then create trust. *The opposite of confidence can be seen as distrust. The opposite of trust can be seen as suspicion.*

Lacking confidence involves a lack of belief or conviction. Lacking trust involves a lack of feeling secure or safe in a relationship or situation.

A lack of confidence can create feelings of uncertainty and, consequently, feelings of distance between people and a lack of collaboration. A lack of trust can create fears of being hurt or betrayed.

Reflect on your closest relationships: with your relatives, a partner, parents, and children. There, trust exists because the relationships are built on __emotions__. In these relationships, you feel <u>pride instead of confidence</u> when someone achieves a success.

According to Bengt and Lotta Wiström, trust is having the courage to act without knowing. To be able to trust and put your life in another person's hands without truly knowing.

To have such strong faith in yourself and others that you dare to take steps without having all the answers or knowing exactly how it will turn out (you remember "the stones").

Striving for a good level of trust as a person and a leader has many advantages. It increases your flexibility and adaptability; you develop your understanding and respect for people's differences and your empathic ability; you are less likely to be suspicious and anxious. Above all, it fosters the atmosphere you want to build in your culture, an atmosphere that includes openness and positive expectation, leading to better communication and feelings of increased belonging and community (level 3 in Maslow's hierarchy of needs).

You now know that trust can be the difference that leads a team member to stop going to work solely for a paycheck and instead go there to share in community and belonging. This is a significant, wonderful step. This is the reward of leadership: to inspire another person to want more in life, to help them understand and realise that there is more to life than they believed. Trust can change people's identities and can transform the most hardened bearer of a negative culture into your most valuable team member. _Imagine if you were the first person to show that individual trust in their life.._

Trust.
I see trust as a prerequisite within an entity to create a culture of self-sufficient team members and long-term motivation, where each team member strives for personal development.

Resistance exists in all forms of entities: at home, in the workplace, in the sports world, in schools and universities, etc. **Your concrete tool to counteract the level of resistance is the degree of trust.**

Your coaching, feedback, and employee discussions, as well as your developmental methodologies, are crucial as they create acceptance of each team member's role.
If a team member does not feel trusted, it may be because they feel they are not in the right place or do not feel fully recognized, valued, seen, or respected. In your conversations, you have the opportunity to create trust, and _when the person tells you their "why," you have taken the step from creating confidence to creating trust_.

The best explanation of what trust is comes from Patrick M. Lencioni: *"Trust is being open and vulnerable and knowing that you are still accepted by your surroundings."*

Where can you be your true self and show vulnerability? That is where you feel trust from those around you. Often, it is with your partner, a relative, a colleague, or perhaps your best friend.

How do you create trust?
I see it as having four methods:

1. When you, as a leader, show vulnerability.
2. When a team member knows that they are allowed to fail.
3. When the realisation occurs within the team member that everyone's unique traits are not a risk but a necessity for harnessing the full potential of the entity. (Alone is not strong.)
4. When the team member demonstrates genuine curiosity in wanting to know more than superficial things about their fellow members in the entity.

Your willingness to show vulnerability as a leader is fundamental to creating trust. You can build trust in an instant during a single situation. This might involve you:

- Sharing mistakes you've made in your life.
- Discussing failures in your professional career.
- Sharing personal experiences that have taught you important lessons you now carry as strengths.
- Talking about significant life events that have shaped your values and moral principles as a person.
- Genuinely listening to people and asking follow-up questions.

- Taking the time to show empathy and genuine understanding when a team member is unwell.
- Clearly standing up against injustices.
- Asking for help.
- Encouraging individual initiatives within clear boundaries.
- Having the courage to delegate challenging tasks.
- Seeking feedback at levels 2 and 4 because you do not see yourself as fully learned.

The Trust Wheel.

"When someone claims to be fully learned, you know that person has much to learn."
- Niclas Timmerby

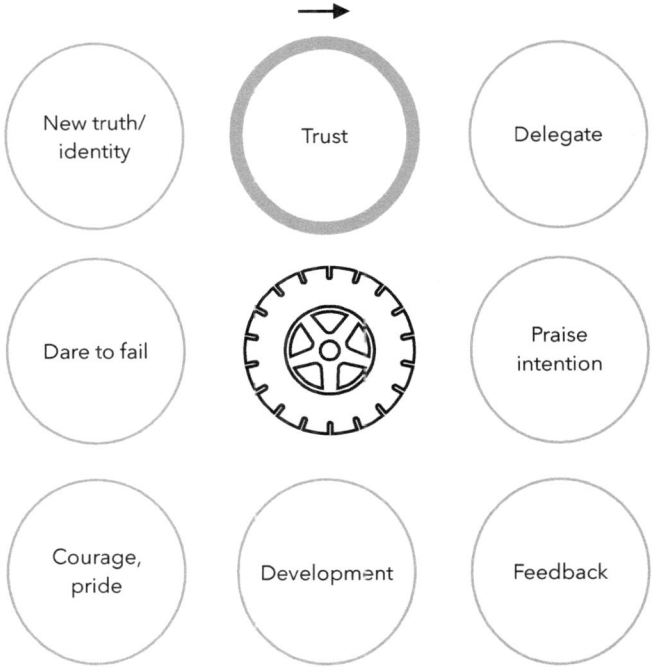

The Trust Wheel on the previous page is a methodology I teach in leadership training. The purpose is to highlight how methodical and strategic work can help team members grow, desire to develop, and contribute more through trust.

The wheel is set in motion when you, as a leader, actively demonstrate _trust_ in the team member by _delegating_ a challenging task. (If the task is not challenging, the person will not grow.) When the work begins and feedback is provided in your follow-up conversations, it is not uncommon for things not to have gone entirely according to plan. This is where you show support by _appreciating intentions_. In conjunction with your early follow-ups, you use _feedback at levels 1 and 2_. Level 2 creates _development_, and the team member grows; level 1 fosters _courage and pride_ within the person, and the team member flourishes. When an individual feels they are developing and possesses courage and pride, they are more inclined to take _initiative_ because they know you allow them to make mistakes along the way, as you correct and adjust through feedback. The team member dares to take initiative and do things they have not done before because they now _dare to fail_. When the task is completed, you can provide feedback at level 3 on the points where the team member has developed and contributed the most.

The team member now has _a new truth, a new identity_ thanks to your strategic leadership.

Trust

Delegate

Praise intention

Feedback

Develop-ment

Courage, pride

Dare to fail

New truth/ identity

Lack of trust.

One of your primary responsibilities as a leader is to cultivate trust within your entity. This is crucial because the risks associated with a lack of trust can quickly diminish the potential of an entity, and the greatest risk is that skilled team members may eave simply because they do not feel a sense of trust.

As everyone fundamentally views their surroundings from a subjective perspective, the unfortunate result is that the differences among team members become a source of tension and conflict. When there is a lack of trust, it has a direct negative effect on the culture.

Patrick M. Lencioni described in his book *"The Five Dysfunctions of a Team"* the risks that arise when there is a lack of trust within a work team.

Step 1: Lack of trust

->

Step 2: Risk of gossip and conflicts

->

Step 3: The entity begins to feel a lack of engagement

->

Step 4: The entity stops holding each other and themselves accountable

->

Step 5: The entity ceases to care about results and the future of the entity and the organization

I see a significant risk with the lack of trust in that the people within the entity do not feel motivated or inspired. They become stuck in their needs hierarchy or, in the worst case, fall downwards. What is the actual potential of your entity, and is there a risk that several will descend to step 2, safety, where they begin to come to work primarily for the paycheck or start seeking other opportunities?

How does a lack of trust arise?

I see micromanagement as the direct operational opposite of demonstrating trust. Micromanagement can take many forms, which everyone perceives differently. The most common scenario is that the immediate supervisor does not allow the team member to work in peace but constantly wants updates about their status, how they are working, and what they are doing throughout the workday.

This creates a very clear impression that there is neither trust nor confidence present.

A manager in a job I held long ago asked all employees questions during our weekly conference calls such as: "What did you do between 3:30 PM and 5:00 PM last Friday? What will you do tomorrow between 8:00 AM and 12:00 PM?" This is a toxic way to lead.

Micromanagement can also manifest as sending texts or emails after working hours. This immediately places the team member in a very difficult situation.

If they read it and do not respond, it generates anxiety.

If they read it and respond, the team member has accepted the micromanagement.

Micromanagement stems from a need for control.
When a manager lacks the courage to lead with trust or confidence, only control mechanisms remain as alternatives. I reiterate my quote from page 229, who are you today, and who do you want to be?
"A manager directs people through controls. A leader develops people, teams, and organisations. A mentor develops leaders."

What are the three most important factors for an entity to achieve good liquidity and solidity while also maintaining a healthy culture and a good working environment?

The answer is simple:
1. The people in the entity, including yourself.
2. The people in the entity, including yourself.
3. The people in the entity, including yourself.

I write this as an extra emphasis on how crucial people are, including yourself. When a team member, due to micromanagement, begins to see themselves as a resource rather than as a human being, micromanagement has gone so far that feelings of trust and confidence are nonexistent.

Creativity is an important factor for growth and development.
As a leader, be mindful of anything that poses a risk that hinders or stops creativity. This is because a creative person finds it easier to think outside the usual comfort zone and has a tendency to want to challenge themselves; they are also more able to see and understand others' perspectives.

*Creativity nurtures and promotes pride and job satisfaction.
Control and micromanagement stifle creativity.*

Factors that can hinder creativity include not allowing failures, not providing time and resources for creative thinking, and structures within the organization/entity that create visible and/or invisible hierarchies that stifle individual initiatives, along with a lack of praise, support, and encouragement. What also hinders creativity is a culture of numerous meetings where participants are expected to listen without having a clear and meaningful purpose.

Another common factor is when an employee is loyal and informs the employer that they risk not being able to complete a specific task in time.

The employer might respond: "You can postpone the task or we will have to give the task to someone else."

At this point, the employee feels inadequate because they sense responsibility and loyalty towards their role, their colleagues, and the company.

Risk: The employee may quit, lose motivation and engagement, experience increased stress, demonstrate decreased effectiveness, exhibit diminished creativity, stop caring about results, and face a higher risk of sick leave.

The employer has two options when this factor arises:
1. **The easy path:** *See it as the employee needing to prioritize their time better and becoming more efficient.*

2. **The right path:** *Ask the employee how they are doing, how their family is doing, and if there are any circumstances the company is*

unaware of that may be affecting their time constraints. Ask the employee to share what their work situation has looked like over the past month or six months. Ask the employee: "What can we do for you to make things easier? We may not be able to conjure up a magical solution today, but you are important and valuable to us, so let's come up with a plan moving forward so you feel you can keep up."

Louise Bringselius, a Swedish associate professor and researcher in organisation and management, has written amazing books and speaks at lectures about psychological safety, trust-based leadership, trust-based governance, management, and shared leadership.

Regarding micromanagement, she wisely stated:
"We must be careful not to measure and follow up too much in detail. It is crucial that we focus more on effects, the significant results of our efforts, what truly matters."

About trust, she wrote:
"Trust is a management philosophy that involves choosing to believe that the people in core operations have the knowledge, judgment, and willingness to carry out their work well without micromanagement."

As a leader, you are building a house.
I came up with this analogy by chance while trying to explain the content of the book to an acquaintance. All of us leaders build houses. Sometimes we get new houses (newly established entities), but most often we receive used houses that have endured various types of weather *(read: leadership, external factors, and strong cultural bearers)*.
 Now the house is our responsibility, and in our first days, we conduct (consciously and unconsciously) a visual inspection of the

"property." Visually, we identify any deficiencies, risks, damages, and maintenance needs to gain an understanding of its current condition. You will also hear a lot of things in those first days that will influence you.

In your leadership role, you need to remain fundamentally objective, impartial, and neutral during this visual phase. *This means listening and being aware of personal feelings and opinions, taking extensive notes, reflecting, and then summarising your impressions based on facts.*

What kind of house do you want, and what house do you have?

You need to lay **the Foundation** and follow strategies that create a forward-leaning **Process**. The visual inspection provides you with visual insights; over the following months, you will have an essential task: to create fact-based documentation so you can see and understand the whole picture.

Your fact-based documentation gives you a clear, objective view of how the house is faring and what strategies you need to adopt to move the house from its current state to your desired state.

Once you have completed this work, you can establish strategies for maintenance and development. This is called a technical inspection in construction terms; you perform an objective and comprehensive assessment of the building's structural integrity, framework, construction, and materials.

With your objective perspective, you have the ability to see details from various subjective viewpoints, opinions, and arguments and, based on this, create an objective, reliable, and fair perspective of the bigger picture.

The foundation you lay is the culture you contribute to the most. There is nothing stronger than culture, which invisibly influences everyone who works, inhabits, or comes into contact with an entity.

If you change the culture, you change everything.
In all cultures, there are tensions, general feelings of anxiety, fears, and various forms of stress, such as social anxiety, performance anxiety, and work-related stress, which can arise from, among other things, stress, conflicts, work methods, overload, and uncertainty regarding work performance and belonging.

It is essential for you as a leader to understand where these feelings and thoughts originate:
- *What has actually happened or is at risk of happening?*
- *How have the strong cultural bearers influenced the atmosphere?*
- *Is everyone secure in their roles?*
- *Has everyone accepted their roles?*
- *Is everyone feeling intrinsic motivation, and if not, why?*
- *How have previous leaders set strategies regarding goals, vision, difficult conversations, staff meetings, and employee reviews?*

In your crucial initial conversations, you will understand who wants change and who resists it. You need to be strong and purposeful; your team members need to see the same leadership qualities in you every day. When you are challenged and provoked, you must remain calm and act in accordance with your self-leadership, daring to show who you are and what you stand for.

Keep your focus on the vision and do not be afraid to say: *"We are heading here; we are all heading here: that is why we come to work."*

377

The decisive factor is trust-based leadership.

For a house to keep all its components in place regardless of challenges inside or out, a sustainable roof is necessary.

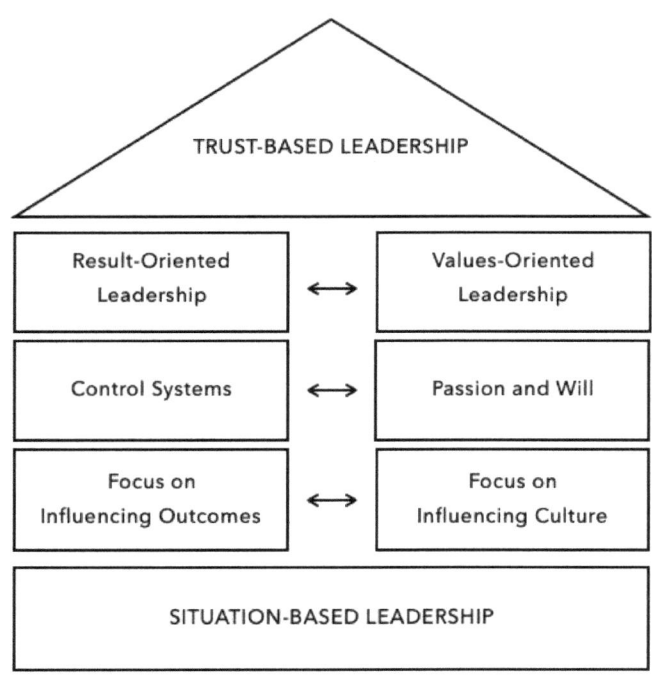

The trust you have within the entity is the roof of your house.

Trust is a fundamental building block for effective, honest, and sustainable leadership. When you, as a leader, demonstrate sincerity, honesty, and transparency, you create an atmosphere of openness and trust, which enables your entity to feel safe and comfortable sharing opinions, ideas, and concerns. Just as a well-constructed roof protects against the elements, trust protects against conflicts, misunderstandings, and poor communication, fostering a healthy work environment, a sustainable atmosphere, and a good culture.

Trust also provides a solid foundation for communication, collaboration, feedback, and coaching both within and outside the entity. When team members feel that they can trust their leader and one another, they naturally become more inclined to work together, share experiences, knowledge, and successes, and support each other on a genuine and human level, both in and out of the workplace.

This creates a positive aspect of the culture in which ideas and innovations can flow freely, much like how a strong, well-built roof offers stability and allows various parts of the house to function together.

A roof provides protection and security for those who live in a well-built house. In the same way, trust creates a sense of security and belonging within an entity. The important success factors of engagement and intrinsic motivation are stimulated by trust, as team members feel that the leadership is genuine and that they are valued and respected. They become even more motivated and inclined to strive toward the vision and mission, uphold the values, and strengthen their willingness to contribute concretely to the success of their entity and organization.

In your leadership role, it is essential to look beyond the current situation. When you learned to ride a bike, you learned to look beyond the front wheel; similarly, when you learned to drive a car, you focused further ahead, allowing you more time to correct and adjust for a safe journey. In sports, the same principle applies: the earlier you can anticipate an opponent's moves or the impact of nature, the more likely you are to win the ball, save a penalty or adjust the sails.

A sustainable roof is built to withstand stresses over a long period. *This is precisely how you should think about trust in your leadership.*

It needs to be able to withstand stress and risks, which is why you must build for the future and be well-prepared to modify, adjust, and correct over time. The essential element for building long-term trust is to continuously dare to be yourself, regardless of the situation. Your team members will then know that they see your true, genuine, authentic self.

Everything builds and strengthens trust over time.

Daring to put yourself out there, acknowledging mistakes, discussing your own failures, demonstrating sincerity, keeping your promises, refraining from spreading gossip, exhibiting trust, delegating, utilizing feedback at all four levels, and providing tailored coaching to create development and courage, along with open communication and transparency within the frameworks you have.

By continuously creating and maintaining a culture of trust, you lay a foundation for the well-being of the entity and the sustainability and success of the organization.

> *"When people have financial interests, they want a return.*
> *When people have emotional bonds, they want to contribute."*
> *- Simon Sinek*

The degree of trust is also felt by customers, suppliers, and partners. What are you as a leader doing strategically and proactively to strengthen trust in your entity? What is your current state; your work environment, atmosphere, and culture? Is the roof tight, or is there any leakage? What strategies do you employ to prevent leaks?

I see trust as the most crucial component of leadership.

If you have an entity where everyone on the team feels trust for one another, there are very few things that can throw the team off balance.

"Trust is like a bridge; it connects people and creates a strong community."
- Mother Teresa

Here is a brief summary to highlight the importance and benefits of your conscious and continuous work on trust.

Stability: Just as a strong roof provides stability and protection for the house, trust provides stability and security for the entity and organization. By creating a culture of trust, you, as a leader, can build a fundamental stability that allows team members to focus on their tasks without worrying or feeling uncertainty or fear.

Sustainability: A sustainable roof is designed to last over time and cope with stresses. Similarly, trust in leadership can be built and strengthened over time. By being consistently honest, transparent, and reliable in your leadership, you can create a sustainable foundation of trust that endures and supports the entity while providing a good basis for the organization's success.

Protection: Just as a roof protects against the elements, trust protects against conflicts, misunderstandings, and poor communication. When your team members feel they can genuinely trust you as their leader and that their opinions and concerns are taken seriously, the risk of conflicts decreases, and the opportunities for effective communication and collaboration increase.

Flexibility: A roof needs to be flexible to adapt to various weather conditions and stresses. Similarly, trust within your leadership needs to be flexible to adjust to changing circumstances and challenges. By creating a sustainable and stable foundation of trust, everyone within the entity can be more flexible and adaptable in their working methods and decision-making. When you then adjust and correct, your entity feels secure in the foundation you have created.

Development: A strong roof can serve as a foundation for building upon and developing the house. In the same way, trust within your leadership can act as a foundation for developing and promoting employees' growth and potential. When your team members feel genuine trust from you and that their contributions and performances are valued, they are more likely to strive for personal and professional development.

"Trust is like a key; it unlocks doors to deep and meaningful relationships."
- Nelson Mandela

"Trust is like a mirror; it shows you your true self-image and how you treat others."
- Mahatma Gandhi

Trust, a foundation for creating a winning culture.

Few words make coaches, leaders, CEOs, COOs, and management teams mouthwatering more than the term winning culture. Everyone wants a winning culture.

My view of how a winning culture is measured is by how frequently the entity wins together.

"Trust is like a seed; when planted and nurtured, it grows into a strong and vital relationship."
- Martin Luther King Jr

The frequency with which the entity achieves goals together is a key factor in creating winning teams, and that is <u>focus</u>.

When a team achieves small goals, large goals, and even nearly impossible goals, it all relies on <u>the entity's collective focus</u>. Everything we accomplish in personal or professional life, alone or as a team, comes down to one thing: focus. It is quite simple; the more focus invested in preparation and in the actual work, the more likely the goal is to be realised. In coaching conversations, I often say: *"If you maintain focus on what you focus on, you will yield the results of that focus. So what are you focusing on right now? What are you focusing on when you arrive at work? When you are speaking with a customer or preparing for a customer visit? When you return home to your family? When you are training for your well-being? How strong is your focus?"*

You may have read a famous quote by Albert Einstein: when I lecture on creativity and innovation, I reformulate it as: *"The definition of genius is to try different methodologies over and over again. Only then can the expectation of different results be realised."* What I mean by this is that the leader must encourage thinking outside the box to foster development within their entity, and this applies strongly to the work of achieving goals. Achieving a goal once can be managed by any entity; achieving success time and again is entirely different.

The very word focus comes from Latin (focus) and literally means "fire" or "bonfire." Originating, focus described the specific point where the sun's rays converged to create the conditions for warmth and fire. In ancient Rome, this central point was a crucial part of the technology for igniting fire and keeping it burning.

*Based on the historical meaning of the word, we can view goal images as **"something that should be ignited."***

A winning culture is created in the entities that have the best common focus. And they do not have this focus just once.
They have this razor-sharp focus over and over and over again.

You, as a leader, have the important task of creating a crystal-clear image of **exactly what** needs to be achieved and **exactly how** it should be achieved. **What exactly should be "ignited," and how will you do that?** It is also crucial that all team members understand what the potential sub-goals are for reaching the main goal; that is, what steps do we, as an entity, need to achieve to know that we are on the right track? What is your plan as a leader when you set a goal? Do you follow up individually or as an entity, or both, throughout the journey? How do you communicate the goal to ensure that everyone understands?

I remember when I did my military service and received an order from my superior. After issuing the order, the officer raised their voice and said, "Repeat 2110, Timmerby!" If I said it correctly, I had understood. I am not suggesting that this is a methodology to use in civilian life, but it does highlight how important it is for everyone to comprehend the goal image.

Backup.

What is fundamentally important for not losing focus or losing the built winning culture is always to be prepared and have one or more backup plans. The world around us is changing at a staggering pace. I had my first real job as a salesperson at KappAhl in Kristianstad in 1991 and have worked in various sales roles throughout my life. I have never experienced such significant changes as we have seen in the past 5-10 years, and it continues to change at an even faster rate. *Therefore, it is important to have well-prepared strategic backup plans that consider various potential scenarios that may arise in the future.*

Risk Assessment and Revision.

When you plan a goal, you also need to conduct a risk assessment. *What could happen along the way that might jeopardise achieving the goal?* Be clear about this when you communicate the goal image.

If it becomes evident during the journey that there is a significant risk of not reaching the goal despite your team members' efforts and your support, you need to revise the goal image.

Few things are as pointless and demotivating for people as working hard when they know they will not succeed.

This is where you excel in your leadership; before they even arrive at that insight or those thoughts, you have already revised the goal.

It may mean lowering expectations or adjusting parameters in the goal image. Every time your team members feel that they are winning is a victory for the entity and for the organisation. *Here to the right, you can read one of my absolute favourite quotes.*

"The pessimist complains about the wind.

The optimist hopes the wind will change.

The leader adjusts the sails."
- John C. Maxwell

Under Working Conditions.

The better the focus, the better the conditions to achieve goal images, greater productivity, and efficiency. The better the focus, the better the conditions for concentration; the better the concentration, the better tasks are performed with precision and engagement.

Once the work is initiated, it is important that you encourage, ask questions, and provide support to adapt the right level of feedback and coaching. Conduct follow-up conversations during the process and ask questions to understand. Observe attitudes and behaviours.

- *Is the goal image/sub-goal crystal clear?*
- *What is going well and less well in the work?*
- *What is easy and what is difficult?*
- *Does the team member feel supported by you?*
- *Does the team member want you to do something differently?*
- *Is the communication clear from you as a leader?*
- *Do you need to tailor follow-ups more to individuals?*
- *Do you show appreciation and give praise even for small victories?*
- *Do you encourage collaboration?*
- *How do you ensure that everyone is on the direction required to achieve the goal?*
- *Are you prepared to handle potential conflicts and other challenges?*
- *Have you allocated the right resources? Evaluate and revise if possible.*

- *How and where do team members direct their energy and attention? Is it on different things?*
- *How easily are your team members potentially distracted?*
- *Why are they distracted?*

Finalise the Goal.

One of the simplest things is often what gets forgotten. When a task is completed, no matter the outcome: How do you communicate to your entity that the task is finished?

Many companies start new goals on top of existing ones but forget to close the old ones. The consequence is a significant risk of creating confusion and reluctance to work with goal images. People cannot have too many goals active simultaneously as it leads to fragmented focus. In section B, I wrote about a study by Stephen Covey that showed:

- With 2-3 active goals at the same time, the entity achieves 2-3 goals.
- With 4-10 active goals at the same time, the entity achieves 1-2 goals.
- With 11-20 active goals at the same time, the entity achieves 0 goals.

People also want closure after they have strived, whether they have worked alone or as part of an entity. Take the time after completing a task to evaluate, reflect, and assess the entire process. What went well, and what can be improved for the next task?

Inform the entity of the results and ask them to identify factors in their own work; this shows that you want to involve them and that you genuinely care about their development.

To truly create trust is to show vulnerability.

You need to be humble and apply the tips I've provided earlier in this book. Building trust can take many years, but it can be destroyed in an instant. The most important thing is to be 100% yourself; don't play a role of how you *think* you should be to create trust. Show that you do not have all the answers by asking, *"What do you think?"*

Demonstrate that you want to develop and are open to feedback by requesting criticism: *"What do you think I could do better?" "If you give me feedback, I would appreciate it; I want to develop in my role." "Can you tell me how you think I can improve?"*

Showing your vulnerability creates trust for you and safety for your team members. As a leader, you need to focus on making your entity feel secure rather than making them feel self-confident. Anyone can appear self-confident, but that does not mean they feel secure inside. A customer, colleague, or family member can immediately tell if you are acting self-confident or if you are secure in the situation. **The beauty of trust is that if you can genuinely create it, your surroundings will feel safe with you, which makes them self-confident.**

When you start meetings with your team, try saying something other than "How are you?" Instead, ask them if they would like to share one thing that is challenging or tough in their personal lives right now. *Sharing within a group that not everything is perfect in life helps to build connections among people and teams, fostering trust.*

The Trust Thermometer.

Imagine that your work of leading with trust is visible on a thermometer. The healthier the culture/atmosphere, the warmer the thermometer becomes. The warmer the thermometer gets, the more development occurs at the individual and group level. This creates a natural positive spiral; *the warmer the thermometer becomes, the stronger and healthier the culture is*. What can you do today to create more trust?

Higher natural and accepted expectations
of each other within the entity

Higher goals can be created and fulfilled

Well-being and results increase

Better communication

More openness and honesty

Genuine personal engagement and ownership

Passion and the willingness to contribute

Fundamental trust creates security and intrinsic motivation

Reflection, Section G

1. How often do you have the courage to show genuine vulnerability to your team members in order to create authentic trust? (You can compare this with how often you show your humanity.)

2. How often do you ask for help, making your team members feel important and valued?

3. How often do you encourage dignity and respect because it is important to you?

4. How often do you talk about your values as a person and the background behind why you feel that way?

5. How often do you delegate tasks to develop people rather than because you are too busy?

6. How often do you take the time to listen empathetically and ask follow-up questions to understand when a team member shows a need to be heard or expresses vulnerability? This creates a deep sense of belonging and human connection.

7. How often do you promote open and honest communication by being transparent and truly listening to your team members' opinions, views, and ideas?

8. When you receive feedback about yourself or the organization, how often do you say that you accept their perspective instead of defending yourself or the organization? A good long-term approach is, if possible, to involve the team member more in the larger perspectives to foster understanding and open up for more questions in staff meetings or employee discussions to create more participation and openness.

9. Do you keep the promises you make to your team members?

10. Do you welcome conflicts to encourage dialogue and collaboration?

11. Do you share examples of your own mistakes and lessons learned to demonstrate genuine vulnerability and openness, which creates a culture of mutual trust and understanding?

"Trust is the glue of life.

It's the most essential ingredient in effective communication.

It's the foundational principle that holds all relationships."
- Stephen R. Covey

H

Continuity, the leader's reflections

If you lose your humility, you risk losing everything.
Niclas Timmerby

I have previously written extensively in this book about the significance of self-reflection for you as a leader and a human being. The reason I am now highlighting this in a separate section is purely out of concern. If there is anything I ask you to take away from this book into your personal and professional life, it is the words *humility and respect.*

I have shared my own methodology G-I-F-T in Chapter 2 and Section F. What I have discovered in my work with myself, in coaching conversations, and in discussions with various entities, is that everything begins and ends with humility. As I mentioned in the quote on the previous page: *If you lose your humility, you risk losing everything.* Be mindful in your life so that you have self-awareness regarding the extent of your humility. Reflect on the other parts of G-I-F-T; how significant is humility?

When you approach all situations in life with humility, you automatically possess self-awareness, which is a gift that <u>always</u> works for you, as you have the ability to understand others' perspectives and emotions.

Humility is closely linked to respect.
Sometimes, when I read and hear how the word respect is used casually today, I become concerned as the true meaning and significance of the word is something beautiful. The word originates from the Latin term *"respectus"*, which was originally used to *show reverence or esteem for someone or something.* Its meaning can also be *to regard* or *to look back upon.*

Respect in its true sense is an essential social and ethical principle for promoting good relationships, mutual understanding, and cooperation between people. It means that we acknowledge and appreciate the worth and rights of all indiv duals, which in practice involves treating everyone we encounter with dignity, consideration, and kindness, regardless of natural differences in background and opinions.

Humility towards yourself.
Within psychology, humility is described as a personality trait that encompasses a humble and respectful attitude towards others <u>as well as towards oneself</u>. Being humble towards yourself is a crucial factor for personal development, psychological health, and well-being. *It involves being open to self-reflection (please feel free to revisit the tools I provided earlier in the book) and continual personal growth, as well as having a realistic and balanced view of your own abilities, strengths, and weaknesses.*

By consciously integrating humility into your self-image, you change your identity and strengthen your self-esteem as you promote a positive and healthy relationship with yourself.

The more you work on being humble towards yourself, the more genuinely humble you can be towards those around you. I have written extensively about self-reflection earlier. Here are some other tools to strengthen your humility towards yourself:

Self-compassion.
You need to cultivate humility towards yourself by being kind and empathetic to yourself when facing difficult challenges or making mistakes. How would you treat a close friend or family member in such a situation? Probably with compassion by showing understanding and kindness; treating yourself the same way fosters a healthy self-image.

Self-acceptance.

Practicing acceptance of yourself with all the flaws and imperfections you have, while striving for personal development and growth, benefits your self-awareness. Be open and willing to see yourself as a whole, including the parts you may not be satisfied with or those you find difficult. When you embrace all sides of yourself, self-acceptance is created, making it easier for you to free yourself from self-criticism and self-condemnation, thus fostering a more loving and compassionate relationship with yourself. Self-acceptance also encompasses the ability to stop comparing yourself to others and instead focus on your own unique qualities and attributes. By fully accepting yourself without trying to live up to unrealistic expectations and ideals, you can create a more authentic and genuine self-image.

Self-forgiveness.

Practicing this by consciously working to let go of past mistakes and self-criticism that create negative feelings can foster humility towards yourself as you build a more forgiving relationship with yourself. You are a person who is significant and important; maintain a balanced view of situations and events to create a more peaceful and harmonious relationship with yourself.

Thankfulness.

The third step in G-I-F-T is naturally included here, as it directly fosters humility towards yourself. By regularly reflecting on what you are thankful/grateful for, from small things occurring in daily life to significant matters, such as the ability to breathe, you directly increase your awareness of the positive aspects of your life. Reflecting on the good and valuable in your existence benefits your self-image.

Risks of not demonstrating true humility.

It is important for you to also be aware of the risks associated with not working on your own development around humility.

Ultimately, it all comes down to becoming aware, which creates the conditions for increased psychological flexibility, better problem-solving abilities, and reduced stress that naturally radiates to your surroundings.

Risk of loneliness in life.

> A person who struggles to display vulnerability and openness risks isolating themselves from others because they do not allow anyone to get close.

Risk of communication difficulties.

> Without genuine humility, a person may be perceived as less inclined to show empathy and understanding, which can lead to difficulties in communication and relationships.

Risk of difficulties in personal development.

> A person lacking humility may be less receptive to criticism and developmental feedback.
> This can result in a difficulty in acknowledging shortcomings and mistakes, hindering personal and professional growth.

Risk of a lack of trust.

> When humility is lacking, a person finds it challenging to ask for help or support when needed, even when it is obvious to those around them. Consistently failing to recognise and acknowledge weaknesses can lead others to lose trust in that person.

Risk of distrust.

> *A person with a lack of humility may excessively focus on themselves, their own needs, and achievements.*
> *This may be perceived by others as narcissistic traits, with a diminished ability to see and value other people's perspectives.*

Don't give up.

There will be situations where you will doubt.

Is all the work worth it, everything you invest in terms of time, resources, and energy? Is this what it means to be a boss or a leader?

When doubt arises, return to the leader's primary task: to create new leaders.

Being a leader means standing at the forefront and showing others the way. It is a tremendous privilege and a significant responsibility.

I want to give you three tips.

1. Use a Winning Culture.
You want to create a winning culture where you consistently achieve common goals over and over. You do this through a strong mindset: *you fight for one another every day, regardless of the situation.*

Together, you create a culture of determination that energises you to face setbacks and challenges.

Use the culture you have built together as your driving force. Observe what you have accomplished and done for others; how you have inspired others to believe in something great, how you have encouraged others to change themselves. You are important, valuable, and significant.

2. Mentorship in reality.
Real mentorship involves being genuinely challenged, which is highly developmental. When you, as a leader, ask someone else to be your mentor, you might express it like this:

- *"I want to develop; I want to improve. Can you help me?*

- *Can you come to my workplace and observe me? How do I come across? What signals do I send out? How well do I focus? How well do I prioritise? How do I treat my entity?*

- *This is how I structure my workdays. What would you do to be more organised and effective?*

- *This is how I describe our vision, my mission, our shared foundation of values. How can I improve this so everyone understands the 'why'?*

- *I want to feel 'this way'; I want to be 'this way' as a leader. What can I do differently? Will you challenge me?"*

3. Let it go!
When I conduct two-day leadership training sessions, I conclude day one, which has focused extensively on self-leadership and personal development, by reading a text with great emotion. It evokes a lot of feelings in the room. You can read the text on the next page.

"We get to dance for a while here on earth.
Ensure that your life has meaning and purpose.

So dance! Laugh! Be brave! Never take crap! Dare to say no!

Be humble, be generous in word and deed,
take responsibility, be grateful.

Dare to give of yourself from your heart to others.
For it is then that you truly touch people.

The moment you touch people, you change people and cultures.
It is then that you are most alive.

I want to share my absolutely strongest tool, which consists
*of three simple words: **Let it go!***

If something goes against you in your personal or professional life:
If you can influence it, do everything in your power to affect it.
If you cannot influence it, let it go!

For in your professional life, you do not have time to dwell on things you
cannot influence, as you need to focus on what you can impact.

And in your personal life, you have a life to live.
You do not have time to let things you cannot influence affect you.
You have a life to live; the more you influence it, the more you truly live."

CONCLUSION

The height of wastefulness is to spend a day without meaning.
Niclas Timmerby

I want to thank you from the bottom of my heart for reading this book.
My ambition is that you have gained concrete tools that you can apply directly in your personal and professional life.

My purpose with this book, has been to give you a sense of purpose.

In 2012, I wrote a quote:
"Life begins when purpose becomes more important than the shell."

At that time, after more than ten years of my own studies in psychology, I understood why I am here on earth. I understood the meaning; I understood the purpose. It was my deepest insight. *The moment we let go of the significance of our shell, our exterior, is the moment we begin to truly live.* When I released the importance of my shell and began to reflect until I found my true purpose: *I want to make a significant difference for other people.*

That is when I truly began to live. I changed how I communicated; I started to weigh my words carefully, both when I spoke and when I wrote, how attentively I listened, how I stood, how I challenged myself and others. Minor problems and concerns lost their significance and impact. I began to let go of things I cannot influence in my personal and professional life.

My conclusion is that the meaning of life is to find your purpose.
When you release the significance of "your shell" and instead focus on your "why" in life, I dare say that you will feel your best. Your shoulders will drop a little as the expected pressure of how you are *supposed* to be drastically decreases. When you find your purpose, you discover a different, more harmonious way to live your life.

Frequently ask yourself: *What can I genuinely give to others in words and actions?* If you make a difference for people, they will never forget what you did for them. Never. This is not about money, gifts, or material things. It is solely about how you treat your fellow human beings.

John McEnroe wisely said, **"You must develop a sharpness to become good at something."** I love that quote because it makes me aware of my own behaviour and attitude. *What can I learn today? How can I improve? Can I listen better? And so on.*

My final quote in this book is about resilience.

> *"Always let who you are influence circumstances*
> *more than circumstances influence you."*

Life is far too fragile and too short to spend energy, time, and focus on circumstances you cannot influence. Your well-being is greatly interconnected with how well you do not allow circumstances to affect you. Can you let things go?

Here, humility also comes into play. The more humble we are, the more we can focus on what truly matters: our purpose.

You can be like the flutter of a butterfly's wings. You always have a choice: *What do you do, what do you spread around you, what traces do you leave behind?*

See the bigger perspective to appreciate the small things.
If you feel that you lack energy, that you feel doubt, then reflect on the largest perspective:

We orbit our G-star, the sun, at about 108,000 km per hour (67,108 mph); at the equator, the Earth's rotation corresponds to 1,674 km per hour (1040 mph). Our solar system travels in its orbit around the centre of the Milky Way at about 840,000 km per hour (521,952 mph), taking our solar system approximately 225-250 million years to complete one orbit. The sun's gravity keeps all the planets in our solar system in their respective orbits.

Is it really the right time to ponder circumstances that have no long-term impact on our lives? Is it really the right time to complain or sulk over trivial matters? So why not dance in the rain, enjoy a red traffic light, be grateful that you can stand in a queue, smile at a parking ticket, or laugh when the Wi-Fi is shaky?

We must never forget that it is an incredible, highly improbable miracle that we can wander around on this green, beautiful planet for a little while.

What do you want to say to yourself on the day you stop working?
I was fair, I was unpretentious, I stood up for equality? I was humble, generous in word and deed, took 100 percent responsibility, and was deeply grateful whenever I had the opportunity? I treated people well and helped them grow, develop, and feel good? I was kind to myself in times of adversity?

For success and development in your self-leadership:
Accept yourself for who you are 100 percent and stand up 100 percent for your human values and moral principles.

Wishing you the best!
Niclas

ABOUT THE AUTHOR

I was born in 1972 in Jönköping, Sweden.

My childhood dream was to become an air traffic controller or a teacher. I can now see that I have achieved my childhood dream, as I am somewhat of a teacher when I train and lecture, and an air traffic controller as I currently manage 23 teams in southern Sweden.

I have three ambitions when I educate and lecture. Number one is to touch people. My second ambition is to challenge old truths and thought patterns. My third ambition is that we should have a lot of fun together.

All to create greater willingness, accountability, and desire for positive change within the team.

When I engage with the participants, something much stronger and more powerful than confidence is created - namely, trust. When trust is established, the conditions for direct change in individuals, teams, and corporate cultures are simultaneously created.

I educate and lecture on leadership, hospitality, team building, and changing corporate cultures.

I listen to your specific needs, conditions, and what you want to gain from our time together. I then adapt and optimise the material and any workshops we mutually agree upon to ensure you get the maximum value from your time and investment.

Companies:
IKEA, Apoteket, BRA-flyg, Cubus, Price Waterhouse Coopers, Choice Hotels, Öresundsbron, St1 Sverige AB, Lindab, MediaMarkt, Brafab, Färdig Betong, Just4Sports, Arjohuntleigh, Mockfjärdsfönster, Furninova, Svea Fireworks, Lexington.

Government, Municipal, and Trade Union:
IF Metall, Gothenburg City, The Public Employment Service, Region Skåne, Norrbotten County, Västerbotten County, Jämtland County, Västernorrland County, Kalmar County, Trelleborg Municipality, Osby Municipality, Karlshamn Municipality, Kristianstad Municipality, Båstad Municipality.

Sport clubs:
Kristianstad DFF, Helsingborgs IF, FC Trelleborg, Skepparslövs Golf Club, Glimma Hockey.

Others:
Akademi Båstad, Nordic Business Institute, Queenia, Livsmedels-akademien, Barncancerfonden (ideellt), Sveriges bagare och konditorer, Helsingborgs business region (Familjen Helsingborg), Ung Företagsamhet, Göinge Näringsliv, Nyföretagarcentrum, Folkuniversitetet.

7 Steps Within Self-Leadership

Foreword by Tina Thörner

432 pages

Every time you are influenced by another person, it shapes you as an individual. It affects your thoughts, behaviour, attitude, well-being, how you act towards your goals, and how you, from that moment on, influence others on your life journey. How does all this affect your everyday life? This book is about how to take control and provides you with 7 steps to live a unique life.

Also available as an e-book.

100 Ways to Genuine Self-Leadership

Foreword by Emerich Roth

612 pages

100 short chapters with insightful principles. Practical advice for your personal life journey to counteract external expectations, negative imprinting, and stress, as well as concrete tools to build a solid reputation in your professional life. A self-assessment questionnaire of 13 pages is included in the book so you can track your own development.

Nominated for "Project Management Book of the Year 2024" by Swedish Project Forum.

Also available as an e-book.

Show Your Gold

376 pages

Finding the meaning of life is not about changing yourself. It is about changing your perception of yourself. When we change how we see ourselves, we simultaneously change how others perceive us. We attract what we are; the better we genuinely feel and thrive within ourselves, the more interested others become in us. This requires insights and courage. The more you challenge yourself and your truths, the more you grow.

Also available as an e-book.

7 Steps Within Self-Leadership

Foreword by Tina Thörner

464 pages

To live a rich and unique life, regardless of our circumstances, we need to reflect to gain self-awareness and empowerment. Who has truly decided how and who you should be? Have you created your own life journey, or could it be that the person you are today is more or less molded and influenced by others and partially by cultures?

1. What life have you learned to live?
2. What is your potential?
3. Who do you want with you on the journey?
4. Live, think, and act in the present.
5. The negative veil.
6. The long-term perspective.
7. The final destination.

Also available as an e-book.